Melville

Melville

Fashioning in Modernity

Stephen Matterson

BLOOMSBURY
NEW YORK • LONDON • NEW DELHI • SYDNEY

Bloomsbury Academic
An imprint of Bloomsbury Publishing Inc

1385 Broadway	50 Bedford Square
New York	London
NY 10018	WC1B 3DP
USA	UK

www.bloomsbury.com

Bloomsbury is a registered trade mark of Bloomsbury Publishing Plc

First published 2014

© Stephen Matterson, 2014

All rights reserved. No part of this publication may be reproduced or transmitted in any form or by any means, electronic or mechanical, including photocopying, recording, or any information storage or retrieval system, without prior permission in writing from the publishers.

No responsibility for loss caused to any individual or organization acting on or refraining from action as a result of the material in this publication can be accepted by Bloomsbury or the author.

Library of Congress Cataloging-in-Publication Data
Matterson, Stephen.
Melville : fashioning in modernity / Stephen Matterson.
pages cm
Includes bibliographical references and index.
ISBN 978-1-62356-367-7 (hardback) – ISBN 978-1-62356-200-7 (paperback)
1. Melville, Herman, 1819–1891–Criticism and interpretation. 2. Clothing and dress in literature. 3. Identity (Philosophical concept) in literature.
4. Civilization, Modern, in literature. I. Title.
PS2387.M34   2014
813'.3–dc23
2014003677

ISBN: HB: 978-1-6235-6367-7
PB: 978-1-6235-6200-7
ePub: 978-1-6235-6606-7
ePDF: 978-1-6235-6055-3

Typeset by Newgen Knowledge Works (P) Ltd., Chennai, India

In memory of my parents, Charles and Mary
They gave this child more of themselves than that

Contents

Acknowledgements	viii
Introduction: Herman Melville's Blue-Jean Career	1
1 So Unspeakably Significant: Melville, Hawthorne and the Shawls	5
2 A Very Strange Compound Indeed: Carlyle, *Redburn* and *White-Jacket*	39
3 He Was a European, and Had Clothes on: *Typee*	85
4 The Dress Befitted the Fate: Israel Potter's Lives	131
5 These Buttons That We Wear: *Billy Budd*	171
Bibliography	213
Index	225

Acknowledgements

It is tempting just to say, in the immortal words of Captain Louis Renault, 'round up the usual suspects'. These would be various colleagues in the School of English here at Trinity College, Trinity colleagues in other disciplines, and friends and colleagues at University College, Dublin. Suspects also include our undergraduate and postgraduate students, who never allow anything to be easy.

Anyone who works on Melville quickly learns that in order to follow the expansive nature of his fiction you really do, like Ishmael, need to swim through libraries. Such swimming incurs its own debts, and I would like to thank librarians at Trinity and at the Phillips Reading Room in Harvard for their considerable help, and the staff at the Houghton Library at Harvard for providing access to the Melville holdings.

Trinity's Faculty of Arts Humanities and the Social Sciences kindly granted me a study leave during the academic year 2010–11, without which this book may never have been started, never mind completed. The friendly encouragement of successive Heads of the School of English, Darryl Jones and Eve Patten, is also much appreciated, and both embody the collegiality that has meant so much to me since I was lucky enough to take up a post here.

I would like particularly to thank the three anonymous readers of my manuscript. Their scholarly, thoughtful and encouraging reports were invaluable in my revising towards publication. Since my very first contact with Bloomsbury, Haaris Naqvi and Laura Murray have been exemplary in their efficiency, courtesy and professionalism.

In what unexpectedly proved to be a most difficult year, the constant love, support and encouragement provided by Jean Nee have been of crucial significance, and she deserves more thanks than anyone. Besides, this is all her fault for giving me *The Portable Melville* and *The Portable Hawthorne* as birthday presents so long ago.

Introduction: Herman Melville's Blue-Jean Career

I recall vividly, though in a slightly embarrassed way, exactly when I started to reflect on the ideas behind this book. One Sunday I was preparing the clothes I was to wear during the week ahead, looking through my diary and deciding which outfit was appropriate to each day's main activity. (This also occasioned some reflection on the varied roles of today's academic.) Ahead was a meeting of University Council for which I usually dressed formally, classes with a small group of first-year students, for which I prefer to dress informally, two lectures to large audiences, a book launch, a Faculty meeting, two advanced seminars, one afternoon that I could spend in the library and a meeting with a prospective student. I began idly to think of how much clothes project a persona, and how at some point they are not merely clothes but are costumes or uniforms or even camouflage. I do not want to dwell too much on this moment, partly for fear of representing myself as Cher at the opening of the film *Clueless* (for one thing I do not own a Junior Gaultier kilt). But it coincided with my rereading a good deal of Melville around that time, particularly *Israel Potter*, and I started to think about Melville's attentiveness to clothing. At times his descriptions of particular items of dress are very detailed; and, after all, he named one of his novels, *White-Jacket*, after an article of clothing. Furthermore, his characters are often wearing the wrong clothes, or are uncomfortable in their clothing. Some characters use clothing as a disguise, concealing their true identity, others promote or even flaunt themselves through their dress. There is a variety of changes of clothing in his novels. In *Typee*, his first, Tommo changes the 'civilized' clothes of the sailor and while he lives with the South Sea natives wears a variation of their dress. *White-Jacket* begins with its main character preparing the jacket that he will wear for the voyage, and ends with the loss of the coat. *Israel Potter* involves a striking number of changes of clothing, and Melville alludes at one point to Israel's 'blue-jean career' which the *OED* records as the first usage of blue-jean as an adjective, a metaphorical representation of the labourer. There are also instances of characters dressing others; the narrator of 'Bartleby, the Scrivener' giving his coat to his employee, Turkey. I was dimly aware of

Melville's indebtedness to the prose of Thomas Carlyle in his development as a writer, and I knew that Carlyle had written *Sartor Resartus*, ostensibly at least about the symbolism of clothing.

As my interest deepened, I was particularly drawn to those characters of Melville who find themselves in the wrong clothing. Their attire may be wrong because it is inappropriate for the circumstances, or because it is no indication of their inner self. The wrong clothes may lead to shame, embarrassment and discomfort. But they may also be signifiers of defiance, expressive of one's individuation. They may be indicators of not belonging, and of a refusal to belong or to conform. Generally, those who are at ease in the wrong clothing, and who even flaunt this, tend not to be the major characters in the novels. They are Melville's versions of the dandy, and their presence usually highlights the anxiety and discomfort felt by the central characters. It is these characters, Tommo, Israel Potter, Captain Vere from *Billy Budd*, who form the main focus of this book, with reference also to White-Jacket and to the ambivalent case of Wellingborough Redburn. The anxiety, discomfort and self-estrangement of these main characters are evident in the disconnection between their clothing and their actual sense of themselves, in some measure between their public identity and their inner reality. This is slightly less evident in the character of Tommo. Melville almost certainly wrote *Typee* and his second novel *Omoo* before his reading Carlyle stimulated further reflections on clothes as symbolic. *Typee* is more concerned with clothing and power, and how it relates to the colonizing that Tommo witnesses, but this also leads Tommo to consider his own costume as a signifier of self.

Typically, Melville represents characters who are struggling in modernity. While modernity is a much-discussed term, I have in mind here not so much the modernity of a specific historical moment or period but an ongoing confrontation with rapid social change leaving the individual dislocated and uncertain. For Melville this could be apparent at any time from the late eighteenth century to his own time. Looking at modernity in this way of course echoes Foucault, who in turn echoes Baudelaire. Foucault wondered

> whether we may not envisage modernity rather as an attitude than as a period of history. And by 'attitude', I mean a mode of relating to contemporary reality; a voluntary choice made by certain people; in the end, a way of thinking and feeling; a way, too, of acting and behaving that at one and the same time marks a relation of belonging and presents itself as a task.[1]

---

[1] Michel Foucault, 'What Is Enlightenment?' in *The Foucault Reader*, ed. Paul Rabinow (New York: Pantheon Books, 1984), p. 39.

As Foucault notes, it was Baudelaire who saw modernity placing the individual in crisis, not just in relation to the age but in relation to oneself. In modernity the self must be created; 'Modern man, for Baudelaire, is not the man who goes off to discover himself, his secrets and his hidden truth; he is the man who tries to invent himself.'[2] Baudelaire involved clothing as part of this self-invention, and for him the figure who most realized modernity's possibilities was the dandy, and *dandyisme* was 'the burning desire to create a personal form of originality, within the external limits of social conventions'.[3] Melville's sense of the relation between self-invention and clothing engages me most in this book, how dress comes to be part of the narrative of the self, to paraphrase Anthony Giddens: 'A person's identity is not to be found in behaviour, nor – important though this is – in the reactions of others, but in the capacity *to keep a particular narrative going*.'[4] Dress may be an important element of that unification of the self, as Elizabeth Wilson asserted in her influential study *Adorned in Dreams*:

> [W]e may view the fashionable dress of the western world as one means whereby an always fragmentary self is glued together into the semblance of a unified identity. Identity becomes a special kind of problem in modernity.[5]

Typically Melville explores those who struggle to keep a narrative going, those who unlike the dandy are objects rather than subjects in modernity.[6] But he also connects some of these anxieties to his own, and this is partly why this book describes and examines Melville's self-positioning during the process of writing. This is especially prominent in the composition of *Typee* and *Billy Budd*, his first and his last novels. The writing of *Typee* involves Melville's own self-invention; indeed, in a letter to Nathaniel Hawthorne he commented that it was from this action that his life truly began: 'From my twenty-fifth year I date my life.'[7] It is as though Melville is playing the

---

[2] Ibid., p. 42.
[3] Charles Baudelaire, 'The Dandy', section 9 of 'The Painter of Modern Life', in *Selected Writings on Art and Artists*, trans. P. E. Charvet (Harmondsworth: Penguin, 1972), p. 420.
[4] Anthony Giddens, *Modernity and Self-Identity* (Stanford, CA: Stanford University Press, 1991), p. 54.
[5] Elizabeth Wilson, *Adorned in Dreams: Fashion and Modernity* (London: Virago, 1985), p. 11.
[6] I here follow the terminology used by Marshall Berman in *All That Is Solid Melts into Air: The Experience of Modernity* (Harmondsworth: Penguin, 1988).
[7] Herman Melville, *Correspondence* (Evanston, IL: Northwestern University Press, 1993), p. 193.

part of the writer in the same way that his protagonist Tommo changes out of his sailor clothes to act out a role with the native population, and is re-dressed (by others) at the end of the adventure. The mode of writing makes it difficult to locate *Typee*'s attitudes with any certainty (and even to be sure of its genre), as Melville records the shifting developing process of his thought, rather than beginning the work having already reached a decided set of conclusions. *Billy Budd* is equally introspective, the more so because the manuscript shows reworking and revisions over five years. It is both introspective and retrospective, as Melville draws on memories of events from forty years ago, and Vere's discomfort in his uniform comes to be suggestive of Melville's own anxieties over the 'Herman Melville' he had begun to create with *Typee*. I certainly see Vere as very much the centre of the novel. In this I agree with those critics who argue that readings which place the central conflict between Billy and Claggart have become normative partly because of influential early critical readings which were actually based on a deeply problematic text. The novels I focus most closely on here represent Melville's own forms of self-invention, his self-dressing, his 'blue-jean career'.

In general, Melville's interest in clothing is in its signification, its symbolism. As we shall see in Chapter 2, although this interest predates his reading of Carlyle, it was certainly further stimulated by it. This study, then, is attentive to the symbolic aspect of dress, rather than to what might be called the material culture of the clothing that features in the works. That is, I am not concerned with the price of clothing, its material particularities or the appropriateness of a particular article of clothing for any given year. There is no doubt that Melville's work invites such an approach, but this is not my focus. Also, while I hope that Melvilleans will find this book interesting, it will be quickly apparent that it is not written with the Melville expert in mind. What I do have in mind is a more general reader who has some interest in Melville, but who may not have thought very much about the Melville beyond *Moby-Dick*.

1

So Unspeakably Significant: Melville, Hawthorne and the Shawls

In August 1852, a few weeks after a visit to Nantucket, Herman Melville wrote a letter to his friend and Massachusetts neighbour Nathaniel Hawthorne. His writing to Hawthorne was far from unusual, and the surviving letters that Melville sent to him between January 1851 and November 1852 are among the most revealing documents we have of his state of mind, especially during the composition of *Moby-Dick*, published in the United States in November 1851. In these letters Melville articulates both his despair at the place of the writer in a materialistic America and his overwhelming sense of accomplishment on the completion of *Moby-Dick*. These are letters characterized by extraordinary mixtures of mood, combinations of self-pity, despair and angry defiance. In a now-famous letter probably written in June 1851 Melville writes:

> In a week or so, I go to New York, to bury myself in a third-story room, and work and slave on my 'Whale' while it is driving through the press. *That* is the only way I can finish it now, – I am so pulled hither and thither by circumstances. The calm, the coolness, the silent grass-growing mood in which a man *ought* always to compose, – that, I fear, can seldom be mine. Dollars damn me; and the malicious Devil is forever grinning in upon me, holding the door ajar. My dear Sir, a presentiment is on me, – I shall at last be worn out and perish, like an old nutmeg-grater, grated to pieces by the constant attrition of the wood, that is, the nutmeg. What I feel most moved to write, that is banned, – it will not pay. Yet, altogether, write the *other* way I cannot. So the product is a final hash, and all my books are botches.[1]

Clearly Melville is exhausted at this point; by the effort of finishing his novel, by the demands of life as a farmer in Pittsfield, and by his uncertain ability

---

[1] Melville, *Correspondence*, p. 191.

to support his family, with his wife Elizabeth now expecting their second child. But while the exhaustion is evident, so too is a particular pride, a belief in his gifts as a writer, despite his sense that his writing is increasingly out of step with the market-place. This self-belief drives this long letter, giving it energy and ferocity unmatched in any of Melville's other available correspondence. In fact, these letters to Hawthorne are themselves unusual for Melville. Melville wrote few letters and he generally did not keep copies of letters that he did write. The authoritative Northwestern-Newberry volume of his correspondence contains texts of only 313 letters, the first dated 1828, when Melville was aged 9, and the last a brief note written in November 1890, 10 months before his death at the age of 72. We know letters from Melville to Elizabeth were destroyed by his family after his death, but it remains true that in sharp contrast to his some of his literary contemporaries, Melville did not conduct a voluminous or a consistent correspondence. This fact alone should indicate some of the difference between Melville and those contemporaries such as Ralph Waldo Emerson, Henry Wadsworth Longfellow and Hawthorne. Unlike them, as the June 1851 letter to Hawthorne articulates, Melville never felt he had the leisure for the 'silent grass-growing mood' deemed essential to composition. This is why the ten extant letters to Hawthorne are so valuable; they are self-revelatory and provide us with insight into a key period of his life.

However, the August 1852 letter is radically different from the 1851 letters. Rather than expressing energetic despair, Melville writes in an almost resigned way. *Moby-Dick* has been published and not as well-received as Melville had anticipated by critics or the public. It is worth pointing out that the reviews were generally favourable – occasionally *Moby-Dick* is represented as being a complete failure; it was not. However his subsequent novel, *Pierre*, was published earlier that August and received some of the worst reviews Melville ever had. In one of them, published on 4 August, *Pierre* was called 'the craziest fiction extant', with an 'almost infinite' amount of 'utter trash' in it.[2] Four more reviews during August matched this damning assessment, and their messages were straightforward enough; Melville should return to the style of his first two books or give up writing altogether. As one reviewer put it:

> [I]f we had any influence with Mr Melville, we would pray him to wash out the remembrance of [*Pierre*] by writing forthwith a fresh romance of the Ocean, without a line of dialogue in it. Thereon he is at home;

---

[2] Watson G. Branch (ed.), *Melville: The Critical Heritage* (London: Routledge and Kegan Paul, 1974), pp. 294, 295.

thereon he earned his literary laurels; thereon he may regain his literary standing, which he must have perilled by this crazy rigmarole.³

It is in this context that Melville wrote to Hawthorne on 13 August, the same day that he sent an inscribed copy of *Pierre* to the Hawthornes.⁴ However his letter makes no mention at all of *Pierre* and is almost entirely focused on some material Melville has come across that he believes can be worked up into a powerful story. But one of the remarkable things about the letter is that Melville is not planning to write this story himself; he is urging Hawthorne to do it. This indicates that Melville has in some measure absorbed what the reception of *Moby-Dick* and the reviews of *Pierre* suggested, and that his writing over the past three years has indeed resulted in 'botches' that pleased no-one. His entire sense of himself as a writer is being questioned over a short period which will initiate the depression from which Melville periodically suffers for the next 25 years and which will lead to his wife's family regarding him as insane.

Read in this context, the 13th August letter to Hawthorne can be seen as an act of relinquishing the role of the writer. He is now resigned to passing on promising material to someone who can do a better job, and Hawthorne is being cast as *il miglio fabbro*, to use Dante's term which T. S. Eliot borrowed to praise Ezra Pound. Melville's sense here of Hawthorne as 'the better craftsman' is complex. It partly has to do with the material for the proposed story and partly to do with Melville's apprehension that Hawthorne could succeed in exactly the manner that Melville had tried and failed. That is, Hawthorne had an enviable way of combining what he felt 'most moved to write' with a popular appeal. Shortly before he met Hawthorne for the first time at a picnic in August 1850, Melville had written perceptively and enthusiastically of him, in an anonymously published essay, mainly devoted to the short-story collection *Mosses from an Old Manse*. The essay, 'Hawthorne and His Mosses', appeared in two parts in the *Literary World*, the issues of 17 and 24 August. In it, Melville combined enthusiasm for Hawthorne with a sense of national pride in the evidence of American artistic maturity. But what he saw in Hawthorne is something like duplicity. Hawthorne's ability to produce a pleasing tale is, Melville asserted, how the public know him: 'Where Hawthorne is known, he seems to be deemed a pleasant writer, with a pleasant style, a sequestered, harmless man, from whom any deep and weighty thing would hardly be anticipated: – a man who

---

³ Ibid., p. 299.
⁴ Hershel Parker, *Herman Melville: A Biography* (Baltimore and London: Johns Hopkins University Press, 1996, 2002), 2, p. 130.

means no meanings.'⁵ But Melville sensed something ominous underneath this surface, a 'Puritanic gloom' or a sense of evil, or a destructive force; a 'great power of blackness':

> [T]his black conceit pervades him, through and through. You may be witched by his sunlight, – transported by the bright gildings in the skies he builds over you; – but there is the blackness of darkness beyond; and even his bright gildings but fringe, and play upon the edges of thunder-clouds. – In one word, the world is mistaken in this Nathaniel Hawthorne. He himself must often have smiled at its absurd misconception of him.⁶

Almost 80 years later, another novelist also recognized this duality in Hawthorne. In *Studies in Classic American Literature*, D. H. Lawrence famously cautioned us to trust the tale, not the artist, and of Hawthorne he remarked: 'That blue-eyed darling Nathaniel knew disagreeable things in his inner soul. He was careful to send them out in disguise.' Reflecting on *The Scarlet Letter*, Lawrence made a claim for its 'marvellous undermeaning! And its perfect duplicity.'⁷

Melville was clearly drawn to this aspect of Hawthorne because it provided a solution to what had become an enduring problem for him: how to combine earning a living from writing while maintaining his ideal of writing as a vehicle of self-integrity. Eventually he was to be defeated by the incompatibility of these ambitions. He published the last novel in his lifetime, *The Confidence-Man*, in 1857. Following various attempts to find employment he took up a post as deputy inspector of customs in New York port in 1866 and worked there until he retired at the end of 1885. Tellingly, though, Melville did not cease writing. As well as the Civil War lyrics that he published in 1866, he allowed his maternal uncle Peter Gansevoort to pay for the publication of his epic 16,000-line poem *Clarel* in 1876. However, the old dilemma between self-expression and market-place was by this time long played out. Whatever his hopes for *Clarel* had been, by 1884, with two-thirds of the print-run now pulped, he described it as 'a metrical affair . . . of several thousand lines, eminently unadapted for popularity'.⁸ As will be detailed in Chapter 5, Melville's commitment to writing was maintained

---

⁵ Herman Melville, *The Piazza Tales, and Other Prose Pieces* (Evanston, IL: Northwestern University Press 1987), p. 242.
⁶ Ibid., pp. 243–4.
⁷ D. H. Lawrence, *Studies in Classic American Literature* (Harmondsworth: Penguin, 1977), p. 106.
⁸ Melville, *Correspondence*, p. 483.

after his retirement with his work on *Billy Budd*, even if his continual revisions to this manuscript suggest a commitment to writing rather than necessarily to publication.

But this resignation was far from evident in the early years of the 1850s, and the example of Hawthorne, and his friendship with him in these years, energized him and was crucial to his self-confidence as a writer. Born in 1804, Hawthorne was 15 years older than Melville, he had self-published a novel titled *Fanshawe* in 1828, and a well-received collection of stories, *Twice-Told Tales*, in 1837. These stories had already appeared in periodicals, and were collected in book form without Hawthorne's knowledge. In 1846, the same year as Melville's first book, his *Mosses from an Old Manse* was published, and *The Scarlet Letter* appeared shortly before the first meeting of the two men in 1850; the novel is referred to briefly in Melville's essay. The few years of their close friendship were crucial ones for both men; Hawthorne published two major works, *The House of the Seven Gables* (1851) and *The Blithedale Romance* (1852); Melville produced *Moby-Dick* (1851) and *Pierre* (1852), before working on the stories, including 'Bartleby, the Scrivener' and *Benito Cereno*, that were eventually collected in *The Piazza Tales* (1856). This collection included a kind of homage to Hawthorne; 'The Bell-Tower' written very much in the non-realist/fantastic vein that Hawthorne often employed in his short fiction. By April 1857, Melville had published what would be his final completed works of fiction, *Israel Potter* and *The Confidence-Man*.

These were, then, years of remarkable creativity for both men, even if Hawthorne was rather more canny about his writing and his career than Melville ever was. Hawthorne's main undertaking for the election year of 1852 was a campaign biography, *The Life of Franklin Pierce*. Hawthorne had known Pierce since they were undergraduates and when Pierce became President Hawthorne was rewarded with the post of consul in Liverpool; just the kind of post Melville himself longed for, and had tried hard to obtain before taking up the job at the port. While Hawthorne held the consulship he and Melville met for what turned out to be the last time, in the spring of 1857. To Melville, Hawthorne was the writer who had successfully negotiated the enduring problem of how to combine artistic integrity with popular appeal. He saw him as someone refusing to conform to the values of the age, even when on the surface he seemed obedient to them. As he wrote to Hawthorne in April 1851:

> There is the grand truth about Nathaniel Hawthorne. He says NO! in thunder; but the Devil himself cannot make him say *yes*. For all men who say *yes*, lie; and all men who say *no*, – why, they are in the happy

condition of judicious, unincumbered [sic] travellers in Europe; they cross the frontiers into Eternity with nothing but a carpet-bag, – that is to say, the Ego.⁹

When he came to write *Moby-Dick* Melville aspired to the kind of dual writing he so admired in Hawthorne. The surface was an exciting tale of adventure, surely designed for popularity, while the undertext with which it is increasingly intertwined provided room for Melville to explore a developing philosophy, sometimes whimsically, sometimes profoundly. This mode of writing was, moreover, a development of a romance, a genre or style that Hawthorne was learning to utilize to great effect. He offered his thoughts on romance, as distinct from the genre of the novel, in two now-celebrated and much-quoted prefaces, to *The Scarlet Letter* and *The House of the Seven Gables*. Hawthorne was inordinately fond of prefaces and of explaining the mechanics of his tales to the reader; a fact which made Emerson, for one, impatient: 'Hawthorn [sic] invites his readers too much into his study, opens the process before them. As if the confectioner should say to his customers Now let us make the cake.'¹⁰

The Preface to *The House of the Seven Gables* introduces a crucial and influential distinction between the romance and the novel:

> When a writer calls his work a Romance, it need hardly be observed that he wishes to claim a certain latitude, both as to its fashion and material, which he would not have felt himself entitled to assume, had he professed to be writing a Novel. The latter form of composition is presumed to aim at a very minute fidelity, not merely to the possible, but to the probable and ordinary course of man's experience. The former – while, as a work of art, it must rigidly subject itself to laws, and while it sins unpardonably, so far as it may swerve aside from the truth of the human heart – has fairly a right to present that truth under circumstances, to a great extent, of the writer's own choosing or creation.¹¹

He ends the Preface by declaring that the work of fiction which follows has 'a great deal more to do with the clouds overhead, than with any portion of the actual soil of the County of Essex'.¹² In 'The Custom-House', the

---

⁹ Ibid., p. 186.
¹⁰ Ralph Waldo Emerson, 'Journal O' (1846), *Selected Journals 1841–47* (New York: Library of America, 2010), p. 319.
¹¹ Nathaniel Hawthorne, *Novels* (New York: Library of America, 1983), p. 351.
¹² Ibid., p. 353.

lengthy semi-detached preface to *The Scarlet Letter*, Hawthorne made more of a claim for the form of romance which requires a synthesizing of the 'actual' and the 'imaginary'. The writer of romance, Hawthorne claims, is best suited by the medium of moonlight, which softens the actual yet also delineates it more clearly than ever. Moonlight may seem to transform the actual, but in doing so it brings out a deeper truth: 'Thus, therefore, the floor of our familiar room has become a neutral territory, somewhere between the real world and fairy-land, where the Actual and the Imaginary may meet, and each imbue itself with the nature of the other.'[13] This insistence on the imagination's capacity to reveal a truth invisible from a realist approach was one of the features that drew Henry James to Hawthorne. As he put it in his 1879 study, 'The fine thing in Hawthorne is that he cared for the deeper psychology, and that, in his way, he tried to become familiar with it.'[14] But the crucial aspect in Hawthorne's formulation of romance is the necessity of balance. A superfluity of imagination (or moonlight) results in excess and a departure from the real; too much mimesis results in a fact-bound and limited work, the major problem, as he sees it, with the novel as a genre.

Again, Melville is attracted to Hawthorne because this desired balance, this synthesis, had so far eluded him. In 1849 *Mardi* had been a critical and commercial disaster. There, Melville had departed considerably from the fact-based narratives of his *Typee* and *Omoo*, in favour of what readers found to be bewildering allegory. *Moby-Dick* was a balance, Melville thought, between the two modes, between the actual and the imaginary. Its dedication to Hawthorne 'In token of my admiration for his genius' indicates the example he found in the older writer, and there is some evidence that Melville altered and considerably revised what had been planned as a more straightforward sea-novel, possibly due to the influence of Hawthorne. There are many echoes of Hawthorne in *Moby-Dick*; the relation between Ahab and Hawthorne's protagonist in the story 'Ethan Brand'; the echo of 'they call me Ilbrahim' from 'The Gentle Boy' with 'Call me Ishmael', the opening words of 'Loomings', the first chapter. He also claimed affinity with Hawthorne's power of blackness. 'I have', he wrote to Hawthorne in November 1851, 'written a wicked book [and yet] feel spotless as the lamb'.[15]

Melville's August 1852 letter to Hawthorne, then, comes at a charged moment for him, after *Moby-Dick*, after *Pierre* and after, in some ways, the

---

[13] Ibid., p. 149.
[14] Henry James, 'Hawthorne', in *Essays, American and English Writers* (New York: Library of America, 1984), p. 168.
[15] Melville, *Correspondence*, p. 212.

absorption of Hawthorne's exemplary 'genius'. But one of the many curious features of this letter, referred to by Melville scholars as the 'Agatha' letter, is that Melville is outlining a potential story not because he intends to write it, but because, he claims, this is material more appropriate for Hawthorne. While in Nantucket in July, Melville was told a story by someone he calls a lawyer from New Bedford, which intrigued him so much that he asked the lawyer to send him a written record of the case. The lawyer was John H. Clifford, a friend of Melville's father-in-law, Chief Justice Shaw. Clifford was at that time the Massachusetts Attorney General and would soon become the State Governor, and the case had taken place many years before, when he was a District Attorney. Melville's letter was supplemented by what is taken to be a transcription of Clifford's notes on the case; usefully, this provides the factual basis that formed a starting-point for Melville's imaginative speculations.[16]

As the Agatha materials tell it, the case concerned the marriage between a young local woman and a sailor called James Robertson. Robertson had been shipwrecked in 1806 on the Massachusetts coast in Plymouth County, near Duxbury. Agatha Hatch nursed him and they were married in 1807, setting up home in Falmouth. However, two years later Robertson deserted Agatha while she was pregnant. He apparently left to look for work, but was entirely absent for 17 years. He unexpectedly reappeared after this time, met his daughter, Rebecca, for the first time, and stayed with the family for a day or so, giving Agatha a 'handsome sum of money' but refusing to inform his family where he was living.[17] He returned about a year later, on the eve of Rebecca's marriage to a Mr Gifford. He then left once again, but, curiously, invited his son-in-law to visit him for a few days in Alexandria, near Washington, DC. Gifford did so, and came back to Falmouth with 'a gold watch and three handsome shawls which had been previously worn by some person'.[18] For Agatha and Rebecca these shawls in particular confirmed their suspicion that Robertson had been married to another woman during the 17-year absence. Finally, Robertson visits Falmouth once more, telling Agatha and Rebecca that he intends moving to Missouri and unsuccessfully tries to persuade the whole family to go with him. Although there was correspondence between Agatha, Rebecca and Robertson, they never met again, and at one point Robertson apparently told Agatha that he intended to marry a Mrs Irvin. After Robertson's death in 1840, the truth about his marriages emerged, primarily because Agatha contested a claim that their

[16] Ibid., pp. 621–5; see also Parker, *Herman Melville: A Biography*, 2, p. 120.
[17] Melville, *Correspondence*, p. 623.
[18] Ibid., p. 624.

marriage was not legal and that Rebecca was illegitimate. In effect, they were laying claim to a share in Robertson's estate, and, with the assistance of Clifford's law firm, were able to prove that the 1807 marriage was legal, and that the other two marriages were invalid. Robertson had bigamously married a woman in Alexandria (the owner of the shawls), as well as Mrs Irvin, though no children issued from these later marriages.

In the account that he gives of Melville's visit to Nantucket and of the Agatha letter, Hershel Parker speculates that the story engaged Melville for a variety of reasons, perhaps among them the idea of the father who disappears and then reappears, which, due to his relationship with his own father, 'could not help stirring up intense feelings in Melville'.[19] The relation between the story and Melville's own childhood may not seem overly compelling as a reason for his interest. Although often absent from the family on business, Melville's father did not disappear (even though there has been constant and perhaps unconvincing speculation that he fathered a child outside marriage), and he died – in debt, as it turned out – in January 1832, when Melville was aged 12.[20] Even without any personal involvement, the theme of disappearance and reappearance is a compelling one, which continues to intrigue. It compels because it is in some measure reflective of belief, or desire to believe, in resurrection, and the concept of return is at the heart of so many myths, not just of the Christian story but also of many older stories such as that of Orpheus and Eurydice and its numerous retellings. The compulsion of the returned is at the heart of many of literature's greatest works. The intrigue is, however, almost equally important; what, for instance, could motivate Agatha to accept the returned husband? Did she simply suppress any suspicion of the other family? Was she driven by the need to provide her daughter with a father?

There is no doubt from the Agatha letter that Melville was drawn to the mystery of the story regarding motivation. But again, it is to Hawthorne that the story is offered:

> I have a little turned the subject over in my mind with a view to a regular story to be founded on these striking incidents. But, thinking

---

[19] Parker, *Herman Melville: A Biography*, 2, p. 115.
[20] The proposal that Melville's father had a child out of wedlock is fuelled very much by the fact this is a main plot in *Pierre* and by a claim, referred to in a letter, apparently made against the father's estate by two women. See Amy Puett Emmers, 'Melville's Closet Skeleton: A New Letter about the Illegitimacy Incident in *Pierre*', *Studies in the American Renaissance* (1977), 339–43; Henry A. Murray, Harvey Myerson and Eugene Taylor, 'Allan Melvill's By-Blow', *Melville Society Extracts*, 61 (1985), 1–6; Philip Young, *The Private Melville* (University Park: Pennsylvania State University Press, 1993) and Parker, *Herman Melville: A Biography*, 1, pp. 62–5.

again, it has occurred to me that this thing lies very much in a vein, with which you are peculiarly familiar. To be plump, I think that in this matter you would make a better hand at it than I would. – Besides, the thing seems naturally to gravitate towards you . . . it seems to me that with your great power in these things, you can construct a story of remarkable interest out of this material . . . you have a skeleton of actual reality to build about with fulness & veins & beauty. And if I thought I could do it as well you, why, I should not let you have it.[21]

The metaphor of the skeleton is notable here. As in Hawthorne's image of the romance-writer in 'The Custom House', the skeleton is actuality, the bare-boned and impoverished real, which Hawthorne is able to transform with the touch of the imaginative. However, Melville does much more than offer a 'skeleton' to Hawthorne. One other remarkable feature of the letter is that Melville sketches out so fully the story that he does not intend to write that Hawthorne must have felt entirely confused about his motivation. Melville suggests starting with a shipwreck ('then there must be a storm'), and he creates the character of Agatha's father, 'an old widower' and suggests generating tension by having her resolve never to marry a sailor.[22] Indeed, the letter is almost comic in Melville's simultaneously insisting the story is a gift to Hawthorne and generating the imaginative touches that testify to his own creative engagement with it. The allusions to Shakespeare's late plays are also unmistakable: from *The Winter's Tale*, with its central family broken for 16 years, to *The Tempest* which starts with a storm and a shipwreck and develops with a castaway, a widowed father and a marriageable daughter.

Why should Melville propose that the Agatha story should be written up by Hawthorne? There is one obvious answer to this, and Melville himself hints at it, but there is a somewhat less obvious reason, which nevertheless testifies to an enduring concern of Melville. The obvious reason is that Hawthorne had already touched on many of the issues raised by the Agatha material in his story 'Wakefield', first published in 1835 and collected in *Twice-Told Tales*. In the Agatha letter, Melville alludes to 'Wakefield', though not by its title: 'And here I am reminded of your *London husband*; tho' the cases so widely contrast.'[23] Set, as Melville observes, in London, 'Wakefield' is the story of a man who one evening, having told his wife he is going on a journey for a few days, leaves his home, takes lodgings in the next street and unknown to his wife lives there for over 20 years. During

---

[21] Melville, *Correspondence*, pp. 234, 237.
[22] Ibid., pp. 235, 237.
[23] Ibid., p. 235.

this time he is declared dead and his estate settled. Then one evening he simply returns to his wife, 'quietly, as from a day's absence, and became a loving spouse till death'.[24] Hawthorne tells us the story of Wakefield as an anecdote in the story's first paragraph. The remainder of the tale is a curious amalgamation of imaginative reconstruction of Wakefield's story and an analysis of the motivation to relinquish one's place in life. Typically, Hawthorne provides a factual prefatory account of the incident, then moves to the subjunctive mood ('Let us now imagine'), blurs this into the present tense then concludes with a return to the subjunctive. This intriguing, and intriguingly managed, tale is, as Melville saw, a 'London' story, where urban alienation, one of modernity's consequences, means that a husband may live in the next street to his wife and not be detected. It is also a Rip Van Winkle story of flight and return and a story about the desire to challenge the restrictions of our lives with an awareness of the cost involved:

> Amid the seeming confusion of our mysterious world, individuals are so nicely adjusted to a system, and systems to one another, and to a whole, that, by stepping aside for a moment, a man exposes himself to a fearful risk of losing his place forever. Like Wakefield, he may become, as it were, the Outcast of the Universe.[25]

The fact that Hawthorne offers no simple moral to the tale ensures that its materials intrigue, and the central idea of voluntary disappearance, a temporary or permanent rejection of a chosen life has intrigued numerous authors, most of whom are male. Beginning again, seizing an opportunity is a staple of a good deal of fiction, and is a notable recurrence in suspense, thriller and detective writing where, usually through an accident a protagonist is reported dead and consequently given the opportunity to choose a new life. Dashiell Hammett uses the trope in the story of Flitcraft from *The Maltese Falcon* (1930), and so does Richard Wright in his existential novel *The Outsider* (1953), in the character of Cross Damon. Flitcraft and Damon are examples of losing place, questioning one's role and identity, and confronting the chance to remake one's life. After his momentary insight into an unordered universe, Flitcraft rebuilds his former life elsewhere; Damon tests the very boundaries of his identity. Disappearance and absent character are also staples in the fictions of Paul Auster, compounded imaginatively by recurring references in his work to various writings by

---

[24] Nathaniel Hawthorne, *Tales and Sketches* (New York: Library of America, 1982), p. 290.
[25] Ibid., p. 298.

Poe, Hawthorne and Melville. E. L. Doctorow reimagined Wakefield as a contemporary in a short story that shares Hawthorne's title. Melville was certainly correct in realizing that the Agatha story was powerful literary material, and in his own lifetime the problematics of absence and return were repeatedly popularized; by Alexandre Dumas père in his retelling of the sixteenth-century case of Martin Guerre, and the publication of Alfred Tennyson's narrative poem 'Enoch Arden' in 1864.

As Hawthorne indicates, what it means to 'step aside for a moment' raises questions of self-dislocation, responsibility to family and community, and the nature of freedom and identity. These are also in some crucial ways questions of modernity, of social transitions and putative ruptures that potentially dislocate and challenge any sense of what one's 'place' is or might be. Consequently, modernity, as an attitude, demands a mode of self-examination which may be unwelcome. In Foucault's formulation, in modernity we are no longer involved in a search for 'formal structures with universal value' but in an analysis of how we are constituted 'as subjects of what we are doing, thinking, saying'. This necessarily involves the possibility of relinquishing our constructed identity as subject, 'the contingency that has made us what we are, the possibility of no longer being, doing, or thinking what we are, do, or think'.[26] Melville scripts this process repeatedly, with dislocated characters such as Bartleby and Israel Potter. Both in some respects are avatars of Pip 'The Castaway' in *Moby-Dick*, who having been deserted in the ocean, gains, like Flitcraft, a new and unwelcome insight into his being; 'He saw God's foot upon the treadle of the loom, and spoke it; and therefore his shipmates called him mad.'[27] Hawthorne wrote also of the individual's need to re-examine identity at a time of transition in 'My Kinsman Major Molineux', an important text used by Melville in *Israel Potter*.

It may be that in reflecting on the Agatha story, Melville perceived a common bond between Agatha's absent husband, Wakefield and Bartleby. These are characters who step aside from a system, and face the consequences. They are also characters whose motivation is either unexplained or misunderstood; 'Bartleby, the Scrivener' is very much a companion piece to 'Wakefield'. Melville's description of Bartleby as a 'bit of wreck in the mid Atlantic' echoes both Pip and Hawthorne's meditation on how one might become 'the Outcast of the Universe'.[28] Both in some

---

[26] Foucault, 'What Is Enlightenment?', p. 46.
[27] Herman Melville, *Moby-Dick* (Evanston, IL: Northwestern University Press, 1988), p. 414.
[28] Melville, *The Piazza Tales*, p. 32.

measure allude to Defoe's *Robinson Crusoe*; a character never, it seems far from Melville's mind – indeed, at one point in the Agatha letter, Melville mistakenly uses the name 'Robinson' when he means Robertson.[29] The sense of being adrift or a castaway recurs in Melville's self-definition in the mid-1850s and becomes so integral to the scene of writing as to multiply the mystery of Melville's motives in writing the Agatha letter. The story that he heard touches and excites him, yet he offers it to Hawthorne, with his advice on how to tell the tale.

Only one letter to Melville from Hawthorne and his wife Sophia survives, and so we simply cannot know of his response to the Agatha letter, though there has been some speculation that he did consider working on the story.[30] We do know, however, that the Agatha case fascinated Melville for many months, and possibly considerably longer. In October 1852 he presented Hawthorne with a few further suggestions on how it should be written up, focusing on Robertson's background as a sailor and Melville's perception of a slowly developing moral responsibility to his deserted first wife. By December, though, it is apparent that Hawthorne had declined the story and that Melville had decided to work on it himself. While many of Melville's letters are lost simply because his correspondents did not preserve them, his wife Elizabeth made copies of some that he wrote. One of these transcribed letters is written to Hawthorne, probably from December 1852, and here Melville states that he will follow the advice to write up the Agatha story himself, and he asks for the return of the material sent in August. Hawthorne clearly did so, and these materials are in the Houghton Library at Harvard. As so often with Melville, a series of puzzling issues proliferates, leading to often intense speculation. When he took back the Agatha materials in December 1852, he had been aware of the case for almost six months, having first heard of it in July. It was simply unprecedented for Melville to have held an idea for a work for such a long time without developing it. In fact, the speed with which Melville composed is rather striking. He completed his first two novels, *Typee* and *Omoo* within about eighteen months, and between 1849 and 1852 he was finishing about one novel a year; and these include three lengthy works, *Mardi*, *White-Jacket* and *Moby-Dick*. The failure to write up the Agatha story may be due to a loss of confidence in his writing or in his sense of a readership after the failure of *Pierre*.

There is also the intriguing possibility that Melville did produce a work of fiction based on the Agatha case. Without an unforeseen manuscript turning up, this of course remains speculative, but there is plausible

---

[29] Melville, *Correspondence*, p. 236.
[30] See ibid., p. 606.

evidence that such a work was produced, and that it was titled *The Isle of the Cross*. Looking at letters within the Melville family, Parker has argued lucidly and increasingly tenaciously, for the existence of the manuscript, and he presents this in his Melville biography. It had been proposed several times that there was a missing manuscript called 'The Story of Agatha', but as Parker discovered, there are two references to a manuscript specifically called *The Isle of the Cross*.[31] Both occur in letters from Melville's cousin Priscilla to his sister Augusta. We do not have the letters that Augusta wrote, but in May 1853 Priscilla wonders when *The Isle of the Cross* will appear: 'When will the "Isle of the Cross" make its appearance? I am constantly looking in the journals & magazines that come in my way, for notices of it.'[32] In June she comments on the coincidence of the book's being finished just as Herman and Elizabeth's third child, Lizzie, is born: 'the "Isle of the Cross" is almost a twin sister of the little one & I think she should be nam'd for the heroine – if there is such a personage – the advent of the two are singularly near together'.[33] Furthermore, on 11 June, Melville's local daily paper, the *Springfield Republican*, reported that 'Herman Melville has gone to New York to superintend the issue of a new work.'[34] Even more fascinating than the putative existence of a manuscript, however, is the possibility that Melville was unable to interest a publisher in it. In November 1853, five months after the supposed visit to New York with the manuscript, Melville writes to his usual publishers, Harper and Brothers (known generally as Harpers). This letter is a request for an advance of $300 on his account, and it promises a future book, on Tortoise Hunting. But there is also a reference to a work not accepted for publication: 'In addition to the work which I took to New York last Spring, but which I was prevented from printing at that time; I have now in hand, and pretty well on towards completion, another book – 300 pages, say – partly of nautical adventure, and partly – or, rather, chiefly, of Tortoise Hunting Adventure.'[35] There are several possible reasons why Harpers, if they indeed did, might have refused to publish a book based on the Agatha story. Perhaps chief among these is the reception that had been given to *Pierre*, which indicated that Melville's critical standing was low; perhaps at the lowest point since his writing career began; although they did give him the $300 for which he asked. There may have also been a legal concern over a story dealing with actual people, the Robertson

---

[31] See Harrison Hayford, 'The Significance of Melville's "Agatha" Letters', *ELH, A Journal of English Literary History*, 13:4 (1946), 299–310.
[32] Quoted in Parker, *Herman Melville: A Biography*, 2, p. 155.
[33] Ibid.
[34] Quoted in Melville, *Correspondence*, p. 249.
[35] Ibid., p. 250.

families, a possibility given some support by Melville's statement that he was 'prevented' from publishing it – that is, the manuscript was perhaps not simply rejected, there was some other barrier to its publication.

Neither reason seems sufficiently compelling. Melville's letter to Harpers, presumably because of the request for an advance, prompted an enquiry into Melville's book sales. *Pierre* had certainly sold fewer copies than Melville's recent work: 1,916 copies compared with 2,771 for *Moby-Dick* and generally the chart of Melville's book sales indicated an author declining in popularity. The high point was *Omoo* (6,328 sold), followed by *Redburn* (4,316) and *White-Jacket* (4,145).[36] While the sales are disappointing, they are solid enough, and there was always the possibility of a return to the early popularity. Furthermore, Harpers were willing to advance Melville the requested money on advance sales and they were soon to encourage him to submit work to their *New Monthly Magazine* (Melville published seven sketches there between 1854 and 1856). On the other hand, it is telling that *Pierre* was the last novel of Melville's that Harpers published. They brought out his collection of Civil War poems, *Battle-Pieces*, in 1866, but his subsequent fiction was published in the United States by G. P. Putnam or by Dix and Edwards. The possible fear of a legal concern is, again, not entirely convincing. After all, a distinguished lawyer, Clifford, had provided the story for Melville and did not appear to see any reason against it forming the basis for a fictional work.

If Harpers did reject the Agatha story (or somehow 'prevent' it from being published), it must have confirmed and compounded Melville's acute sense of alienation and failure, perhaps to the point that he was wholly discouraged from seeking another publisher. Parker suggests that *The Isle of the Cross* was a dark work and speculates that at some point Melville gave up any attempt to publish it but allowed it to stand as a kind of lonely triumph, consoled by its existence if not its publication – he cites the aesthetic upheld by Hawthorne in his short story 'The Artist of the Beautiful' as a support for this.[37] It may also be, as several critics have suggested, that Melville used

---

[36] See ibid. The figures for *Typee* are misleading in this account, because while Harpers sold 1,779, it had first been published by Wiley and Putnam, for whom it had strong sales.

[37] See Parker, *Herman Melville: A Biography*, 2, pp. 160–1. Melville highlighted the following passage in his copy of *Mosses from an Old Manse*: 'It is requisite for the ideal artist to possess a force of character that seems hardly compatible with its delicacy; he must keep his faith in himself while the incredulous world assails him with its utter disbelief; he must stand up against mankind and be his own sole disciple, both as respects his genius and the objects to which it is directed'. See Jonathan A. Cook, 'Introduction to Melville's Marginalia in Nathaniel Hawthorne's *Mosses from an Old Manse*' at <http://melvillesmarginalia.org/UserViewFramesetIntro.php?id=16> [accessed 31 October 2013].

the reworked Agatha material elsewhere in his fiction. For example, one of the sketches in 'The Encantadas' from *The Piazza Tales* deals specifically with desertion and endurance; and there are also a few tortoises and a bit of tortoise hunting. The eighth of the sketches set in the Galápagos Islands, 'Norfolk Isle and the Chola Widow' relates the story of Hunilla, a Peruvian woman who had been stranded alone on an island for an unspecified period of time following the deaths of her husband and brother.[38] The group had gone to the island to collect tortoise oil but the French captain who promised to collect them did not return, and the men were killed in an accident. The obvious connections to the Agatha story are seen in the consequences of betrayal and in Hunilla's endurance, but also in the mysterious aspects of the story, of the narrator's withholding something from us, and Hunilla's silence; it is implied that she was raped by a crew of whale-men during her ordeal, and that they simply left her on the island to die. However, whatever connects *The Isle of the Cross* and 'Norfolk Isle and the Chola Widow' is oblique and a matter for speculation.

The Agatha letter and a possible lost manuscript are among many intriguing episodes and incidents of Melville's career, and one likely to continue to interest; it is even a plotline in Sheridan Hay's 2007 novel, *The Secret of Lost Things*. Lost works, unpublished works, destroyed works, hold a strong fascination for us, and the story of the lost or endangered manuscript appears so often in novels that it is almost a subgenre of fiction. There are numerous famous lost works in literary history. Byron's publisher burnt his *Memoirs*; a suitcase containing a large amount of Hemingway's work was stolen in 1922; Malcolm Lowry had to reconstruct *Ultramarine* after the manuscript was stolen from his publisher; the working manuscript of the novel Sylvia Plath was working on at the time of her death has disappeared, and she destroyed a novel that predates *The Bell Jar*. A missing manuscript excites not only because of the status of the author, but because it teases with possibility, a kind of romance quest. When manuscripts that were thought lost turn up unexpectedly, the event often makes headline news; the finding of the Boswell papers at Malahide Castle; an unpublished poem by Tennyson, Thomas Hardy's notes for a novel. And there is always the possibility that supposedly lost manuscripts or manuscripts that no-one knew existed, will turn up. This happened in 1983 when a partial manuscript for *Typee* was discovered in Gansevoort, New York. The existence of this manuscript will require a revision of the then authoritative Northwestern-Newberry edition of the novel that appeared in 1968; it is also a starting-

---

[38] See Basem L. Ra'ad, '"The Encantadas" and *The Isle of the Cross*: Melvillean Dubieties, 1853–54', *American Literature*, 63 (1991), 316–23.

point among Melville scholars for a fundamental challenge to the concepts and practices of textual editing, as John Bryant has shown in his 2008 book *Melville Unfolding* and in his pioneering work on the 'fluid text'. The idea of Melville unfolding, continually developing in the very act of writing, offers important fresh approaches to his work.

But there is much more to the Agatha story than the tale of a missing manuscript, exciting though this is. In effect, the Agatha letters are the manuscripts that we have, and they illuminate a good deal about Melville's work and his practice as a writer. As noted earlier, in Clifford's report on the case, the shawls are of great importance. Robertson gives these three shawls to his son-in-law Gifford, along with the gold watch, during Gifford's visit to Alexandria. When Gifford returns to his wife and mother-in-law, it is evident that the shawls 'had been previously worn by some person'.[39] This is of course the moment when the suspicion of Robertson's bigamy grows stronger and is apparently confirmed, since these are not new shawls. The shawls, then, form a crucial moment in the plotting of the tale, and in his advice to Hawthorne, Melville draws particular attention to them: 'The narrative from the Diary is instinct with significance. – Consider the mention of the *shawls* & the inference derived from it'.[40] Melville sees the shawls as representing not only the moment of realization, indicative of Robertson's character and motivation. His passing on the shawls to his first family is an attempt at some kind of reparation, and acknowledgement in some measure of his neglect of them. The gift also suggests a reluctance to waste the clothing. After drawing attention to the shawls in the letter, Melville goes on to offer some thoughts about Robertson's character.

As suggested, one of the reasons for Melville's alerting Hawthorne to the Agatha story lies in its similarity to the story of the voluntarily absent Wakefield. But there is a further reason for choosing Hawthorne, and it is one that opens up a somewhat neglected aspect of Melville's own work. In one respect, Melville's advice about the shawls is curiously redundant; if he did decide to write up the story, Hawthorne could hardly have missed their significance. But in a more important regard, Melville's attentiveness indicates another of the attributes that the two writers shared; an alertness to the symbolism and significance of clothing. The shawls are not simply the literal clue in the detective story; they are also symbolic, indicating a history, an attitude, a relation. In 'Wakefield', Hawthorne conveys the ordinariness of the evening on which the husband leaves by a description

---

[39] Melville, *Correspondence*, p. 624.
[40] Ibid., p. 237.

of the clothes he wears: 'Let us now imagine Wakefield bidding adieu to his wife. It is the dusk of an October evening. His equipment is a drab great-coat, a hat covered with an oil-cloth, top boots, an umbrella in one hand and a small portmanteau in the other.'[41] The outfit is notable for not being notable at all; it is the ordinary and anonymous outfit of a man going away for a few days – not for more than 20 years. It is an outfit that will draw no attention to himself, will allow him to 'melt into the great mass of London life'.[42] But while Wakefield is dressed to give no clue to his intentions, Hawthorne does provide us with a glimpse of his life with this one-sentence description. It is his 'drab' predictable existence that Wakefield is countering, seeking to challenge or test the limits of his ordinary and self-protecting life, represented by his encompassing great-coat, protective oil-cloth, umbrella and top-boots. This is a man who needs to step outside the forces that have constituted him as a particular subject. Hawthorne imagines Wakefield's homecoming as an impulsive gesture, a sudden desire during a rainstorm for, in effect, his old clothes: 'Shall he stand, wet and shivering here, when his own hearth has a good fire to warm him, and his own wife will run to fetch the gray coat and small-clothes, which, doubtless, she has kept carefully in the closet of their bed-chamber?'[43] To resume his former life is just the act of putting his old comfortable clothes on; particularly the overcoat but also the knee-breeches (small clothes), tellingly kept, he believes, by the wife he deserted. The adventure or lacuna, whatever it was, is over and he is realigning himself with the familiar.

As might be expected, Hawthorne's use of clothing as symbolic is most fully represented in *The Scarlet Letter*, where he creates a particular relation between clothing, identity and sexual transgression, all of which could have been readily adapted to tell the story of Agatha and her errant husband. From the very first appearance of the convicted adulteress Hester Prynne, Hawthorne engages us with the association of clothing as an issue of submission and transgression, obedience and defiance. Hester, carrying her 3-month-old daughter Pearl, who has no publicly acknowledged father, leaves the prison to stand on public display in the market-place. According to the Puritan statutes of seventeenth-century Boston, Hester must publicly wear a token denoting her adultery. Although Hawthorne is occluding a complex history, this being after all a romance, he makes it clear that the

---

[41] Hawthorne, *Tales and Sketches*, p. 291.
[42] Ibid., p. 292.
[43] Ibid., p. 297.

crowd expects her to wear a modest badge bearing the letter *A*.[44] However, Hester appears wearing a very different kind of letter:

> On the breast of her gown, in fine red cloth, surrounded with an elaborate embroidery and fantastic flourishes of gold thread, appeared the letter A. It was so artistically done, and with so much fertility and gorgeous luxuriance of fancy, that it had all the effect of a last and fitting decoration to the apparel which she wore; and which was of a splendor in accordance with the taste of the age, but greatly beyond what was allowed by the sumptuary regulations of the colony.[45]

Hester's knowing defiance of sumptuary laws, of course, marks her out immediately as transgressive, even where she appears obedient to the demands and other laws of her community. Furthermore, her transgression intensifies to the point where it wholly defines her as a person. The fact that she earns a living by her needlework, and that her work is highly prized, allows Hawthorne to develop fully the most important theme of his romance; the relationship between idealism and actuality, between obedience and self-expression. Clothes are deeply part of this relationship; for whom do we wear clothes? Do they express our inner self or our social self? How do we find the balance between these often (and in Hester's case, corrosively) conflicting desires?

For all Hawthorne sets the romance in the historical past, it is interesting to think of *The Scarlet Letter* as a kind of dystopia, since a common feature of dystopian fiction – of George Orwell's *Nineteen Eighty-Four* or Margaret Atwood's *The Handmaid's Tale* – is control over clothing, and the use of

---

[44] Puritan attitudes and laws regarding adultery have occasioned much debate, and have drawn attention to the departures that Hawthorne made from historical actuality. For some time, the statute book dictated the death penalty for adulterers, and Hawthorne alludes both to this and to the practice of branding (Hawthorne, *Novels*, p. 162). There are historical records for both branding and execution in Massachusetts, and punishment by whipping and by fines. It is not until 1694 that a law is passed, in Salem, which requires a woman convicted of adultery to wear a badge with the letter A sewn on her clothes. Since *The Scarlet Letter* is set in the period 1642–9, it is obvious that Hawthorne wants to make a specific, though ahistorical, association between clothing, transgression and punishment. See Frederick Newberry, 'A Red-Hot "A" and a Lusting Divine: Sources for *The Scarlet Letter*', *The New England Quarterly*, 60 (1987), 256–64. Hawthorne notes that the uncertainty over whether Hester was guilty of adultery or fornication (a less serious offence) determined against the death sentence. Several commentators have noted the parallels between Hester Prynne and the historical Hester Craford, who in Salem in 1688 was sentenced to be whipped for fornication, which had resulted in her bearing a child. The Craford case is especially intriguing because Hawthorne's great-great grandfather, William Hathorne [sic], was the sentencing magistrate.

[45] Hawthorne, *Novels*, p. 163.

dress to signify not an inner identity but the subordination of identity to a political or ideological reality. Today recurring debates on banning the burka or the hijab frequently focus on the issue of freedom and control.⁴⁶ In *Nineteen Eighty-Four*, Orwell has Julia articulate the belief that freedom to choose her mode of dress is not *symbolic* of freedom, an analogy; it *is* freedom, freedom expressed in the most fundamental of ways. After she and Winston have claimed their private room, she declares:

> And do you know what I'm going to do next? I'm going to get hold of a real woman's frock from somewhere and wear it instead of these bloody trousers. I'll wear silk stockings and high-heeled shoes! In this room I'm going to be a woman, not a Party comrade.⁴⁷

Atwood has drawn particular attention to how dress rules in dystopias are actually extensions of often unwritten codes of all societies: 'Utopias and dystopias both take a lot of pleasure in describing costume. What is worn and what is forbidden? What cannot be worn, who can wear what and under what circumstances? This is of course just an exaggerated variant on what goes on anyway.'⁴⁸ In fact, all societies and cultures have codes regarding clothing, sometimes written as laws, sometimes unwritten – one of the first records of a sumptuary law is from Greece in the sixth century BC.⁴⁹ Hawthorne of course draws attention to Puritan sumptuary laws when he first introduces Hester. For the most part these were modifications of English laws that first had come into existence in the fourteenth century, where the focus was on the requirement to dress appropriately to one's class. The Puritans were to develop these hierarchical laws further, adding the stipulation that with the assertion that certain materials were illegal because

---

⁴⁶ In Orwell's Oceania, there are no sumptuary laws, there are actually no laws at all, but dress denotes rank in the party and consequently one's social role. O'Brien wears the black overalls of the Inner Party (George Orwell, *Nineteen Eighty-Four*, (Harmondsworth: Penguin, 1974), p. 12), and the young 'Spies' have a uniform of 'blue shorts, grey shirts and red neckerchiefs' (ibid., p. 22). In an ironic allusion to its history as a signifying colour, members of the Junior Anti-Sex League wear a scarlet sash to denote chastity. In Atwood's theocratic Republic of Gilead, there are strict sumptuary laws and all must be dressed in colours that represent their social function.

⁴⁷ Ibid., p. 117.

⁴⁸ Quoted in Cynthia Kuhn, '"Clothes Would Only Confuse Them": Sartorial Culture in *Oryx and Crake*', in *Styling Texts*, ed. Cynthia Kuhn and Cindy Carlson (Youngstown, NY: Cambria Press, 2007), p. 396.

⁴⁹ See Alan Hunt, *Governance of the Consuming Passions* (Basingstoke: Macmillan, 1996), p. 18. Many sumptuary laws were to do with protectionism and containing threats to certain trades.

they were indicative of vanity and luxury. Thus, the Sumptuary Law passed in Massachusetts in October 1651 includes both the by now conventional requirement to dress according to one's social position and income, but also declares that dressing inappropriately is an offence against God:

> Although seuerall declaratjons and orders have binn made by this Courte against excesse in apparrell, both of men and weomen … wee cannot but to our greife take notice that jntollerable excesse and bravery hath crept in vppon vs … to the dishonnor of God, the scandall of our profession, the consumption of estates, and altogether vnsuiteable to our pouertje; and although wee acknowledge it to be a matter of much difficultje, in regard of the blindnes of mens mindes and the stubbornes of their willes, to sett downe exact rules to confjne all sorts of persons, yett wee cannot but account it our duty to comend vnto all sorts of persons the sober and moderate vse of those blessings which, beyond expectation, the Lord hath bin pleased to affoard vnto vs in this wildernes, and also to declare our vtter detestation and dislike that men or weomen of meane conditjon should take vppon them the garbe of gentlemen, by wearing gold or silver lace or buttons, or points at their knees, or to walk in great bootes, or weomen of the same rancke to weare silke or tiffany hoodes or scarfes, which though allowable to persons of greater estates, or more liberal education [are] jntollerable in persons of such like condition: itt is therefore ordered by this Courte, and the authoritje thereof, that no person within this jurisdiccon … whose visible estates, reall and personall, shall not exceede the true and indifferent valew of two hundred pounds, shall weare any gold or silver lace, or gold and silver buttons, or any bone lace above two shillings p yard, or silk hoods or scarfes, vppon the pcenaltje of tenn shillings for euery such offence, and euery such deljnquent to be presented by the graund jury.[50]

The five-volume collection, *The Records of the Governor and Company of the Massachusetts Bay* is a fascinating sourcebook for many issues, including the repeated attempts to control what people wore. Massachusetts had introduced sumptuary laws in 1619, as soon as it had a representative assembly. Especially pertinent to Hester's transgression is the law of 1634:

> The Court, takeing into consideracon the greate, superfluous, & unnecessary expences occaconed by reason of some newe & immodest

---

[50] Nathaniel Shurtleff (ed.), *The Records of the Governor and Company of the Massachusetts Bay in New England* (New York: AMS Press, 1968), 4, pp. 60–1.

fashions, as also the ordinary weareing of silver, golde, and silke laces, girdles, hatbands, etc. hath therefore ordered that noe person, either man or woman, shall hereafter make or buy any apparell, either wollen, silke, or lynnen, with any lace on it, silver, golde, silke or threed, under the penalty of forfeiture of such cloathes.[51]

Hester's fantastic embroidery is offensive in itself, but Hawthorne's suggestions of fantastic orientalist luxuriance, silk and gold, are an affront to the laws of her society. Indeed, Increase Mather proclaimed that King Philip's War of 1675–6 was God's retribution for the community's clothing transgressions.[52] While Hester herself dresses modestly, apart from the luxurious *A*, her dressing of Pearl compounds her rebellion:

> Her own dress was of the coarsest materials and the most sombre hue, with only that one ornament – the scarlet letter – which it was her doom to wear. The child's attire, on the other hand, was distinguished by a fanciful, or, we might rather say, a fantastic ingenuity, which served, indeed, to heighten the airy charm that early began to develop itself in the little girl, but which appeared to have also a deeper meaning.[53]

Hester's rebellion is not *represented* by the act of clothing herself and Pearl as she chooses; it *is* the rebellion. It is the statement of her wilful difference, but also of her sense of a secret kinship with others, as Hawthorne makes clear in 'Hester at her Needle'. Hester makes clothes for almost all, sewing charitably for the poor but earning her living by supplying the decorative materials that all secretly desire. Clothing and consideration of clothing is central to Hawthorne's purposes in *The Scarlet Letter*, and he exploits the fundamental ambivalence towards clothing and our attitudes towards it. As Elizabeth Wilson has expressed it, the 'strangeness of dress' is the link it makes between 'the biological body' and the 'social being', requiring us to see that the human body is not just a 'biological entity' but 'an organism in culture, a cultural artefact'.[54] The essential function of clothing is modesty, a covering for nakedness and a protection against the elements. But dress is simultaneously self-adornment, a means of attracting others, the body made alluring not by revealing nakedness but by its artful concealment.

---

[51] Ibid., 1, p. 126.
[52] See Ruth Mayer, '"Intollerable Excesse and Bravery": On Dressing Up in Puritan New England', in Kuhn and Carlson (eds), *Styling Texts*, pp. 91–110.
[53] Hawthorne, *Novels*, p. 189.
[54] Wilson, *Adorned*, p. 2.

Ostensibly dress represses and conceals the sexual, but it actually may flaunt it. Hawthorne extends this ambivalent function of clothing to a consideration of the consequences of Puritanical attempts to suppress sexual expression, and this is of course a key theme of *The Scarlet Letter*. It is also central to one of the first important studies of dress, J. C. Flügel's *The Psychology of Clothes*, published in 1930. Despite their function as serving modesty, Flügel declares that the 'ultimate purpose' of clothes is, 'to add to the sexual attractiveness of their wearers and to stimulate the sexual interest of admirers of the opposite sex and the envy of rivals of the same sex'.[55] Of course, clothes serve many more social and personal purposes than the sexual, but Flügel's comments are apposite for Hawthorne's use of clothing in *The Scarlet Letter*. As we shall see, Melville represents clothing in more ways than the sexual. He considers the ambivalence of clothing in its capacity both to represent and simultaneously conceal a self, to suggest a self that is coherent rather than fragmented, to indicate one's membership of a group and one's difference from it. In this respect he explores the paradox of fashion; 'to dress fashionably is both to stand out and to merge with the crowd, to lay claim to the exclusive and to follow the herd'.[56]

The Scarlet Letter is Hawthorne's fullest examination of clothing as symbolic, partly because his interest in dress has become integral to his fascination with the Puritans. The account that he gives in 'The Custom-House' of encountering the elaborately embroidered scarlet letter and its history makes the letter charged with the kinship that he feels to it. Certainly, the letter fascinated Hawthorne, and he referred to it in 'Endicott and the Red Cross', a story published in 1838. His use of dress was actually noted by Henry James, himself keenly alert to the economic and social messages that clothing provides. In his study of Hawthorne, he calls *The Scarlet Letter* 'the finest piece of imaginative writing yet put forth in the country', and claims that with its publication, America had at last 'produced a novel that belonged to literature, and to the forefront of it'.[57] Oddly, James recalls that as a boy his first memorable encounter with the book was not in reading it (he was too young to access the family's copy), but by being powerfully impressed at seeing a portrait of Hester. Taken to the annual exhibition at the National Academy, he

> encountered a representation of a pale, handsome woman, in a quaint black dress and a white coif, holding between her knees an elfish-

---

[55] J. C. Flügel, *The Psychology of Clothes* (London: Hogarth Press, 1930), p. 26.
[56] Wilson, *Adorned in Dreams*, p. 6.
[57] James, 'Hawthorne', pp. 402–3.

looking little girl, fantastically dressed and crowned with flowers. Embroidered on the woman's breast was a great crimson *A*, over which the child's fingers, as she glanced strangely out of the picture, were maliciously playing. I was told that this was Hester Prynne and little Pearl, and that when I grew older I might read their interesting history. But the picture remained vividly imprinted on my mind; I had been vaguely frightened and made uneasy by it; and when, years afterwards, I first read the novel, I seemed to myself to have read it before, and to be familiar with its two strange heroines.[58]

The Scarlet Letter inspired several paintings, but it is likely that James is referring to Tompkins Harrison Matteson's *The Scarlet Letter*, which was shown at the National Academy of Design in 1860, when James was aged 17.[59] Matteson consulted with Hawthorne on the painting. If this is the painting to which James alludes, his memory is not entirely accurate. The painting includes Dimmesdale and Chillingworth as well as Hester and Pearl; it is in fact a representation of the episode in chapter 12, 'The Minister's Vigil', when Hester, Pearl and Dimmesdale stand on the scaffold at night, as Chillingworth looks on, and the letter *A* appears in the sky. Pearl's head is not covered with flowers, and she is not touching the letter, since Dimmesdale stands between Pearl and her mother. What is interesting is not that James is misremembering, but that his recollection creates an image cluster that Hawthorne provides in the fiction. This is not just in terms of the vivid pictorial qualities of his representation, but in the very communication of meaning and suggestion through clothing. James's discomfort is visually stimulated, deriving from a sense of the incongruities in the painting, the contradiction of clothing, the 'ungrammatical' nature of the dress. How might the woman's 'quaint black dress' be reconciled with her wearing the 'great crimson *A*' and with the 'fantastically dressed' child with the flowers on her head? James's study of Hawthorne is in some respects an examination of his own understanding of fiction, and this is a key moment in finding an origin for his attention to the signification of dress.

So, one reason for Melville's suggestion that Hawthorne write the Agatha story stems from Hawthorne's interest in the symbolism of

---

[58] Ibid., p. 402.
[59] Another candidate is Hugues Merle's 1861 'Hester et Perle', which does concentrate on the two figures, representing them in the Madonna and child pose (Chillingworth and Dimmesdale are distant background figures). However, James does specifically state that the painting he saw was at the National Academy, whereas Merle's painting was shown in Paris in 1861 and bought by an American collector, William Walters and shipped to the United States in 1865.

clothes, evident in *The Scarlet Letter* and elsewhere. But Melville himself was considerably interested in clothing and symbolism. This is partly because reflections on clothing are expressive of his major preoccupation as a writer; the relation between one's inner life and public behaviour. At times these elements are in conflict and the blending of an inner reality with the external world is a necessary aspiration. Hawthorne seemed to have solved this problem by developing a style of writing that was publicly acceptable and attractive while being true to his own feelings. Clothing always involves a negotiation between the needs and desires of the self and social acceptability, and Melville's repeated engagements with matters concerning dress frequently involve urgent issues regarding the self in society and in modernity. It is also important to note how constant Melville's interest in clothing was. Melville scholars have often remarked on the importance of Thomas Carlyle's 1834 book *Sartor Resartus* on the development of his prose style and his increasingly complex sense of narrative effect. This work is indeed of major significance, as will be detailed in Chapter 2. Carlyle, among many other things, considers the very meaning of clothes, remarking at one point, 'Clothes, as despicable as we think them, are so unspeakably significant.'[60] The phrase 'unspeakably significant' is particularly striking in its connotations. Clothes do not of course communicate orally, but we cannot avoid the fact that they do communicate and they may communicate significant truths; hence Henry James's recalled discomfiture at the purely visual clash of clothing in the Scarlet Letter portrait. While *Sartor Resartus* and Carlyle's thought generally came to mean a great deal to Melville, his attention to the unspeakable meanings of dress are evident long before that, and are central to an understanding of *Typee*.

By the time Melville was drawing Hawthorne's notice to the shawls, he had developed a way of looking at clothing that required the recognition of its symbolic as well as literal meanings. The desire to clothe another is rooted in concepts of hospitality, of family, of kinship, so Robertson's provision of the shawls suggests to Melville the acceptance of the abandoned family. To provide clothes is also to nominate oneself as a host; it is a gesture of hospitality and in some measure a claim to equality. Indeed, as Jacques Derrida emphasized, hospitality is a form of power, since it can be exercised only when the host is sovereign.[61] In *Robinson Crusoe*, Robinson effectively

---

[60] Thomas Carlyle, *Sartor Resartus*, ed. Kerry McSweeney and Peter Sabor (Oxford: Oxford University Press, 2008), p. 56.
[61] See Jacques Derrida and Anne Dufourmantelle, *Of Hospitality*, trans. Rachel Bowlby (Stanford, CA: Stanford University Press, 2000).

claims dominion over Friday by clothing him in his own image. Thus the naked Friday is transformed and made subservient; indeed, in an episode that has special resonance for *Typee*, Defoe makes the scene of clothing Friday (which causes him some discomfort) an act of civilizing, coming immediately after Robinson believes he has seen Friday's cannibalistic, savage tendencies.[62]

There is another striking example of the relation between power and the provision of clothing in a novel chronologically closer to Melville, *Oliver Twist*, which Dickens published in book form in 1838. In his preface to the third edition of 1841, Dickens defends his choice of the poor and the criminal as his subject matter, for which he had been much criticized, and clarifies what the reader will not find in the novel: 'Here are no canterings upon moonlit heaths, no merry-makings in the snuggest of all possible caverns, none of the attractions of dress, no embroidery, no lace, no jack-boots, no crimson coats and ruffles.'[63] But Dickens was always alert to clothing, and in his fiction social mobility is always signalled by changes of dress, and clothes do play a significant role in Oliver's story. After Oliver leaves the workhouse Dickens sets up the question of his future identity within two possibilities: the criminal underworld of Fagin or Brownlow's middle-class gentility. For a period Oliver oscillates between these two, and it is striking that in each identity, one of the first acts of the host is to claim him through an act of hospitality. In this regard, providing Oliver with the clothes appropriate to the identity ascribed to him is an act of power over someone unable to clothe himself, and both Fagin and Brownlow effectively claim ownership and possession through the right to dress him in their own image. These switches of clothes, and, by implication, of family and of communal identity, cause confusion for Oliver; in fact they generate what one fashion analyst has called clothing's 'identity ambivalence'.[64] Dickens emphasizes this confusion as sartorial as well as moral. In chapter 16, Oliver is kidnapped and returned to Fagin's gang, where of course his Brownlow clothes are radically out of place:

> 'Look at his togs, Fagin!' said Charley, putting the light so close to his new jacket as nearly to set him on fire. 'Look at his togs! Superfine cloth, and the heavy swell cut! Oh, my eye, what a game! And his books, too! Nothing but a gentleman, Fagin!'

[62] Daniel Defoe, *Robinson Crusoe*, ed. J. Donald Crowley (Oxford: Oxford World's Classics, 1990), pp. 207–8.
[63] Charles Dickens, *Oliver Twist* (Bloomsbury: Nonesuch Press, 1937), p. xviii.
[64] See chapter 2 in Fred Davis, *Fashion, Culture and Identity* (Chicago: University of Chicago Press, 1992).

'Delighted to see you looking so well, my dear', said the Jew, bowing with mock humility. 'The Artful shall give you another suit, my dear, for fear you should spoil that Sunday one.'[65]

The emphasis on clothing in *Oliver Twist* was remarked on by Emerson. Having been persuaded to read the novel, Emerson grumbled that it lacked insight into character and he thought Dickens (like Hawthorne) had no 'dramatic talent'. But, with *Sartor Resartus* fresh in his mind, he did note with approval Dickens's 'acute eye for costume' commenting 'he sees the expression of dress'.[66] As Emerson notes, it is about *costume*; that is, Oliver's identity within each group is determined by costume rather than clothing. Being reclothed by another as an act of reclamation recurs in Dickens's work, and it can be framed within poignancy or menace. What is especially interesting with regard to *Oliver Twist* is the association that Dickens thereby creates between Brownlow and Fagin. Of course Brownlow acts from generous benevolence while Fagin is morally reprehensible, but both are motivated to own Oliver and to dress him accordingly.

As noted, providing clothes can also be seen as a claim for equality or even, to use Derrida's terms, mastery. There's a notable example of this in William Faulkner's 1948 novel, *Intruder in the Dust*, a work deeply concerned with concepts of justice, deference, racial equality and the boundaries of identity. Early on, the white adolescent Chick Mallison is helped from an icy creek into which he has fallen, by Lucas Beauchamp, an elderly man descended from slaves who is legally defined as black. Lucas takes him back to his cabin, where he dries, warms and feeds him, and treats him exactly as a host treats a guest. This includes Chick's stripping out of his wet clothes and being wrapped up for a time in a quilt provided by Lucas's wife Molly. Being cocooned in the quilt entirely alters Chick's perception of the other, and will precipitate for him a crisis that is deliberately engineered by Lucas. Lucas in effect claims equality through being the host: a claim compounded by his refusing a tip from Chick. This sets in motion a series of initially comical attempts by Chick to make Lucas conform to their unequal status, but gradually evolving into a crisis for

---

[65] Dickens, *Oliver Twist*, p. 113.
[66] Ralph Waldo Emerson, 'Journal D' (1839), *Selected Journals 1820–42* (New York: Library of America, 2010), p. 698. As will be detailed in Chapter 2, Emerson greatly admired Carlyle and was instrumental in getting *Sartor Resartus* published (and acclaimed) in the United States.

him. Chick needs 're-equalization, reaffirmation of his identity and his white blood'; he must, he believes, reject the kinship and claim to equality that providing the quilt represents.[67]

To clothe someone else indicates some sense of kinship; after all, it is one of the fundamental duties of a parent to a child, and in St Matthew's Gospel, Christ specifies the provision of clothing as one of the characteristic actions of those who will be redeemed on the last day: 'I needed clothes and you clothed me.'[68] While the clothing of the other may be an act of charity, at a deeper level it is an acceptance of equality, community and kinship; the righteous are those who have accepted the other as an equal and act upon this acceptance. Melville suggests that Robertson's gift of the shawls is also recognition of kinship, responsibility and a reform of a personality. In 'Bartleby, the Scrivener', probably written in the summer of 1853, Melville makes intensive use of clothing and of these gospel verses in exploring themes of hospitality, power and social injustice.

Melville's attentiveness to the shawls is not an *ad hoc* gesture born out of a particular feature in the Agatha case. Throughout his fiction he draws the reader's attention to clothing: inappropriate clothing, clothing as the mark of the civilized, clothing as power, clothing as symbolic of identity (either stable or in crisis), clothing as an image of writing. In work spanning more than 40 years, from *Typee* right through to the unfinished *Billy Budd*, Melville notices dress, uniform, the choice of clothing, and makes these central to what is being developed in his fictions. On the face of it, this seems odd. For one thing, Melville generally showed little interest in his own clothing, travelling as lightly as he could, at times refusing to dress up for costume parties, and so on. Even though he had something of a penchant for oriental clothing, dressing informally at home in loose flowing robes (and Turkish slippers; he attended at least one costume party dressed as a Turk), he was no dandy.[69] Furthermore, unlike his contemporary Walt Whitman, Melville did not promote a crafted image of himself as a writer through his choice of clothing, and notably unlike Whitman, he made no use of photographic technology to further that image, actively resisting requests to be photographed or to have daguerreotypes made of him. While abroad he could be embarrassed by his choice of clothing, for instance, on a trip to

---

[67] William Faulkner, *Intruder in the Dust* in *Novels 1942–1954* (New York: Library of America, 1994), p. 303.
[68] Matthew 25.36–7.
[69] See Timothy Marr, *The Cultural Roots of American Islamicism* (Cambridge and New York: Cambridge University Press, 2006), p. 219; Parker, *Herman Melville: A Biography*, 1, pp. 760–1.

London in 1849 he felt his green jacket was making him a spectacle and he bought a more appropriate one.[70] A few years later he seems to have cared less, and to be travelling rather more lightly. In 1856 he spends a few days in Scotland on his way to Europe and the Holy Land, and he records a list of clothes to be laundered in Edinburgh:

Washing Edinburgh
----
9 Shirts
1 Night Shirt
7 Handkerchiefs
2 Pair Stockings
Draws & undershirts[71]

He also left his trunk of belongings at the American Consulate in Liverpool, and set off for the Holy Land, a trip that was to last six months, with only a carpet-bag.[72] While in Liverpool, he spent a few days with Hawthorne, who was then in post in the city as American Consul, though his home was a few miles along the coast, in Southport. The two had not met for four years, and in his lengthy Journal entry dated 20 November, Hawthorne noted Melville was 'a little paler, and perhaps a little sadder', wearing 'a rough outside coat'.[73] The two men made several trips together, walking along the sands at Southport, visiting Chester, and looking for a ship in Liverpool to take Melville to the continent. Melville brought very few clothes with him; 'the least bit of a bundle' Hawthorne noted, containing 'a night shirt and a tooth-brush'.[74] This prompted him to reflect that Melville was 'a person of very gentlemanly instincts in every respect, save that he is a little heterodox in the matter of clean linen'.[75]

In this 20th November record of what turned out to be the final meeting between Hawthorne and Melville (most of which is taken up by a description of Chester), Hawthorne could not resist articulating an

---

[70] Herman Melville, *Journals* (Evanston, IL: Northwestern University Press, 1989), pp. 39–40.
[71] Ibid., p. 140.
[72] Melville, *Correspondence*, p. 303.
[73] Quoted in Melville, *Journals*, p. 628.
[74] Ibid.
[75] Ibid. Hawthorne is echoing Samuel Johnson's statement of empathy with the poet Christopher Smart, who had been confined in an asylum for the insane; 'Another charge was, that he did not love clean linen; and I have no passion for it.' James Boswell, *The Life of Samuel Johnson* (London: Oxford University Press, 1966), p. 281.

analogy between Melville's habitually travelling light with his intellectual independence:

> This is the next best thing to going naked; and as he wears his beard and moustache, and so needs no dressing-case – nothing but a toothbrush – I do not know a more independent personage. He learned his travelling habits by drifting about, all over the South Sea, with no other clothes or equipage than a red flannel shirt and a pair of duck trowsers.[76]

This persistent lack of regard for his own clothing, however, should not lead us to believe that he took no interest in what other people wore, or that we need not pay attention to what his fictional characters are wearing – he is, after all, one of the very few writers to have used an article of clothing as the title for a novel. In fact, the anxieties, identities and, indeed, pathologies, of his fictional characters are made evident in their clothing. Frequently his characters are in the wrong clothes, wrong for the time, for their occupation, for the social moment, wrong as an expression of their own sense of identity. This may be a source of embarrassment but also of defiance; it may also indicate their own uncertain identity, an anxiety closely linked to the scrutiny of oneself as a subject in modernity.

Perhaps the lack of critical recognition of the role of clothes in Melville's work has to do with the kind of characters about whom he generally wrote. It may also have a good deal to do with the assumption that dress refers to the representation of women rather than to men, indeed studies of clothing and fashion in literature tend to be concerned with women's dress, except where specifically focused on the figure of the dandy.[77] Melville's work demonstrates little interest in women's clothing; this marks him as very different from, say, James, who wrote astutely of fashion and used fashion as way of delineating his female characters. Melville wrote so often of men only, and, with few exceptions, of men whose choice of clothing is severely restricted and who are very far from driven by fashion: whalers, merchant sailors, sailors in uniform, and so on. As Alison Lurie rather crudely puts it these are groups of people whose 'sartorial vocabulary' is limited;

> [The sartorial resources] of a sharecropper, for instance, may be limited to five or ten 'words' from which it is possible to create only a few 'sentences'

---

[76] Quoted in Melville, *Journals*, p. 633.
[77] See, for example, Clair Hughes, *Dressed in Fiction* (New York and Oxford: Berg, 2006); Kuhn and Carlson, *Styling Texts*; and Peter McNeil, Vicki Karaminas and Catherine Cole (eds), *Fashion in Fiction* (New York and Oxford: Berg, 2009).

almost bare of decoration and expressing only the most basic concepts. A so-called fashion leader, on the other hand, may have several hundred 'words' at his or her disposal, and thus be able to form thousands of different 'sentences' that will express a wide range of meanings.[78]

Presumably Lurie's offensiveness in equating actual vocabulary and intelligence with whatever sartorial vocabulary is available is unintended – though it is in fact compounded in her text by including photographs of a 1940 Ozark mountain family in poverty and a tramp ('a person of low status') on a London park bench.[79] But Melville's abiding concern with such persons of low status does not mean that they have no sense of the power, meaning and vocabulary of dress, of the unspeakable significance of clothing. As is evident from the example of Faulkner's Lucas Beachamp, who is a 1940s sharecropper with limited sartorial resources, sophisticated knowledge of what clothing means is not restricted to the wealthy and their walk-in wardrobes filled with expensive clothes. In fact, the very limitation of sartorial resource may make one more aware of this power, and more alert to nuance than to extravagant statement.

Melville's concentration in his fiction on the worker and the marginalized, with their limited opportunities for dress, may be one of the reasons why the functions of clothing in his work has been generally overlooked by critics, in contrast with say, that of James, whose work typically involves the upper-middle class, the leisured classes or the aristocracy. The roles played by clothing in James's work have been richly scrutinized, notably by Clair Hughes, and particularly with regard to class, manners and transgression.[80] A study such as Hughes's requires careful attention to the minutiae of dress that James provides, and an awareness of fashion and customs, of the material culture of the period. But it also involves recognition of the insistent if vexed relationship between clothing and identity on a symbolic as well as literal level, on the power of clothing both to convey identity and to conceal it. This is examined very specifically in a passage from *The Portrait of a Lady* (1881). Here the sophisticated American expatriate Madame Merle articulates her sense of clothing's revelatory power in conversation with Isabel Archer, the younger American innocent abroad. This is one of their earliest sustained conversations, as they move towards an intimacy, and James marks the difference between the characters in their attitude to clothes. Madame Merle insists that in

---

[78] Alison Lurie, *The Language of Clothes* (New York: Random House, 1981), pp. 4–5.
[79] Ibid., pp. 5, 9.
[80] See Clair Hughes, *Henry James and the Art of Dress* (New York: Palgrave, 2001).

assessing character, one must consider the external, the materiality of representation as a figuration of the self:

> When you have lived as long as I, you will see that every human being has his shell and that you must take the shell into account. By the shell I mean the whole envelope of circumstances. There is no such thing as an isolated man or woman; we are each of us made up of a cluster of appurtenances. What do you call one's self? Where does it begin? Where does it end? It overflows into everything that belongs to us – and then it flows back again. I know a large part of myself is in the dresses I choose to wear. I have a great respect for *things*! One's self – for other people – is one's expression of one's self; and one's house, one's clothes, the books one reads, the company one keeps – these things are all expressive.[81]

Ostensibly, this is an invitation to trust, an overt denial of clothing's power to mislead. All that you see is all I am, Madame Merle is saying: the shell is the self, my clothes are a true expression of me, my inner self. On another level, Madame Merle is in effect warning Isabel. Since identity depends on appearances, she must learn to read appearance in order to reach an understanding of character. The sophisticate's corollary of this, of course, is that since clothing represents a performative identity then appearance can be manipulated in order to present a particular character, and this is Merle's undertext: if you learn to believe that I am what I appear to be, then I will hold a certain power over you. Melville's characterization of Benjamin Franklin in *Israel Potter* focuses exactly on this, Franklin's manipulative self-presentation through dress as a form of authority.

Compared to Madame Merle, Isabel may be an innocent but she is in fact keenly aware that clothes are social signifiers rather than necessarily expressions of an inner identity. In response to Madame Merle's remark that Isabel dresses 'very well' she comments:

> 'Possibly; but I don't care to be judged by that. My clothes may express the dressmaker, but they don't express me. To begin with it's not my own choice that I wear them; they're imposed upon me by society.'
>
> 'Should you prefer to go without them?' Madame Merle enquired in a tone which virtually terminated the discussion.[82]

---

[81] Henry James, *The Portrait of a Lady* in *Novels 1881–86* (New York: Library of America, 1985), pp. 397–8.
[82] Ibid., p. 398.

In fact, Isabel would (symbolically) prefer to go without, an assertion of nakedness as honesty, a truth accessible without the distracting messages that clothes convey. Clothes are social requirements, a matter of manners and of belonging rather than of one's own identity. Inevitably they send out a message, but they must not be confused with the genuine self beneath. This conversation significantly prefigures the climactic confrontation between the two women late in the novel, when an exasperated and confused Isabel asks Madame Merle 'Who are you – what are you?' This is followed by what for her is the most crucial question of all: 'What have you to do with my husband?'[83]

In the first discussion between Madame Merle and Isabel, James is not so concerned, as he often is elsewhere, with the materiality of clothing in the time and space that form the novel's setting. He is concerned with its symbolic import and with its power. Indeed, underneath the conversation between Madame Merle and Isabel is the ancient association of nakedness with innocence, clothing as guilt, Adam and Eve only covering their nakedness after the Fall. In spite of Madame Merle's sarcasm, Isabel does possess an innocence that she will seek to preserve throughout the events of the novel. In fact, as in other James novels, such as the cluster of *What Maisie Knew* (1897), *The Awkward Age* (1899) and *The Golden Bowl* (1904), the preservation of perception of innocence are central plot drivers. Nakedness is innocence but clothing is both an inevitable social requirement and a means of controlling (or confusing) the identity we convey to others. Often in James's fiction those who dress well and self-consciously are alert to the power of dress and manipulate this to their own ends, fully aware that they are participating in a game. This contrasts sharply with characters such as Daisy Miller, Isabel Archer and Catherine Sloper who lack this insight and consequently do not possess the power it confirms.

Again, moving away from the minutiae, the details of clothing, this is the level on which Melville also explores the often incongruent relations between clothing and identity, representing clothing as symbolic as well as material. Indeed, Howard P. Vincent noted this in his excellent 1970 study *The Tailoring of Melville's White-Jacket*, and in a footnote he quotes part of Madame Merle's speech to illuminate his point.[84] *White-Jacket* has a special place in Melville's consideration of clothing. Vincent was alert to this, and to the fact that attending to this representation opens up afresh some of the works that critics have attended to the least. These include

---

[83] Ibid., p. 723.
[84] Howard P. Vincent, *The Tailoring of Melville's White-Jacket* (Evanston, IL: Northwestern University Press, 1970), p. 16n.

the books that Melville himself apparently dismissed, and it allows us to approach in a new way his most consistently overlooked novel, *Israel Potter*. This is one of the reasons why the Agatha letter is so important. In telling Hawthorne to look at the unspeakable significance of the shawls, Melville is also directing us to recognize a particular aspect of his fiction; that he attended to shawls.

2

A Very Strange Compound Indeed: Carlyle, *Redburn* and *White-Jacket*

On the evening of 19 June 1790 an event occurred that Thomas Carlyle, in his *History of the French Revolution*, was to call 'a spectacle such as our foolish little Planet has not often had to show'.[1] A Prussian baron who had adopted the name Anacharsis Cloots (sometimes spelled Clootz) led a 'deputation of foreigners' to the French National Assembly. There he proclaimed that the French Revolution had been a herald of the freedom of people everywhere, that it was a revolution for all nations, for all humanity, and therefore requested that he and his group be allowed to participate in the celebrations of Bastille Day the following month. Styling himself 'the Orator of the Human Race' Cloots wore a mixture of clothing, while his group of 36 followers sported a variety of national costumes – whether they were foreigners or not. The Assembly's official record has the group comprising 'English, Prussians, Sicilians, Dutch, Russians, Poles, Germans, Swedes, Italians, Spaniards, Brabanters, Liegois, Avignonese, Swiss, Genevans, Indians, Arabs, Chaldeans, etc'.[2] In his picturesque representation, Carlyle details the occasion: Cloots enters 'the august Salle de Manége, with the Human Species at his heels, Swedes, Spaniards, Polacks; Turks, Chaldeans, Greeks, dwellers in Mesopotamia; behold them all; they have come to claim place in the grand Federation, having an undoubted interest in it'.[3]

To the members of the Assembly it was all rather frivolous. One historian comments: 'For their part, the deputies ... either laughed the affair off as harmless lunacy, or they saw no harm in accepting the flattery of the deputation.'[4] However playful the event might have seemed, Cloots was very

---

[1] Thomas Carlyle, *The French Revolution* (London: Chapman and Hall, 1896), 2, p. 51.
[2] Quoted in William Doyle, *Aristocracy and Its Enemies in the Age of Revolution* (Oxford: Oxford University Press, 2009), p. 3.
[3] Carlyle, *The French Revolution*, 2, p. 51.
[4] Michael Rapport, *Nationality and Citizenship in Revolutionary France* (Oxford: Clarendon, 2000), p. 114.

serious in his cosmopolitan aspirations and in his commitment to social equality. Although born into aristocracy and wealth, Jean-Baptiste du Val-de-Grâce, Baron de Cloots became a disciple of Voltaire, renounced his Prussian title, borrowed a name from a character in a romance by Jean-Jacques Barthélemy, became a French citizen, and in 1792 a member of the National Convention. He had resolved to live according to the dictates of reason, which included a deep hostility towards any form of religious faith, and to work for a post-nationalistic 'Republic of the World'. He also saw clothing as divisive, the visible and powerful actualizing of inequality and misplaced authority. Again, Carlyle expresses this sentiment in his florid style:

> A dashing man, beloved at Patriotic dinner-tables; with gaiety, nay with humour; headlong, trenchant, of free purse; in suitable costume; though what mortal ever more despised costumes? Under all costumes Anacharsis seeks the man; not Stylites Marat will more freely trample costumes, if they hold no man. This is the faith of Anacharsis: That there is a Paradise discoverable; that all costumes ought to hold men.[5]

Whatever the National Assembly thought of him in June 1790, Cloots's various intrigues and alliances with extremist groups led to his expulsion from the National Convention in 1793, along with Thomas Paine. After a term in prison he was sent to the guillotine in March 1794, and publicly executed with seventeen others who were associated with anti-government conspiracies. The public execution was a spectacle, of exactly the kind Foucault describes in *Discipline and Punish*, and was attended by 'the biggest crowd ever to surround the guillotine'.[6] Ever true to his nature, Cloots addressed the crowd with a brief exhortation: 'Hurrah for the fraternity of nations! Long live the Republic of the World!'[7]

Cloots's preoccupation with dress as a token of inequality and a signifier of nationality might seem quaint or strange in the twenty-first century, when our statute books hold very few sumptuary laws that regulate dress and the materials that may be worn by each class, and where globalization increasingly effaces differences in national modes of dress – you could hardly say today of someone that they 'dress like a Belgian' with any sure sense of what that means. But informal and de facto sumptuary laws or expectations remain, and some sense of national dress has been maintained by most nations. The belief may be latent most of the time, or

---

[5] Carlyle, *The French Revolution*, 2, p. 23.
[6] William Doyle, *The Oxford History of the French Revolution* (Oxford: Oxford University Press, 2002), p. 270.
[7] Rapport, *Nationality and Citizenship*, p. 2.

expressed mainly in pageants or historical displays at folk-museums, but it does surface prominently every two years at the most widely viewed of all international spectacles, the parade of athletes at the opening of the summer and the winter Olympic Games. Guidelines state that the athletes should wear clothing that reflects their nation, culture and history, and in multicultural nations this stimulates much debate about representation. It often also provokes anxiety and uncertainty, or even unintentional comedy when the dress seems like a caricature; the British team for the Mexico summer Olympics in 1968 wore raincoats and carried rolled-up umbrellas. Nor have we lost the sense that dress represents class or social position. This seems obvious when we think of the formal uniforms worn by professions or services, but many offices and businesses have formally stated codes of dress, and some professionals feel anxiety when these codes are relaxed, either through a policy of permitting relaxed wear one day a week ('dress down Friday') or during the summer months. It is obvious from the advice sought by employees that the dress code is not a problem; what is a problem is the uncertainty occasioned by the relaxation of the code. In effect, the replacing of a written code by an unwritten one stimulates anxiety. Freedom in dress is more problematic than regimented dress because it requires individual decisions which still have to do with conformity and acceptability but the onus for deciding these is on the employee. If clothing is a decision we have to make every day, it is often easier to have it made for you. Even uniforms stimulate debate concerning the identity of the wearer. This was especially apparent in the United Kingdom during the summer of 2011, when a conservative 'think-tank' called Policy Exchange suggested that police officers should wear their uniforms while travelling to and from work in order to give the impression of a large public police presence. The idea, admittedly fatuous in itself, was widely ridiculed and was rejected by the Police Federation. However, it raises interesting questions about when you are a police officer and when you are not. Are you always an officer or only when wearing the uniform that shows that you are and carrying the equipment essential to the role? Even a superficial reflection, then, suggests that some of Cloots's preoccupations with dress and social identity retain validity today even when the terms of the debate may have changed.

    Melville's recurring references to Cloots are varied. However obliquely, they indicate his own idealism and political radicalism, and more directly they chart his developing interest in the relation between dress and identity, uniform and self, costume and performance. This interest was evident, as we shall see, in his first two novels, *Typee* and *Omoo*, but it deepened after he had read Carlyle's 1834 book *Sartor Resartus*, probably before composing his third novel *Mardi*, published in 1849. This is probably when he read Carlyle's book because the change in his prose clearly shows a debt to Carlyle's stylistic exuberance, and reviewers of the novel picked up on this.[8] Melville was probably led to Cloots by reading Carlyle's *French Revolution*, and he first alludes to him towards the end of chapter 27 of *Moby-Dick*, the second of two chapters titled 'Knights and Squires'. Ishmael comments on the cosmopolitan make-up of the *Pequod*'s crew, and the odd fact that the men are, mostly, islanders:

> They were nearly all Islanders in the Pequod, *Isolatoes* too, I call such, not acknowledging the common continent of men, but each *Isolato* living on a separate continent of his own. Yet now, federated along one keel, what a set these Isolatoes were! An Anacharsis Clootz deputation from all the isles of the sea, and all the ends of the earth, accompanying Old Ahab in the Pequod to lay the world's grievances before that bar from which not very many of them ever come back.[9]

The name Cloots is here shorthand for the *Pequod*'s crew as representative of all nations. This cosmopolitanism is staged in chapter 40, 'Midnight, Forecastle' with Melville's own Cloots-like deputation of followers. The reference also intensifies the idea of the ship's mission as heroic, embodying an essentially human aspiration, while simultaneously suggesting that like Cloots's enterprise, it is also doomed. The isolatoes may be brought together but they are, with the exception of Ishmael, headed for death.

Appropriately for a text that includes a character called the Cosmopolitan, Melville next refers to Cloots in the second chapter of *The Confidence-Man*. Having opened with a chatter of unidentified voices, the narrator likens the voyagers on the river-boat *Fidèle* to Chaucer's Pilgrims, emphasizing their variousness, another version of the representatives of humanity on the *Pequod*:

> Natives of all sorts, and foreigners; men of business and men of pleasure; parlor men and backwoodsmen; farm-hunters and fame-hunters; heiress-hunters, gold-hunters, buffalo-hunters, bee-hunters, happiness-hunters, truth-hunters, and still keener hunters after all these hunters. Fine ladies in slippers, and moccasined squaws; Northern speculators

---

[8] Melville borrowed Carlyle's *Sartor Resartus* and *On Heroes* from Evert Duyckinck in June and July 1850. See Merton M. Sealts, Jr, *Melville's Reading: Revised and Enlarged Edition* (Columbia: University of South Carolina Press, 1988), p. 59; Mark Cumming (ed.), *The Carlyle Encyclopedia* (Cranbury, NJ: Fairleigh Dickinson University Press, 2004), p. 317.

[9] Melville, *Moby-Dick*, p. 121. There is some discussion as to whether the concluding phrase 'from which not very many of them ever come back', as it appears in the novel's first editions, should be 'from which not very many of them ever came back'. See p. 852.

and Eastern philosophers; English, Irish, German, Scotch, Danes; Santa Fé traders in striped blankets, and Broadway bucks in cravats of cloth of gold; fine-looking Kentucky boatmen, and Japanese-looking Mississippi cotton-planters; Quakers in full drab, and United States soldiers in full regimentals; slaves, black, mulatto, quadroon; modish young Spanish Creoles, and old-fashioned French Jews; Mormons and Papists; Dives and Lazarus; jesters and mourners, teetalers and convivialists, deacons and blacklegs; hard-shell Baptists and clay-eaters; grinning negroes, and Sioux chiefs solemn as high-priests. In short, a piebald parliament, an Anacharsis Cloots congress of all kinds of that multiform pilgrim species, man.[10]

Comparable though this is to the allusion in *Moby-Dick*, there is a noticeable shift from a Cloots-like congress that involves varied nationalities to one that involves a variety of roles. The passengers that the *Fidèle* picks up at different points on its 1,200-mile journey are cosmopolitan ('Natives...and foreigners') but Melville's low-key Whitmanesque catalogue notably refers to the roles that the passengers play, and to the clothing by which they are to be identified: slippers, moccasins, striped blankets, gold-coloured cravats, the 'full drab' of the Quakers and the 'full regimentals' of the American soldiers. That is, Cloots's motley sartorial attire now represents the various roles that we can occupy in life, the costumes we wear for our performance. This is a key aspect of *The Confidence-Man*, with its emphasis on the fluidity of character, the manipulation of appearance and the relation between performance and identity.[11]

Melville's final reference to Cloots is in the unfinished *Billy Budd*. As in the case of *The Confidence-Man*, he makes his appearance very early on in the text – in the second paragraph, in fact. By way of introducing Billy Budd to us, the narrator reflects on the phenomenon of the 'Handsome Sailor', the crew member who is universally loved and whose fellow-sailors take to their hearts. The narrator recalls an incident witnessed in Liverpool 'fifty years ago'.

> I saw a common sailor... so intensely black that he must needs have been a native African of the unadulterate blood of Ham.... The two

---

[10] Herman Melville, *The Confidence-Man* (Evanston, IL: Northwestern University Press, 1984), p. 9.
[11] The name of the steamboat, *Fidèle* has a transvestite connotation, since it calls to mind various characters who assume the name along with a disguise. These include Imogen in Shakespeare's *Cymbeline*, the lover in Wycherley's *The Plain Dealer* and Leonora in Beethoven's *Fidelio*. Melville does mention transvestitism on several occasions in his writing, and the uneasiness occasioned by blurring the fundamental male/female binary.

ends of a gay silk handkerchief thrown loose about the neck danced upon the displayed ebony of his chest, in his ears were big hoops of gold, and a Highland bonnet with a tartan band set off his shapely head . . . he rollicked along, the center of a company of his shipmates. These were made up of such an assortment of tribes and complexions as would have well fitted them to be marched up by Anacharsis Cloots before the bar of the first French Assembly as Representatives of the Human Race.[12]

Cloots here sustains a dual reference. As in *Moby-Dick* the motley crew resembles the cosmopolitanism of Cloots's delegation, here emphasizing the universality of the Handsome Sailor. But the remembered sailor is himself an image of the cosmopolitan, the dandyesque flaunting of silks, golden earrings and a Scotch bonnet representing a sartorial mixed metaphor, a fluid transnational identity lacking fixed boundaries, combining masculinity with the femininity implied by the silks. This is in sharp contrast with Billy, whose stability of identity, despite his altered circumstances (impressed into the Royal Navy from a merchant vessel), is crucially important to the text. Unlike his Captain (and judge), Vere, Billy senses no conflict between his self and his uniform. The early allusion to Cloots is also significant for a text that is very much concerned with conspiracy, mutiny, rebellion, and of course, judicial execution. Although they are not laboured, Melville's deft allusions to Cloots indicate prolonged interest in him as an historical and aspirational figure. More specifically he may be aligned with Melville's recurrent concerns, with internationalism, utopianism, rebellion against authority, role-playing and the fluid possibilities of identity.

As noted, Melville had almost certainly encountered the story of Cloots from his reading of Carlyle's *French Revolution*. His engagement with Carlyle profoundly affected him, involving a fundamental reappraisal of the meaning of literature, the possibilities of fiction and the role of the author. It is possible that Melville first read some work by Carlyle in *The Edinburgh Review* long before his own writing career began. This is suggested by a brief allusion to the *Review* as early as December 1837 in a letter to his uncle, Peter Gansevoort.[13] It is certain, though, that at the end of the 1840s, as Melville starts to think of himself as a

---

[12] Herman Melville, *Billy Budd, Sailor* (London and Chicago: Chicago University Press, 1962), pp. 43–4.
[13] After commenting on a book about pedagogy given to him, we assume, by his uncle, Melville remarks 'But I have almost usurped the province of the Edinburgh Reveiw [sic]'. Melville, *Correspondence*, p. 9.

writer and is reading voraciously and widely, he develops an interest in Carlyle. This may have arisen from his reading work by Emerson and Thoreau that elucidated Carlyle's thinking; it may also have started with his reading some of Carlyle's work that was reprinted in a multivolume set titled *Modern British Essayists*, which he bought in February 1849.[14] However, the remarkable shift in Melville's style with *Mardi*, which he had completed by the end of 1848, suggests that he felt especially liberated after reading Carlyle. The first-person fact-based narratives of *Typee* and *Omoo* are swept away in *Mardi*, with its exuberant wide-ranging free play, its evident delight in the very power of fiction-making, its extension of the possibilities of first-person narration and its mode of self-consciousness. In noting these shifts, *Mardi*'s reviewers attributed them to the heady influence of Carlyle (the first appearance of his name in reviews of Melville), while also citing Emerson, Rabelais, Ossian, Sterne and Thomas Browne among many others.[15] In 1849, when Melville is planning a trip to London to find a publisher for his fifth novel, *White-Jacket*, he writes to his father-in-law, Lemuel Shaw asking him to obtain a letter of introduction from Emerson that will enable him to meet Carlyle.[16] It is almost certain that he did not get the hoped-for letter from Emerson, and we do know that he did not manage to meet Carlyle. Nevertheless, the request for an introduction to another writer was untypical of Melville, and in itself testifies to the esteem in which he held Carlyle.[17]

Carlyle was a figure of major importance for the direction and development of American literature in the mid-nineteenth century, not only directly through his own writing, but also by the interactions with and mediation of his ideas by contemporaries such as Emerson. For various reasons, it is difficult for us today to appreciate the status

---

[14] Parker, *Herman Melville: A Biography*, 1, p. 618.
[15] For instance, the review in the *Athenaeum* warns readers that Melville 'has been drinking at the well of "English bewitched" of which Mr Carlyle and Mr Emerson are the priests'. Branch, *Melville: The Critical Heritage*, p. 139. The reviewers' repeated attempts to find analogies for *Mardi*'s style by invoking a wide range of writers testify not only to Melville's style shift but also to the intensity and range of his reading from about 1847. This exuberance was sharply reined in for his next novel, *Redburn*.
[16] Melville, *Correspondence*, pp. 136–7.
[17] Shaw did obtain letters of introduction to Richard Monckton Milnes, the poet and influential literary figure, the poet and critic Samuel Rogers (known as the 'banker-poet'), and the French magistrate and penal reformer Gustave de Beaumont, today mainly known as De Tocqueville's friend who accompanied him to the United States on the trip that resulted in *Democracy in America*. R. H. Dana also wrote a letter of introduction to the publisher Edward Moxon. Of these Melville seems to have used only the letter to Rogers, whom he met on 20 December.

that Carlyle held in the mid-nineteenth century. It is not that he had a particular paraphrasable philosophy, or a single masterpiece, but that in an important series of essays, lectures, histories and reflections published over a period of more than 30 years, he articulated the sense of crisis as well as the possibilities of the Victorian age. He thought deeply about the role of religion, the nature of social authority, power, capitalism, nationalism and the duty of the writer to engage with a sense of the nation. Some of Carlyle's major preoccupations, such as the duty of actualizing one's beliefs in a social reality, the role of religious faith in relation to doubt and unbelief, the function of the writer in the formation of national identity, the need for social conscience, were directly and effectively taken up by American writers. Emerson was the most notable and influential of these. He had met Carlyle at his home in Scotland in 1833, and the two shared a sometimes uneasy friendship and a correspondence that was to last almost 40 years. Emerson's intellectual engagement with Carlyle underpins some of his most influential works, notably 'Self-Reliance', 'The Divinity School Address', 'The Poet', 'The Over-Soul' and *Representative Men*. In fact, the importance of Carlyle's presence in the development of American literature – its so-called Renaissance – in the middle of the nineteenth century can hardly be exaggerated. In an essay reacting to Carlyle's death in 1881, Walt Whitman highlighted his 'launching into the self-complacent atmosphere of our days a rasping, questioning, dislocating agitation and shock'.[18] In a further reflection on Carlyle's life and influence, he also accurately forecast the puzzlement that future generations may feel about this:

> It will be difficult for the future – judging by his books, personal dissympathies, &c., – to account for the deep hold this author has taken on the present age, and the way he has color'd its method and thought. I am certainly at a loss to account for it all as affecting myself. But there could be no view, or even partial picture, of the middle and

---

[18] 'Death of Thomas Carlyle', in Walt Whitman, *Complete Poetry and Collected Prose* (New York: Library of America, 1982), p. 887. As Whitman suggests in this essay, Carlyle's views became more marginal and socially conservative from the mid-1850s. He became increasingly detached from, and in some respects antagonistic towards, liberal intellectual thought, and two essays in particular, 'Shooting Niagara' and 'Occasional Discourse on the Nigger Question' (1849) seriously damaged his reputation. This was further tarnished by his extravagant praise for Frederick the Great (for which he was honoured by Bismarck) and his increasing attacks on democracy and a growing belief in the need for strong authority, which, in the twentieth century, was considered a precursor to German fascism.

latter part of our Nineteenth century, that did not markedly include Thomas Carlyle.[19]

In this context, Melville's desire to meet Carlyle was not only understandable, but seemingly inevitable. Like other critics, F. O. Matthiessen draws attention to the influence of Carlyle evident in the fanciful conversations in *Mardi*, and 'Etymology' and 'Extracts' in *Moby-Dick*, with their teasing quotations from invented authors.[20] But on a different level Carlyle's ideas are there in the very shaping of Melville's thought. The core theme of 'Hawthorne and His Mosses' is very much drawn from Carlyle, and some of the phrases in the letters to Hawthorne are direct allusions to Carlyle. The examination of the heroic in *Moby-Dick* is in part an imaginative engagement with Carlyle's 1841 collection of six lectures *On Heroes and Hero-Worship*. Importantly, at a crucial time in his career, Carlyle's writings inspire Melville to an intense commitment to a sense of himself as a writer.[21] Tellingly, Hawthorne drew on Carlyle's conceptual vocabulary to summarize his sense of Melville, after what turned out to be their last meeting:

> He can neither believe, nor be comfortable in his unbelief; and he is too honest and courageous not to try to do one or the other. If he were a religious man, he would be one of the most truly religious and reverential; he has a very high and noble nature, and better worth immortality than most of us.[22]

While Carlyle was an important figure for Melville as he redirected his sense of himself as a writer, it is specifically *Sartor Resartus: The Life and Opinions of Herr Teufelsdröckh*, to give its full title, that stimulated Melville to explore the relation between clothing and identity in ways markedly different from *Typee* and *Omoo*.[23] The title *Sartor Resartus* means 'the tailor re-tailored' (Carlyle's working title was the less unwieldy 'Thoughts on Clothes'). The book itself defies categorization under a single genre.

---

[19] 'Carlyle from American Points of View', in Whitman, *Complete Poetry*, p. 890.
[20] F. O. Matthiessen, *American Renaissance* (New York: Oxford University Press, 1941), p. 384n.
[21] See Jonathan Arac, *Commissioned Spirits* (New Brunswick: Rutgers University Press, 1979), p. 148. This is an important study of the influence Carlyle had on the development of the nineteenth-century novel, and pages 139–63 are specifically devoted to Melville and Carlyle.
[22] Quoted in Melville, *Journals*, pp. 628–9.
[23] Teufelsdröckh means 'devil's dung'; 'dung' being less coarse than the 'Teufelsdreck' of Carlyle's original manuscript.

It is an amalgamation of essay, polemic, fantasy, pedantic scholarship and pseudo-scholarship, metaphysics, fiction, comic absurdity, nonsense, satire, transposed autobiography, social commentary and spiritual self-examination. In a letter to the magazine editor James Fraser, Carlyle described it as:

> put together in the fashion of a kind of Didactic Novel; but indeed properly *like* nothing yet extant. I used to characterize it briefly as a kind of 'Satirical Extravaganza on Things in General'; it contains more of my opinions on Art, Politics, Religion, Heaven Earth and Air, than all the things I have yet written.[24]

While its most obvious precursors are two books that Carlyle greatly admired, Jonathan Swift's *A Tale of a Tub* (1704) and Laurence Sterne's *The Life and Opinions of Tristram Shandy* (1767) – echoed of course in Carlyle's full title – it outstrips even these in its expansive range of topics and in its variety of shifting tones. It is also a book that changed remarkably during the very act of writing. Carlyle began composing it as an article on the subject of clothing (one of Swift's subjects in *A Tale of a Tub*), but it grew and was transformed into something well beyond this. Although he had completed the book by July 1831 he was unable to interest a publisher in it, probably because of its genre-defiant wild originality (John Murray, whose firm was later to publish Melville's first book, came closest to accepting *Sartor Resartus* but ultimately declined). Carlyle then broke the narrative into segments and these were published serially in *Fraser's Magazine* from 1833 to 1834. Its poor critical reception encouraged no other publisher, though, and the manuscript rather languished until Emerson persuaded the Boston firm headed by James Munroe to take a chance on bringing it out in book form, appearing in 1836 with a print-run of 500. Emerson wrote a Preface for this, in which he warned the reader of its eccentricities and its potential to offend, while recommending it highly as evidence of an original intellect confronting the transitions of the age.

Given its indifferent British reception, *Sartor Resartus* proved a surprise success in the United States. The first edition quickly sold out, and a second swiftly appeared in 1837; by 1846 there had been five American editions and many reprintings, with an English edition published in 1838.[25] It is

---

[24] Letter to James Fraser, May 1833, in McSweeney and Sabor (eds), *Sartor Resartus*, pp. 227–8.
[25] See Cumming, *The Carlyle Encyclopedia*, p. 415, and *Sartor Resartus*, ed. Rodger L. Tarr and Mark Engel (Berkeley: University of California Press, 2000), p. xxxi.

worth remarking on how unusual this was in terms of publishing between Britain and the United States. Well up until the 1860s it was common for American writers to publish their books first in London, since British copyright provided more protection than American laws did from pirated editions. Yet here, at a time when a distinctively American literature was considered to be undeveloped, the man who would become a major British author has one of his most influential books published first in Boston and then in London. The main reason for this, and Emerson plays a key role here, is that one theme of *Sartor Resartus* struck a particular chord with American thinkers. The book is often characterized as marking an intellectual transition from Romanticism to Victorianism, and stylistically embodying that shift and its dislocations.[26] The issues that the Victorians were to face over the next 60 years are generated by modernity itself. The crisis of Christian faith, the radical transformation of society through industrialism and a changing sense of self in relation to society and community are Carlyle's major themes at the very beginning of Victoria's reign.[27] Once it was brought to their attention, British readers took to *Sartor Resartus* throughout the nineteenth century. As late as 1900, 20 years after Carlyle's death, it was available in 9 separate English editions, and it had a profound influence on the major intellectuals of the age.[28] To its American readers, though, one of its chief attractions was that in making the shift from a Romantic sensibility to Victorianism, Carlyle was in effect rethinking the central ideas of Romanticism so that they could form the ideological basis of social reform. That is, one of his core investigations was into how the tenets of Romanticism, a mystical sense of elsewhere, a belief in an inner truth and in human perfectibility, could become a force applied to everyday living in a specific social reality. This is why *Sartor Resartus* is typically referred to as the founding text of American Transcendentalism; it addressed the possibility of making what might otherwise be merely escapist abstractions into something worthwhile and pragmatic.[29]

---

[26] McSweeney and Sabor (eds), *Sartor Resartus*, p. vii.
[27] Technically, just prior to it, since the composition and first publication predate Victoria's accession in 1837.
[28] Julian Symons, *Thomas Carlyle: The Life and Ideas of a Prophet* (London: House of Stratus, 2001), p. 131. Symons's study was first published in 1952 and he points out that in spite of a proliferation of editions *Sartor Resartus* was virtually unknown just 50 years later.
[29] Cf. Tarr and Engel (eds), *Sartor Resartus*, p. xxxi: 'there is no doubt whatsoever that *Sartor Resartus* became the foundational text of the American Transcendental Movement'.

While it is by its very nature a text that resists both singular generic definition and easy summary, the overall narrative trajectory of *Sartor Resartus* is the working through of a personal spiritual crisis towards a reawakened sense of one's place in the world and of harmony and confluence, rather than conflict, between individual desire and God's design. Not that this trajectory is immediately apparent. Masquerading as an unnamed editor's commentary on a manuscript written by Professor Diogenes Teufelsdröckh (Professor of Things-in-General at the University of Weissnichtwo), it also explores the professor's career and personality.[30] The book is divided into three parts. Broadly speaking, the first outlines Teufelsdröckh's career and relates how the manuscript came to be in the editor's hands; the affinity with *Tristram Shandy* is most in evidence here. The second explores Teufelsdröckh's background and personality (partially Carlyle's comically transposed autobiography) and the third is an analytical explanation and commentary on Teufelsdröckh's Philosophy of Clothes. The book's importance for American readers and for the development of Transcendentalism was chiefly contained in four consecutive chapters in part 2: 'Sorrows of Teufelsdröckh' (an echo of Goethe's *Sorrows of Werther*); 'The Everlasting No'; 'Centre of Indifference' and 'The Everlasting Yea'. One chapter from part 3, 'Natural Supernaturalism' was also influential and much-cited. The four sequential chapters in part 2 narrate Teufelsdröckh's being rejected by his beloved, Blumine, in preference for one of his friends, and his consequent despair and sense of alienation from the world. In depicting a personal spiritual journey they represent a modernized reconsideration of Bunyan's *Pilgrim's Progress*. 'The Everlasting No' articulates his sense of despair and spiritual nihilism:

> [I]n our age of Downpulling and Disbelief, the very Devil has been pulled down, you cannot so much as believe in a Devil. To me the Universe was all void of Life, of Purpose, of Volition, even of Hostility: it was one huge, dead, immeasurable Steam-engine, rolling on, in its dead indifference, to grind me limb from limb. O the vast, gloomy, solitary Golgotha, and Mill of Death! Why was the Living banished thither companionless, conscious? Why, if there is no Devil; nay, unless the Devil is your God?[31]

---

[30] The pseudo-commentary has commonly led critics to claim Vladimir Nabokov's *Pale Fire* as one of the book's literary heirs, and one could add Flann O'Brien's *The Third Policeman* and *The Dalkey Archive*.

[31] McSweeney and Sabor (eds), *Sartor Resartus*, p. 127.

The chapter concludes with Teufelsdröckh's stirring of defiance and rebellion against this condition:

> [T]hen was it that my whole ME stood up, in native God-created majesty, and with emphasis recorded its Protest. Such a Protest, the most important transaction in Life, may that same Indignation and Defiance, in a psychological point of view, be fitly called. The Everlasting No had said: 'Behold, thou art fatherless, outcast, and the Universe is mine (the Devil's)'; to which my whole Me now made answer: '*I* am not thine, but Free, and forever hate thee!'[32]

This negation is followed however by the apathy and self-alienation expressed in the following chapter, 'Centre of Indifference'. Carlyle's title is actually a scientific term describing the midpoint between two magnetic poles; that is, a point neither positive nor negative. This explains the chapter's final sentence: 'This . . . was the CENTRE OF INDIFFERENCE I had now reached; through which whoso travels from the Negative Pole to the Positive must necessarily pass.'[33] In this stage, Teufelsdröckh tries to ignore or find indifference to his inner turmoil by attending to external reality, travelling through the social world; in effect distracting himself from his own condition: 'Thus can the Professor, at least in lucid intervals, look away from his own sorrows, over the many-coloured world, and pertinently enough note what is passing there.'[34]

'The Everlasting Yea' contains the most resonant and influential of all of Carlyle's writing, and it was to have special meanings for a whole generation of active readers. Here Teufelsdröckh revisits the inevitable war between 'necessity' and our individual will which had led at first to negation and then withdrawal. But through struggle and a kind of self-annihilation he comes to a vision of oneness between his inner self and God's design. This gives him a vision of harmony between self, nature and God.

> Here, then, as I lay in that CENTRE OF INDIFFERENCE; cast, doubtless by benignant upper Influence, into a healing sleep, the heavy dreams rolled gradually away, and I awoke to a new Heaven and a new Earth. The first preliminary moral Act, Annihilation of Self (*Selbsttödtung*), had been happily accomplished; and my mind's eyes were now unsealed, and its hands ungyved.[35]

---

[32] Ibid., p. 129.
[33] Ibid., p. 139.
[34] Ibid., p. 134.
[35] Ibid., p. 142.

Self-annihilation is essential for the fullest acceptance of God and of the world, for overcoming defiance and realizing the unity between God, self and nature.

> [T]he Self in thee needed to be annihilated. By benignant fever-paroxysms is Life rooting out the deep-seated chronic Disease, and triumphs over Death. On the roaring billows of Time, thou art not engulphed, but borne aloft into the azure of Eternity. Love not Pleasure; love God. This is the EVERLASTING YEA, wherein all contradiction is solved: wherein whoso walks and works, it is well with him.[36]

At the heart of Carlyle's blazing rhetoric here is a familiar mystical theme of self-abnegation. But there is more than that, and it is this which moves this part of *Sartor* beyond a conversion narrative and beyond a restatement of high Romanticism's validation of individual subjectivity. Carlyle takes us one stage further. We cannot rest in this moment of harmonious vision. It must be seen only as the starting-point for our acceptance and fulfilment of duty; individual regeneration is meaningless unless it is made to be socially transformative. 'Conviction, were it never so excellent, is worthless till it convert itself into Conduct. Nay properly Conviction is not possible till then.'[37]

This is what makes *Sartor* a founding text for Transcendentalism, extending romanticism from subjectivity to social utility and helping to justify Carlyle's reputation for creating the transition from Romanticism to Victorianism. While he was never a Transcendentalist, in Melville's work there is a significant thematic strand that picks up directly from both this No to Yea movement in *Sartor* and parts of *On Heroes and Hero-Worship*, but which rejects the optimism and world-view of the ultimate movement to Yea. Indeed, in his introductory study of Melville, Tyrus Hillway used 'The Everlasting No' as the title for the chapter covering *Mardi*, *Moby-Dick* and *Pierre*.[38] Captain Ahab is the defiant Promethean No-sayer, refusing to accept that the world cannot be shaped to his will. Ishmael begins his narrative as the man living at the 'centre of indifference' between No and Yea, someone with 'nothing particular to interest' him on shore and who goes to sea as an alternative to suicide.[39] ('Worldlings puke up their sick existence,

---

[36] Ibid., p. 146. Melville echoes this passage in his description of the death (or ascension) of Billy Budd, indicating how long *Sartor Resartus* stayed in his consciousness. See Melville, *Billy Budd*, pp. 123–4.
[37] Ibid., p. 148.
[38] Tyrus Hillway, *Herman Melville* (Boston: G. K. Hall, 1979).
[39] Melville, *Moby-Dick*, p. 3.

by suicide' wrote Carlyle in 'The Everlasting No'.⁴⁰) While his indifference is countered by his relationship with Queequeg and his absorption in whaling, it remains Ishmael's fundamental state. A recent study of Melville has foregrounded the theme of boredom in his work, but the terms in which this is discussed, as 'joylessness in/of God' strongly recall Carlyle and the centre of indifference, and also of modernity 'Melville's concern with boredom emphasizes a growing tendency toward a modern sensibility: joylessness in life itself.'⁴¹ Bartleby too is at this apathetic centre of indifference; the narrator believes his condition to be a spiritual apathy ('it was his soul that suffered') and that he is a 'victim of innate and incurable disorder', a phrase directly echoing Carlyle.⁴² But instead of moving to Yea, Bartleby enacts his own quiet rebellion, his own individuated version of No; 'I would prefer not to' and his refusal to work exactly inverts the logic of Carlyle's progress from No to Yea to Action. A good deal of Melville's writing develops from *Sartor*, thematically and stylistically. Both 'The Whiteness of the Whale' and Ahab's celebrated speech have their origins there.

> All visible objects, man, are but as pasteboard masks. But in each event – in the living act, the undoubted deed – there, some unknown but still reasoning thing puts forth the mouldings of its features from behind the unreasoning mask. If man will strike, strike through the mask! How can the prisoner reach outside except by thrusting through the wall?⁴³

Ahab is directly echoing Teufelsdröckh's desire 'To look through the Shows of things into Things themselves', and his saying: 'All visible things are Emblems; what thou seest is not there on its own account; strictly taken, is not there at all: Matter exists only spiritually, and to represent some Idea, and *body* it forth.'⁴⁴

As enormously influential as they undoubtedly were, *Sartor Resartus* is not wholly represented by these chapters from book 2. It is not that they are untypical of the text, but they need to be contextualized in light of the book's main preoccupation, Teufelsdröckh's clothes-philosophy. Hence the movement to Everlasting Yea is not the book's climax; it is a movement within the text's larger trajectories; it can even be considered to burst in

---

⁴⁰ McSweeney and Sabor (eds), *Sartor Resartus*, p. 124.
⁴¹ Daniel Paliwoda, *Melville and the Theme of Boredom* (Jefferson, NC: McFarland, 2010), p. 24.
⁴² Melville, *The Piazza Tales*, p. 29.
⁴³ Melville, *Moby-Dick*, p. 164.
⁴⁴ McSweeney and Sabor (eds), *Sartor Resartus*, pp. 155, 56.

upon them. The 'Everlasting Yea' is followed by a chapter titled 'Pause', ending book 2. Here Teufelsdröckh's editor self-consciously works to resume the clothes-philosophy investigation and make links to the beliefs articulated at the culmination of the previous chapter. Thus the editor draws attention to Teufelsdröckh's

> peculiar view of Nature, the decisive Oneness he ascribes to Nature. How all Nature and Life are but one *Garment*, a 'Living Garment', woven and ever a-weaving in the 'Loom of Time:' is not here, indeed, the outline of a whole *Clothes-Philosophy*; at least the arena it is to work in?[45]

This prepares us for the marvellous introduction of George Fox at the beginning of book 3, in a passage so typical of the mixture of comedy and seriousness that runs throughout *Sartor*. The chapter's title 'Incident in Modern History' is quickly explained:

> 'Perhaps the most remarkable incident in Modern History', says Teufelsdröckh, 'is not the Diet of Worms, still less the Battle of Austerlitz, Waterloo, Peterloo, or any other Battle; but an incident passed carelessly over by most Historians, and treated with some degree of ridicule by others: namely, George Fox's making to himself a suit of Leather. This man, the first of the Quakers, and by trade a Shoemaker, was one of those, to whom, under ruder or purer form, the Divine Idea of the Universe is pleased to manifest itself; and, across all the hulls of Ignorance and earthly Degradation, shine through, in unspeakable Awfulness, unspeakable Beauty, on their souls.'[46]

Teufelsdröckh is typically exaggerating here: Fox did not make a leather suit, but a set of trousers (breeches), and he did so mainly for pragmatic purposes. Fox became an itinerant preacher around 1648, at the age of 24, and a few years later started wearing the leather trousers. Although he had been an apprentice shoemaker and was used to working with leather, there is no indication that he made the trousers himself, despite Teufelsdröckh's claim. To Fox, the leather trousers were actual and practical, rather than the symbols that Teufelsdröckh sees – although of course what Teufelsdröckh sees is that Fox's bringing rational pragmatism to clothing is the point. Fox was certainly famous for the trousers. Although leather trousers were not

---

[45] Ibid., p. 155.
[46] Ibid., p. 158.

especially unusual, they became an identifying signifier for him: 'the man in leathern breeches' is his own self-description.[47] As Carlyle indicates, Fox was ridiculed for this, notably by Voltaire.[48] The association of Fox with the leather trousers has been fairly constant; Joyce represents him thus in *Ulysses*, and in one of George Bernard Shaw's 'discussion plays', *In Good King Charles's Golden Days* from 1939, Fox is immediately identifiable by the trousers.[49]

For all its characteristic exaggeration, Carlyle's choice of Fox's trousers as signifiers of a new age is far from unjustified. This is the clothes-philosophy of *Sartor Resartus* in action. When Teufelsdröckh claims that 'Matter exists only spiritually, and to represent some Idea, and *body* it forth' he continues:

> Hence Clothes, as despicable as we think them, are so unspeakably significant. Clothes, from the King's-mantle downwards, are Emblematic, not of want only, but of a manifold cunning Victory over Want. On the other hand, all Emblematic things are properly Clothes, thought-woven or hand-woven: must not the Imagination weave Garments, visible Bodies, wherein the else invisible creations and inspirations of our Reason are, like Spirits, revealed, and first become all-powerful; – the rather if, as we often see, the Hand too aid her, and (by wool Clothes or otherwise) reveal such even to the outward eye?[50]

Clothes are much more than coverings for nakedness; they are the spiritual and imaginative made physical; this recalls Ralph Lauren's famous remark, 'I don't design clothes, I design dreams.'[51] To become at all meaningful, abstractions must enter into our reality as things. Hence, clothes are a bodying-forth of abstractions such as will, inner self, desire. In making the leather trousers, Fox is creating the perfect physical analogue for what is otherwise an abstraction. His beliefs in equality, craft, practicality in the service of God, usefulness, are expressed in these trousers.

---

[47] George Fox, *The Journal*, ed. Nigel Smith (London: Penguin, 1998), p. 95.
[48] '[O]ne *George Fox* ... took it into his head to preach, and, as he pretended, with all the requisites of a true apostle – that is, without being able either to read or write. He was about twenty five years of age, irreproachable in his life and conduct, and a holy mad-man. He was equipp'd in leather from head to foot, and travell'd from one village to another exclaiming against war and the clergy'. Voltaire, *Letters Concerning the English Nation*, ed. Nicholas Cronk (Oxford: Oxford University Press, 1999), p. 17.
[49] Joyce refers to 'Christfox in leather trews', in *Ulysses* (Richmond: Alma Classics, 2012), p. 142.
[50] McSweeney and Sabor (eds), *Sartor Resartus*, p. 56.
[51] Quoted in *The New York Times*, 19 April 1986.

For Teufelsdröckh, Fox is the pioneer of modernity because in making the trousers he is fashioning his appearance, that is, expressing his whole social self, from his inner conviction and not from someone else's desire or expectation. While Carlyle represents Fox as able to fashion himself in modernity, Melville cannot take this wholly to his heart. He may be drawn to it as an aspiration for his own fictive characters, but typically they are abject in modernity, their clothing not expressing an inner conviction but this abjection. The leather trousers, and this is why it is crucial for Teufelsdröckh that they are 'self-sewn', are a claim to self-definition, unrestricted by class or social or religious orthodoxy, a state unattainable for some of Melville's major characters.

The realization of the abstract as the actual is of course also to be the difference between Romanticism and Transcendentalism, Romanticism's inner lights finding social expression. Teufelsdröckh thus hails Fox as 'the greatest of the Moderns' because his self-styling will herald social transformations. While on the face of it, the Quaker founder's leather breeches are a long way from those worn in the twentieth century, notably by motorcyclists and, iconically, by Jim Morrison of The Doors, there is a connection through the sense that they embody transgression, the refusal to accept the styles and sartorial customs dictated by society, the usually implicit and sometimes explicit rule that you must wear only clothing (or uniform) appropriate to your class, profession or social station.[52] Indeed, in a celebrated 1967 essay for *New Society*, Angela Carter saw the connection between the new freedom of dress in the 1960s and political radicalism: 'Clothes are our weapons, our challenges, our visible insults.'[53] One example she provides is reminiscent of Hester Prynne, standing defiant before the law flaunting her embroidered letter: 'The Rolling Stones' drug case was an elegant confrontation of sartorial symbolism in generation warfare: the judge, in ritually potent robes and wig, invoking the doom of his age and class upon the beautiful children in frills and sunset colours, who dared to question the infallibility he represents as icon of the law and father

---

[52] E. L. Doctorow's short story 'Leather Man' focuses also on the need to see the familiar from another's view, the value of temporary estrangement. His Leather Man is an itinerant, 'colossally dressed, in layers of coats and shawls and pants, all topped off with a stiff-hand-fashioned leather outer-armour, like a knight's, and a homemade pointed hat of leather' (p. 68). One of the characters explains his function: 'What is the essential act of the Leather Man? He makes the world foreign. He distances it. He is estranged. Our perceptions are sharpest when we're estranged. We can see the shape of things'. E. L. Doctorow, *The Lives of the Poets* (London: Picador, 1985), p. 74.

[53] Angela Carter, 'Notes for a Theory of Sixties Style', in *Shaking a Leg* (London: Chatto & Windus, 1997), p. 105.

figure'.[54] For Carlyle, to challenge established authority from your inner convictions is to endorse modernity, and modernity's core tenet which is, as Anthony Giddens puts it, that the world is 'open to transformation by human intervention'.[55] This is why Teufelsdröckh climaxes his endorsement of Fox's sewing so grandly:

> Stitch away, thou noble Fox: every prick of that little instrument is pricking into the heart of Slavery, and World-worship, and the Mammon-god. Thy elbows jerk, as in strong swimmer-strokes, and every stroke is bearing thee across the Prison-ditch, within which Vanity holds her Workhouse and Ragfair, into lands of true Liberty; were the work done, there is in broad Europe one Free Man, and thou art he![56]

As noted earlier, it is relatively easy to see Melville's absorption of Carlyle in a number of ways. But his use of the clothes-philosophy from *Sartor* is less obvious even if it is pervasive. As we saw in the 'Agatha' letter, Melville was attentive to clothing as carrying a symbolic value. He uses this symbolism variously; as representing transgression, inappropriateness and the potential for self-fashioning. He also occasionally makes an analogy between writing and making clothes. While it seems on the face of it that Melville's repertoire of characters have limited sartorial choices, his detailing of clothing and dress is significant. In his naval fiction he often draws attention to the fact that sailors are always mending and sewing; for instance, White-Jacket complains that he can find no seclusion on the *Neversink* because 'an irruption of tars, with ditty-bags or sea-reticules, and piles of old trowsers to mend, would break in upon my seclusion, and, forming a sewing-circle, drive me off with their chatter'.[57] White-Jacket's own attempt at self-fashioning is a key aspect of this novel, troped on the opening page through

---

[54] Ibid., p. 107. Justine Picardie uses the first quotation when she writes about buying a pair of 'leather' (actually plastic) trousers in 1997 when she was 16; they made 'an immediate and definite improvement in my life'. *My Mother's Wedding Dress* (London: Picador, 2005), p. 53.
[55] For Giddens, modernity has three core concepts or conditions: the world is open to transformation by human intervention; there is a complex of economic institutions, and 'a certain range' of political institutions, 'including the nation-state and mass democracy'. Anthony Giddens and Christopher Pierson, *Conversations with Anthony Giddens* (Cambridge: Polity Press, 1998), p. 94. Human intervention includes 'the transformation of tradition'.
[56] McSweeney and Sabor (eds), *Sartor Resartus*, p. 160.
[57] Herman Melville, *White-Jacket* (Evanston, IL: Northwestern University Press, 1970), p. 323.

his self-tailoring of the jacket with 'Quakerish amplitude'.[58] Melville's allusion to Carlyle's representation of Fox is especially evident, though, in Ishmael. In the chapter 'The Mat-Maker' he starts to daydream as he and Queequeg are working together, weaving a 'sword-mat':

> so strange a dreaminess did there then reign all over the ship and all over the sea, only broken by the intermitting dull sound of the sword, that it seemed as if this were the Loom of Time, and I myself were a shuttle mechanically weaving and weaving away at the Fates. There lay the fixed threads of the warp subject to but one single, ever returning, unchanging vibration, and that vibration merely enough to admit of the crosswise interblending of other threads with its own. This warp seemed necessity; and here, thought I, with my own hand I ply my own shuttle and weave my own destiny into these unalterable threads.[59]

Ishmael dreams of fashioning his own fate, of self-mastery that proves elusive for him; and 'The Mat-Maker' emphasizes his entire lack of authority as it concludes with the first sighting of Sperm whales and the appearance of Ahab's phantom crew. But Melville is also continuing an association he often made between weaving, or sewing, and creating a text – the first chapter of *Moby-Dick* being titled 'Loomings'. For all his longing, Ishmael may be unable to shape his own destiny, but he does give us this text, and names himself for it. The text is woven as the world is; later on Ishmael will describe Pip's appalling abandonment and near-drowning as an experience giving him an insight into providence itself: 'He saw God's foot upon the treadle of the loom, and spoke it; and therefore his shipmates called him mad.'[60] Pip sees that one cannot shape one's own self; our lives are determined for us, however much Ahab rebels against this.

Melville's association of the text with fabric is developed in different ways, most notably in *White-Jacket*, and this figuration will be explored later. But there is in several of his works a significant emphasis on characters who are wearing the wrong clothing, an indicator of 'identity ambivalence'.[61] In *Typee* Tommo dispenses his sailor clothes for the duration of his stay on the island. He dresses like the natives do, resuming his seaman's clothes when he flees the island on another ship. These are the right clothes for the purpose, even if the wearing of tappa means a temporary destabilizing of his

---

[58] Ibid., p. 3.
[59] Melville, *Moby-Dick*, pp. 214–15.
[60] Ibid., p. 414.
[61] See Davis, *Fashion, Culture and Identity*, pp. 20–35.

character. But by the time of Melville's fourth novel, *Redburn*, published in 1849, there seems to be a determination to have characters inappropriately dressed for their activities. Among others, a significant precursor text for *Redburn* is R. H. Dana's *Two Years before the Mast*, published anonymously in 1840. Melville greatly admired the book, which in fact revolutionized American maritime narrative by focusing on the experiences of the common sailor rather than the officer class, as had been the case with, for example, the work of James Fenimore Cooper. Dana also utilized first-person narration, a tactic emulated by Melville in his first novels. Although his class background qualifies him for officer status, Dana chooses to enrol as a common sailor, interrupting his studies at Harvard for the two years. The opening of his narrative shows him swapping his student attire for that of the sailor: 'the tight dress coat, silk cap and kid gloves of an undergraduate at Cambridge, to the loose duck trowsers, checked shirt and tarpaulin hat of a sailor'.[62] While it is interesting to note as an aside that in the mid-nineteenth century, student dress was as regulated and recognizable as that of the sailor, the main point is that Dana almost unthinkingly accepts the need to wear the clothes that delineate his station. This is partly pragmatic and partly a demonstration of a commitment, however temporary, to his new life. As he nears the end of the voyage, which had involved gathering and curing hides on the California coast (this Western dimension is crucial to the narrative), Dana throws overboard the clothing acquired for this purpose:

> Having got through the ship's duty, and washed and shaved, we went below, and had a fine time overhauling our chests, laying aside the clothes we meant to go ashore in, and throwing overboard all that were worn out and good for nothing. Away went the woollen caps in which we had carried hides upon our heads, for sixteen months, on the coast of California; the duck frocks, for tarring down rigging; and the worn-out and darned mittens and patched woollen trowsers which had stood the tug of Cape Horn.[63]

Dana's wholehearted commitment to the two-year voyage is evident through his choice of the right clothing, as clearly as it will be discarded as he resumes the uniform of an undergraduate. *Two Years before the Mast* is an important work for many reasons, including its sense that for men, true education

---

[62] Richard Henry Dana, Jr, *Two Years before the Mast and Other Voyages* (New York: Library of America, 2005), p. 5.
[63] Ibid., p. 339.

requires physical exertion as well as college attendance, and that it also needs to incorporate an understanding of the West. This will be developed by key figures later in the nineteenth century, notably by Theodore Roosevelt, but already with Dana there is the sense that a tour of the West is a true alternative to the grand tour of Europe that gentlemen were expected to make as part of their complete education. Melville is not being ironic when he has Ishmael claim that 'a whaleship was my Yale College and my Harvard'.[64]

However, in sharp contrast to Dana's careful preparations, Melville has Wellingborough Redburn seem almost determined to undertake his first voyage in the wrong clothes. This is apparent from the very first paragraphs:

> 'Wellingborough, as you are going to sea, suppose you take this shooting-jacket of mine along; it's just the thing – take it, it will save the expense of another. You see, it's quite warm; fine long skirts, stout horn buttons, and plenty of pockets.'
>
> Out of the goodness and simplicity of his heart, thus spoke my elder brother to me, upon the *eve* of my departure for the seaport.
>
> 'And, Wellingborough', he added, 'since we are both short of money, and you want an outfit, and I *have* none to give, you may as well take my fowling-piece along, and sell it in New York for what you can get. – Nay, take it; it's of no use to me now; I can't find it in powder any more.'[65]

Wellingborough is not just going to sea in the wrong clothes; the detail of the skirts implies a feminine aspect indicating a compromised manhood. Subsequently a series of mistakes on Wellingborough's part means that he is unable to exchange the shooting-jacket for more suitable clothing. The effect is partly comic in a typically Melvillean way, though it also indicates how far Melville is writing a counter-text to Dana's narrative. This is intensified because Redburn's voyage is to the East, to the old world of Europe, and it will incorporate a consideration of the relation between modernity and the past. Dana's journey is an interlude in his life, but is also about the West and the American future.

---

[64] Melville, *Moby-Dick*, p. 112. On the West as education, see Stephen Fender, *Plotting the 'Golden West': American Literature and the Rhetoric of the California Trail* (Cambridge: Cambridge University Press, 1981). Fender points out that Western activities that men today engage in recreationally without women – dude ranches, hunting, fishing, and so on – are 'gestures' to a legendary Western past (p. 61); they also function as recuperative masculinity.

[65] Herman Melville, *Redburn* (Evanston, IL: Northwestern University Press, 1969), p. 3.

When he eventually reports to his ship, the *Highlander*, the chief mate cannot envisage Redburn as a potential seaman:

> [T]he chief mate approached in a great hurry about something, and seeing me in his way, cried out, 'Ashore with you, you young loafer! There's no stealings here; sail away, I tell you, with that shooting-jacket!'
> Upon this I retreated, saying that I was going out in the ship as a sailor.
> 'A sailor!' he cried, 'a barber's clerk, you mean; *you* going out in the ship? what, in that jacket? Hang me, I hope the old man hasn't been shipping any more greenhorns like you – he'll make a shipwreck of it if he has. But this is the way nowadays; to save a few dollars in seamen's wages, they think nothing of shipping a parcel of farmers and clodhoppers and baby-boys.'[66]

Again, the clothes are read as indicative of unmanliness, the 'barber's clerk' implying effeminacy. Immediately, he is renamed by the chief mate, as the unwieldy 'Wellingborough Redburn' is replaced by a metonymic reduction: '"Who had the baptizing of ye? Why didn't they call you Jack, or Jill, or something short and handy. But I'll baptize you over again. D'ye hear, sir, henceforth your name is *Buttons*. And now do you go, Buttons, and clean out that pig-pen in the long-boat; it has not been cleaned out since last voyage."'[67] Redburn's inappropriate clothing is in a sense generic, as Melville utilizes the familiar narrative of a greenhorn or country bumpkin whose inexperience is rendered comically. But it is not merely generic. For one thing, his lack of the right clothing is aligned with more complex aspects of the novel, notably Redburn's nascent manhood and uncertain identity, his search for his dead father, or, more specifically, for the guidance that his absent father might posthumously offer him as he attempts to make his own way in the modern world. As an importer, the father had crossed the Atlantic 'several times' on business, and Redburn recalls the profound impact his stories had on him:

> [H]he used to tell my brother and me of the monstrous waves at sea, mountain high; of the masts bending like twigs; and all about Havre, and Liverpool, and about going up into the ball of St Paul's in London. . . . I tried hard to think how such places must look of

---

[66] Ibid., p. 28.
[67] Ibid.

rainy days and Saturday afternoons; and whether indeed they did have rainy days and Saturdays there, just as we did here; and whether the boys went to school there, and studied geography, and wore their shirt collars turned over, and tied with a black ribbon; and whether their papas allowed them to wear boots, instead of shoes, which I so much disliked, for boots looked so manly.[68]

While the father's tales tell of a world elsewhere, they also provide a script for manliness, complete with the right boots. It is also a world that is represented aesthetically, as Redburn recalls the oil paintings and prints that his father had brought back from his travels, as well as a glass model ship, *La Reine*. The model represents an ideal world, the art that has perfected and remedied nature, making it immune from temporal flux. It is this controllable and fixed world that Redburn seeks on his voyage. This is most readily mirrored in his attempts to follow his father's guidebook in modern Liverpool. Melville dwells a good deal on this guidebook. Chapter 30 is a consideration of old guidebooks, and the next has Redburn attempting to use his father's book, now almost half a century out of date, to guide him through contemporary Liverpool. Redburn puts his faith in this moroccan-bound green book, memorizing it during the voyage in the expectation that when he arrives he will already know the as yet-unvisited city:

> In short, when I considered that my own father had used this very guide-book, and that thereby it had been thoroughly tested, and its fidelity proved beyond a peradventure; I could not but think that I was building myself up in an unerring knowledge of Liverpool; especially as I had familiarized myself with the map, and could turn sharp corners on it, with marvelous confidence and celerity.[69]

As might be expected, the book is quickly seen as redundant, with more recent landmarks in the city, such as the Nelson memorial, and the demolition of buildings that had been conspicuous. Like *La Reine*, the book is fixed in an earlier moment, and while this provides reassurance, it cannot possibly be of practical use to another age. When this is brought home forcibly to him, Redburn reflects:

> The book on which I had so much relied; the book in the old morocco cover; the book with the cocked-hat corners; the book full of fine old

[68] Ibid., p. 5.
[69] Ibid., p. 152.

family associations; the book with seventeen plates, executed in the highest style of art; this precious book was next to useless. Yes, the thing that had guided the father, could not guide the son.[70]

This moment of disillusion is closely linked in the novel with another, and with a further attempt to follow a script generated in childhood. Redburn's childlike dream of travel is one of return and restoration, of selfhood.

> As I grew older my thoughts took a larger flight, and I frequently fell into long reveries about distant voyages and travels, and thought how fine it would be, to be able to talk about remote and barbarous countries; with what reverence and wonder people would regard me, if I had just returned from the coast of Africa or New Zealand; how dark and romantic my sunburnt cheeks would look; how I would bring home with me foreign clothes of a rich fabric and princely make, and wear them up and down the streets, and how grocers' boys would turn back their heads to look at me, as I went by.[71]

Far from a reality in which he must accept his brother's old jacket, his dream of self-accomplishment includes the dandiacal exotic, the cynosure showing off clothes that express his self and his travels. But in a fundamental sense *Redburn* is about growing up and finding that there is no script for your life, and that you must fashion your own. This is what it shares with the Hawthorne's colonial tale published in 1832, 'My Kinsman Major Molineux'. There the country boy Robin comes to town to visit his kinsman, the royally appointed governor, with the expectation of social advancement. Naively unable to read the signifiers of what is happening during the night, he is caught up in a series of nightmarish events during which the governor is tarred and feathered. Lost and disconcerted, Robin resolves to flee the town and return home, but is approached by a 'gentleman' who has taken an ambiguously protective interest in him. He is offered a choice: 'Some few days hence, if you continue to wish it, I will speed you on your journey. Or, if you prefer to remain with us, perhaps, as you are a shrewd youth, you may rise in the world, without the help of your kinsman, Major Molineux.'[72] At a moment of personal as well as historical rupture his choice is between returning to the past and a reality that can exist for only a little longer, or to accept the challenge of the nascent republic and start to make his own way.

[70] Ibid., p. 157.
[71] Ibid., p. 5.
[72] Hawthorne, *Tales and Sketches*, p. 87.

Although Hawthorne suggests he will choose to stay, Robin is at the end of the story in an aporia between two worlds, that of tradition and the past and the future with all of its uncertainties, anxieties and possibilities. To use Marshall Berman's terms, Robin is confronting modernity:

> There is a mode of vital experience – experience of space and time, of the self and others, of life's possibilities and perils. . . . I will call this body of experience 'modernity.' To be modern is to find ourselves in an environment that promises us adventure, power, joy, growth, transformation of ourselves and the world – and, at the same time, that threatens to destroy everything we have, everything we know, everything we are.[73]

At the moment he realizes the uselessness of the guidebook, Redburn is poised at the same moment. *Redburn* is very much concerned with the helpfulness or relevance of a prior script to the reality of modernity; it is not just the father but the father's 'stories' that Redburn believes to have scripted his future. As he says of the guidebook, it 'might have done good service in its day, yet it would prove but a miserable cicerone to a modern'.[74]

Melville will address this question more cogently and more obliquely a few years later in 'The Piazza', whose first-person narrator must move outside the worlds of romance imaginary to apprehend the actuality (and poverty) of his hitherto imagined neighbour; an actuality that resists the romantic and transformative power of the imagination. As a novel about becoming, *Redburn* is, like 'My Kinsman Major Molineux' about a self in transition, suspended between the reassurance of an identity provided by family and a sense of personal lineage, and recognition of the responsibility of creating an identity removed from these, between being an object and a subject. But Redburn does not remain suspended, nor is he simply a victim of self-delusion and of circumstance. For instance, we see his developing agency, especially apparent in the harrowing sequence in chapter 37 when, moving well outside the now-irrelevant guidebook, he confronts a Liverpool of appalling poverty and public indifference and attempts, vainly, to help one family. Similarly, Redburn's inappropriate clothing for the voyage is more complex than a series of unfortunate accidents and misjudgements. There is an element of defiance in Redburn that very much complicates and refutes any sense of him as a victim – the defiance and stubbornness, close to desperation, that drove him to

---

[73] Berman, *All That Is Solid Melts into Air*, p. 15.
[74] Melville, *Redburn*, p. 152.

resist paying his full fare on the journey on the Hudson River to New York. That is, his inappropriateness is willed; an act of refusal to adapt that, though unarticulated as such, is one expressive of fashioning individuation, being a subject. The ambivalence of Redburn's clothing is especially pronounced when he prepares for his first solitary 'stroll' in Liverpool one Sunday:

> I rose bright and early; from head to foot performed my ablutions 'with Eastern scrupulosity', and I arrayed myself in my red shirt and shooting-jacket, and the sportsman's pantaloons; and crowned my entire man with the tarpaulin; so that from this curious combination of clothing, and particularly from my red shirt, I must have looked like a very strange compound indeed: three parts sportsman, and two soldier, to one of the sailor.[75]

Rather than having a sense of an entire identity, Redburn thinks of himself as compounded. When Dana exchanges one 'uniform' for another, he enters wholeheartedly into the working sailor's role he has adopted. Redburn's 'compound' identity is strange in being partly voluntary and partly imposed. As is to be expected, Redburn is mocked both by his fellow *Highlanders*, and by incidental passersby in the city. But it is also clear that while his wardrobe is severely limited, he has dressed in this manner by choice. His motley clothing, with its mixed messages and contradictory grammar, is an expression and an acceptance of the 'strange compound' that he is, representing the variety and complexity of identity that would be suppressed by the adoption of sartorial uniformity, by obedience to the grammar of clothing. There is a certain stubbornness in maintaining this compound identity rather than relinquishing it to an ultimately false whole; false, that is, in not expressing a true self. Although he dreams of being a dandy flaunting 'foreign clothes of a rich fabric and princely make' Redburn is not quite the dandy that Melville will characterize in later works, notably John Paul Jones in *Israel Potter*.[76] Redburn walks about Liverpool in mixed dress, as does the recalled Handsome Sailor from *Billy Budd*, but the contrast between the two is instructive. Where the Handsome Sailor is admired and adored, Redburn simply lacks the self-confident flamboyance that would enable him to flaunt mixed-metaphor clothing – hence the mockery from those who see him. The *haute couture* designer Jean Paul Gaultier has remarked that those who make sartorial mistakes are the true

---

[75] Ibid., p. 153.
[76] Ibid., p. 5.

stylists; 'It's always the badly dressed people who are the most interesting.'[77] But to flaunt these 'mistakes' requires an inner self-belief, even a certain arrogance, which Redburn lacks. It may also require a sense of being of the correct class, having the 'right' to wear such clothes: to use contemporary parlance, two women in the same outfit may result in one described as 'chav' and the other as 'chic'.[78]

Redburn's motley represents an articulated but not enacted awareness of the multidimensionality (the compounds) of his self, and this aspect of the novel represents a notable development of Carlyle's clothes-theories. But there is another that is especially significant and will have a bearing on Melville's developing fictions. This is the oblique representation of the self in the fiction, the process of writing and the relation between clothing and fiction. The surface autobiographical aspects of *Redburn* are obvious to us today, for whom so much of Melville's life is now available.[79] These include the entire narrative frame, since Melville draws on his first experience of life at sea when in 1839, aged 19, he was a greenhorn on the New York merchant ship *St Lawrence* when she sailed to Liverpool and back. Some of Redburn's experiences in Liverpool, notably seeing the Nelson memorial, were Melville's own and were to be refashioned elsewhere in his fiction. More importantly, Redburn's family situation closely resembles Melville's. Like Redburn's father, Melville's had been a merchant and an importer, had travelled to Liverpool and his death left the family in difficult financial circumstances. Although there are some modifications, there is a close resemblance between Redburn's family and Melville's, somewhat intensified by his dedicating the novel to his younger brother Thomas. Intriguing though they are, these autobiographical origins for *Redburn* are superficial when set against both the text's interiority, that is, Melville's exploration of the psychological conflict and development of Redburn in relation to his father, and the circumstances of its composition. In both of these areas, Melville's development of ideas from *Sartor Resartus* is clearly evident. Some of this intensity of feeling is evident in Redburn's fear of being utterly consumed by grief for the dead father, and the dread of

---

[77] *Harpers and Queen*, September 1984, quoted in Wilson, *Adorned in Dreams*, p. 10.
[78] Justine Picardie reflects on this with regard to the footballer Wayne Rooney's working-class teenage girlfriend Coleen McLoughlin modelling for *Vogue* in 2005; see *My Mother's Wedding Dress*, pp. 218–26.
[79] William H. Gilman's *Melville's Early Life and* Redburn (New York: New York University Press, 1951) is invaluable for discriminating between the autobiographical and the fictional in the novel. Although *Redburn* is based on actual experience, much is invention, or is taken from other sources, notably descriptions of the dreadful hardships endured by the Irish emigrants.

losing himself to it entirely. As the *Highlander* passes the fort at New York Harbour, Redburn recalls a childhood family visit there:

> It was noon-day when I was there, in the month of June, and there was little wind to stir the trees, and every thing looked as if it was waiting for something, and the sky overhead was blue as my mother's eye, and I was so glad and happy then. But I must not think of those delightful days, before my father became a bankrupt, and died, and we removed from the city; for when I think of those days, something rises up in my throat and almost strangles me.[80]

As noted earlier, Redburn's mixture of clothing and his inappropriate dress signal his otherwise unarticulated defiance, his sense of difference from others. But this also reflects in an important way on *Redburn* itself. In writing it Melville was returning to a familiar narrative mode after the disastrous reception of the excessively Carlylean *Mardi*, whose unexpected mixture of styles had dismayed reviewers and alienated readers. *Redburn* was welcomed by reviewers as a return to 'form' – the recuperation of the style of *Typee* and *Omoo*. But while apparently obedient to what he perceived as readers' demands, Melville suggests through his clothing imagery that this is a performance, the undertaking of a role that does not fully encompass his own actuality. That is, in contrast to his earlier novels, Melville suggests that *Redburn* is a measured performance.

This is evident from the association between Redburn's clothing and the book itself, in that both are compounded identities. At one point, Melville discusses the various tasks on board ship, with the sailors continually repairing the ship's sails, and he comments, 'For material, they use odds and ends of old rigging called "*junk*" the yarns of which are picked to pieces, and then twisted into new combinations, something as most books are manufactured.'[81] He is not here so much drawing attention to the materiality of his own novel, but to its imaginative provision, his own twisting and reshaping. Like Redburn, Melville is wearing the wrong clothing, putting on a show that cannot properly reflect the true self, as this is in the process of being formed. The mixed grammar of Redburn's clothing for public display in Liverpool is a Carlylean emblem for the mixing of styles in this novel. Melville's subtitle for *Redburn*, 'Sailor-Boy Confessions and Reminiscences', suggests that it is not fiction at all. But it does have its narrative shifts and its clearly fictional elements, and the reviewers who likened it to *Robinson Crusoe* clearly had

---

[80] Melville, *Redburn*, p. 36.
[81] Ibid., p. 114.

noticed this. As one wrote 'If this volume be an imaginary narrative then it is the most life-like and natural fiction since Robinson Crusoe's account of his life on the island of *Juan Fernandez*.'[82] Though *Redburn* lacks the stylistic extremes of *Mardi*, it is still a dynamic, changing narrative.

Reflecting on them now, with what we know of Melville's subsequent career, we could say that both *Redburn* and *White-Jacket* are transitional works by an author who still believed in the possibility of his making a living by writing; or, to put it another way, was driven by the necessity of at least trying to do this. He was accordingly reluctant to attempt once again the imaginative (and economic) risks undertaken in the composition and publication of *Mardi*. The intermediary status of *Redburn* and *White-Jacket* is apparent when we consider the immense differences between them and Melville's next work, *Moby-Dick*; this also confirms and intensifies the powerful influence that Hawthorne (both the man and the writer) had on Melville. As suggested in Chapter 1, having met Hawthorne in the summer of 1850, Melville was encouraged fully to invest himself imaginatively once again in his writing. There is a long-held supposition that *Moby-Dick* began in the factual obliquely autobiographical style of *Redburn* and *White-Jacket*, but developed in a radically different direction under the influence of Hawthorne, to whom it is dedicated. *Redburn* and *White-Jacket* are written expressly with a particular potential readership in mind, and Melville allows his sense of that readership to shape the narrative. At the same time, though, Melville through his clothes imagery tells us of this fact. This is subtly performed in *Redburn* and more overtly in *White-Jacket*, which is after all a novel that takes its title from a singular piece of clothing.

Perhaps it is partly this sense of them as intermediary works, both to be overshadowed by *Moby-Dick*, which has led to the comparative critical neglect of both *Redburn* and *White-Jacket*. Certainly, Melville's written statements about them seem to give license for critical dismissal. Writing to Dana in response to his praise for the books, and repeating almost verbatim phrases he had used in an earlier letter to his father-in-law, Melville commented that he saw both as a job of work. They were written he claimed 'almost entirely for "lucre" – by the job, as a woodsawyer saws wood'.[83] Earlier, in December 1849 he had written to Evert Duyckinck in what has become a much-quoted letter:

> I did not see your say about the book Redburn, which to my surprise (somewhat) seems to have been favorably received. I am glad of it – for

---

[82] Brian Higgins and Hershel Parker (eds), *Herman Melville: The Contemporary Reviews* (Cambridge: Cambridge University Press, 1995), p. 286.
[83] Melville, *Correspondence*, p. 160.

it puts money into an empty purse. But I hope I shall never write such a book again – Tho' when a poor devil writes with duns all round him, & looking over the back of his chair – & perching on his pen & diving in his inkstand – like the devils about St. Anthony – what can you expect of that poor devil? – What but a beggarly 'Redburn'![84]

But 'beggarly' *Redburn* and the equally dismissed *White-Jacket* have a special importance in Melville's development and in particular in the path he takes out of Carlyle's clothes-theory. Furthermore, as well as being significant works on their own terms, a genuine match for the sea-narratives of Cooper and Dana, they contain many of the seeds of Melville's later work, and not only in the attention that Melville pays to the clothing symbolism. For instance, in *Redburn* there is a consideration of defiant nonconformity and its consequences that will be picked up again and again by Melville, especially in the creation of Ahab and of Bartleby. Redburn's sartorial quirkiness has its counterpart in the bullying and mean-spirited Highland crewmate Jackson, who also refuses to dress like a sailor; but where Redburn undergoes a moral growth, Jackson, self-consumed by his hatreds, is killed. The name that Melville chooses for the erstwhile narrator of *Moby-Dick* also originates here, as Redburn reflects on his deracinated reality; 'at last I found myself a sort of Ishmael in the ship, without a single friend or companion; and I began to feel a hatred growing up in me against the whole crew – so much so, that I prayed against it, that it might not master my heart completely, and so make a fiend of me, something like Jackson'.[85] Captain Riga of the *Highlander* anticipates some aspects of *Billy Budd*'s Captain Vere in their implied temperamental unsuitability for their roles – Riga dresses as a captain should while ashore, nicely playing the role, but switches to 'old shabby clothes' for the voyage.[86] There is even a glimmer of what would appeal to Melville about the Agatha anecdote, as he relates the story of 'Dutch' Max, with a New York wife and a Liverpudlian wife, both 'equally well-behaved, discreet, and reputable; and equally devoted to the keeping in good order Max's wardrobe'.[87]

White-Jacket continues both the story of Tommo after *Typee* and *Omoo* and Melville's new found vein of factual/fictive writing with a strain of the Carlylean clothes-theory. For several reasons, it is easy to consider *Redburn* and *White-Jacket*, like *Typee* and *Omoo*, as twinned texts. Melville wrote them very closely together – and quickly; it is estimated that *Redburn* was

---

[84] Ibid., pp. 148–9.
[85] Melville, *Redburn*, p. 62.
[86] Ibid., p. 71.
[87] Ibid., p. 129.

completed in about ten weeks, and *White-Jacket* took only a little longer.[88] Both texts have an autobiographical core, although with much fictional addition. *White-Jacket* has its basis in Melville's 14-month passage on the American naval frigate *United States*, called *Neversink* in the novel. He had temporally enlisted in the Pacific in order to get home, and left the ship on her return to the United States. It is also likely that Dana had suggested Melville write of his naval experience, since Melville's letter to him in October 1849 states 'Your hint concerning a man-of-war has in anticipation, been acted upon. A printed copy of the book is before me.'[89] More importantly, *White-Jacket* continues in the same style as *Redburn*, a first-person narration encompassing a variety of styles and moods, written with a clear sense of what his readership was interested in – and with a good deal of emphasis on the symbolism of dress. This is of course apparent from the very title, and then from the novel's opening sentences:

> It was not a *very* white jacket, but white enough, in all conscience, as the sequel will show. The way I came by it was this. When our frigate lay in Callao, on the coast of Peru – her last harbor in the Pacific – I found myself without a *grego*, or sailor's surtout; and as, toward the end of a three years' cruise, no pea-jackets could be had from the purser's steward; and being bound for Cape Horn, some sort of a substitute was indispensable; I employed myself, for several days, in manufacturing an outlandish garment of my own devising, to shelter me from the boisterous weather we were so soon to encounter.[90]

From the first, then, the jacket is a statement of difference, 'an outlandish garment of my own devising'. It is like Redburn's skirted moleskin shooting-jacket in being emblematic of a refusal to have one's identity subsumed. But it is actually one stage further than that shooting-jacket. Redburn's jacket was handed down from his brother, but even though White-Jacket emphasizes the lack of other available clothing, he does stress that the coat was of his own design. This is particularly telling in that, as Melville was fully aware,

---

[88] Melville's wife Elizabeth recalls the summer of 1849; 'We remained in New York – he wrote "Redburn" and "White-Jacket."' Quoted in Melville, *White-Jacket*, p. 403. Summer likely meant the period from early May until mid-September.

[89] Melville, *Correspondence*, p. 140; the 'printed copy' was likely to have been the proofs. Melville refers to Dana in the text, recalling his description of rounding Cape Horn for the first time: 'But if you want the best idea of Cape Horn, get my friend Dana's unmatchable "Two Years Before the Mast." But you can read, and so you must have read it. His chapters describing Cape Horn must have been written with an icicle'. Melville, *White-Jacket*, p. 99.

[90] Ibid., p. 3.

there was an increasing expectation that personnel in the navy should wear uniforms. This move to uniformity was part of an overall modernization of the naval service, and 1841 saw the publication of a 14-page guide titled *Regulations for the Uniform and Dress of the United States Navy*. Although the guidelines were for the uniforms of officers only, they were part of the increasing standardization for all naval ranks, and not only in terms of dress. These regulations would eventually be developed to incorporate regulations governing general appearance, specifically body and facial hair. These developing rules provide a context for *White-Jacket*'s chapter 85, 'The Great Massacre of the Beards', and the admirable (and effective) defiance of the ancient seaman, Ushant: 'According to a then recent ordinance at Washington, the beards of both officers and seamen were to be accurately laid out and surveyed, and on no account must come lower than the mouth, so as to correspond with the Army standard.'[91] In spite of these developing modern regulations, *Neversink*'s Captain Claret is notably lax regarding their application. 'In the matter of overseeing the men's clothing . . . he was remarkably indulgent, compared with the conduct of other Navy Captains, who, by sumptuary regulations, oblige their sailors to run up large bills with the Purser for clothes.'[92]

White-Jacket is the closest Melville comes to writing realist 'documentary' fiction in the style of Dana, and fiction which also had a clear social import, publicizing the brutality of flogging and the severe nature of discipline in the navy. This again is reminiscent of *Two Years before the Mast*, whose concluding discursive chapter considered the welfare of the common sailor and the harsh regime of the merchant service. Melville hoped to write himself back into public favour in the aftermath of *Mardi* while highly conscious of the tastes of a reading public, specifically here the taste for factual and descriptive passages concerned with naval life. Indeed there is a good deal of very fine writing in *White-Jacket*, as well as a notable consistency of tone and a powerful narrative line, and the episode in which White-Jacket is almost completely unnerved at the prospect of being flogged is among Melville's finest work. This comes about as White-Jacket (in spite of having been on the ship for at least a year) is unaware of the station he is meant to occupy when the hands are required to alter sail so that that ship may tack. Consequently, the ship almost misses the tack, and the Captain witnesses this. While interrogating White-Jacket, the Captain is enraged by his lack of deference, his claim to ignorance of his assigned station, and his contradicting the word of an officer; all serious naval offences. Condemned

[91] Ibid., p. 356.
[92] Ibid., p. 357.

for the first time to a flogging, White-Jacket is shaken to the core of his being:

> The Captain stood on the weather-side of the deck. Sideways, on an unobstructed line with him, was the opening of the lee-gangway, where the side-ladders are suspended in port. Nothing but a slight bit of sinnate-stuff served to rail in this opening, which was cut right down to the level of the Captain's feet, showing the far sea beyond... though he was a large, powerful man, it was certain that a sudden rush against him ... would infallibly pitch him headforemost into the ocean, though he who so rushed must needs go over with him. My blood seemed clotting in my veins; I felt icy cold at the tips of my fingers, and a dimness was before my eyes... through that dimness the boatswain's mate, scourge in hand, loomed like a giant, and Captain Claret, and the blue sea seen through the opening at the gangway, showed with an awful vividness. I cannot analyse my heart, though it then stood still within me. But the thing that swayed me to my purpose was not altogether the thought that Captain Claret was about to degrade me, and that I had taken an oath with my soul that he should not. No, I felt my man's manhood so bottomless within me, that no word, no blow, no scourge of Captain Claret could cut me deep enough for that. I but swung to an instinct in me – the instinct diffused through all animated nature, the same that prompts even a worm to turn under the heel. Locking souls with him, I meant to drag Captain Claret from this earthly tribunal of his to that of Jehovah and let Him decide between us. No other way could I escape the scourge.[93]

To a readership familiar with the slave narratives, this is a particularly powerful passage. As he will later do in *Israel Potter*, Melville makes use of the slave narrative paradigm and its common constituents. The comparison between the naval crewman and the slave is explicitly made in the novel: 'I was not born a serf, and will not live a slave!' is White-Jacket's recoil when he reflects on the absolute authority of the Articles of War.[94] Melville also considers the practice of enlisting slaves into the navy, with the masters receiving the wage, even though this is forbidden by Congress. The Purser, a Virginian, has brought a slave known as Guinea aboard as his body-servant, and is receiving Guinea's pay. In a neat reversal of a common slave narrative motif, Melville has the crew envying Guinea for his relatively privileged

[93] Ibid., p. 280.
[94] Ibid., p. 295.

position.[95] Partly because of this ongoing trope, *White-Jacket* is in some measure a 'state of the nation' novel. White-Jacket avoids the flogging and is saved from becoming a murderer and a suicide because of the extraordinary intervention of Colbrook, the corporal of marines. Colbrook's intercession is supported by Melville's ideal sailor Jack Chase, the lowly ranked captain of the maintop who will be the dedicatee of *Billy Budd* over 40 years in the future.

But in spite of the documentary realism and such intense moments, there is a core metaphysics in *White-Jacket* that is a development of Carlyle's primary concepts. Thematically this has to do with Melville's increasing preoccupation with identity and technically is concerned with writing itself, and specifically with *White-Jacket*'s scene of writing. Teufelsdröckh's thesis is that at some moment of modernity (again, Fox's leather trousers are significant), clothing was no longer a matter of ornament or of utility but of individuation, a choice that sought to express inner character: 'Clothes gave us individuality, distinctions, social polity; Clothes have made Men of us.' But, he continues, clothes simultaneously provide the opportunity for dissembling, for dressing in a way that screens rather than reveals the self; 'they are threatening to make Clothes-screens of us'.[96] This ambiguous dynamic between revelation and deception, or, to see it another way, of simultaneously potentially revealing one's inner identity and yet disguising it, is very much at the heart of *White-Jacket*. It is in fact intensified because Melville is writing for the first time of a world in uniform, even if relatively informal as US naval dress at this time actually was. Wearing a uniform is at its essence an act of de-individuation; a uniform's very function is to supersede a self. As Alison Lurie puts it:

> The extreme form of conventional dress is the costume totally determined by others: the uniform. No matter what sort of uniform it is . . . to put on such livery is to give up one's right to act as an individual – in terms of speech, to be partially or wholly censored. . . . What one does, as well as what one wears, will be determined by external authorities. . . . To wear a uniform is to give up your right to free speech in the language of clothes[.][97]

Wearing a uniform, though, is not so much a surrender of identity as the provision of one; the new identity is the uniform. Melville will explore

---

[95] Ibid., p. 379.
[96] McSweeney and Sabor (eds), *Sartor Resartus*, p. 32.
[97] Lurie, *The Language of Clothes*, pp. 17–18, 19.

the conflict between the uniform and the inner self in the character of Captain Vere in *Billy Budd*, a novel very much rooted in *White-Jacket*. This conflict is touched on when White-Jacket considers the supernumerary Commodore, who has been promoted to the point of discomfort and is consequently alienated from the crew; 'I thought myself much happier in that white jacket of mine, than our old Commodore in his dignified epaulets.'[98] What comes across is White-Jacket's profound ambivalence in his attitude towards the uniform. It is too simplistic to claim that his wearing of the white coat is an expression of individuation, consciously or unconsciously designed to mark off his difference from the other crew members, as is largely the case with Redburn. White-Jacket is himself deeply torn between wanting to belong, to be part of a community, and to remain himself, apart, a man signed up only until the frigate returns to the United States. Melville is touching here on clothing's fundamental ambivalence, seen at its most extreme in fashion; it expresses both our sense of belonging to a group and our individuation. He had written of this kind of conflict before; it is a notable aspect of Tommo's character in *Typee*, as will be explored in the next chapter. But here, bearing in mind the influence of Carlyle, more is at stake. *White-Jacket* is about a character in crisis – the measure of which may be seen in his contemplation of murder and of suicide. The problem with the white jacket is not only that it marks him off as not belonging but that it gives him a specious identity in the eyes of the other sailors. It is in fact an embarrassment, and it frustrates White-Jacket in his repeated attempts to find kinship.

On the face of it, it is puzzling that White-Jacket should feel at all ostracized, cut off, another Ishmael, to repeat Redburn's self-nomination. It is never made clear how long White-Jacket has been on board the *Neversink* during its three-year voyage. The fact that he joined her prior to Callao is equally non-explicit: the impression loosely given is that he has just joined the ship at Callao.[99] The novel starts not with White-Jacket's first boarding the frigate but with his shaping of the jacket and the consequent alteration of his standing. It is as White-Jacket that he is assigned to the series of places that he must attend and, as we have seen, somehow turns out not to know his place for tacking, in spite of having been at this point on board for almost a

---

[98] Melville, *White-Jacket*, p. 22.
[99] In the chapter where White-Jacket is threatened with the flogging, it is stated that he has been a crew member for 'upward of a year' (p. 279) but this does not match the chronology from chapter 1, as a voyage from Callao to Charleston would be made in two or three months. Melville himself signed up to the *United States* in August 1843 in Hawaii. The ship called at Callao in December 1843, and returned there in June 1844, where she stayed a month before departing for the United States on 6 July.

year, during which the ship has tacked hundreds of times. That is, whatever he had been, the white coat represents the assignation of a different identity and, another parallel with Redburn, with his being given a new name. This is not at all welcomed by White-Jacket as his jacket turns into an embarrassment. It allows the crew to condescend to him through the convenient metonymic that it provides, and his frustration with the coat is evident throughout. Even where the narrator has sought to reserve privacy, symbolized by the coat's pockets, the jacket proves deficient. This is the subject of two very short chapters, 9 and 10. They begin with a lament of the lack of privacy on a ship housing over five hundred men: '[T]o a common sailor, the living on board a man-of-war is like living in a market; where you dress on the door-steps, and sleep in the cellar. No privacy can you have; hardly one moment's seclusion. It is almost a physical impossibility, that you can ever be alone.'[100] However, in designing his coat, White-Jacket has resolved to make it amenable to privacy, with pockets that conceal his possessions from the eyes of the 'market': 'I proposed, that not only should my jacket keep me warm, but that it should also be so constructed as to contain a shirt or two, a pair of trowsers, and divers knickknacks – sewing utensils, books, biscuits, and the like. With this object, I had accordingly provided it with a great variety of pockets, pantries, clothes-presses, and cupboards.'[101] As usual with this jacket, though, things quickly go awry. The pockets' contents, including a 'pocket-edition of Shakspeare', are ruined after a heavy rain, and while attempting to dry them out, they are picked over by the crew.[102]

These chapters of *White-Jacket* are deceptive, in that they appear to obey the surface style Melville is employing, but actually point to a symbolic order, particularly to a set of referents to the novel itself. The same happens at the climax of the story, when White-Jacket is almost killed and must save his own life by freeing himself from the garment. The chapter 'The Last of the Jacket' (with its echo of *The Last of the Mohicans*) contains some of the finest writing in the whole novel. White-Jacket, reefing the top-mast sail in the night, loses his footing because his jacket flaps over his face, and he falls headfirst for more than a hundred feet into the ocean: 'Great God! this is Death!' he thinks.[103] About to surrender to it, he is touched by what appears to be a shark 'some inert, coiled fish of the sea' and starts to fight for his life.[104] At this point the jacket's buoyancy lifts him to the surface; a

---

[100] Melville, *White-Jacket*, p. 35.
[101] Ibid., p. 36.
[102] Ibid., p. 37.
[103] Ibid., p. 392.
[104] Ibid., p. 393.

precursor of Ishmael's survival, and he sees *Neversink*'s crew trying to aid him. But then the jacket starts to weigh him down, dragging him to death, and he must violently cut himself free from it in order to survive:

> I whipped out my knife, that was tucked at my belt, and ripped my jacket straight up and down, as if I were ripping open myself. With a violent struggle I then burst out of it, and was free. Heavily soaked, it slowly sank before my eyes. Sink! sink! oh shroud! thought I; sink forever! accursed jacket that thou art![105]

The crew then mistakes the jacket for a white shark and repeatedly harpoons it, and it sinks to the ocean's bottom.[106]

This is in effect the end of the white jacket and of *White-Jacket*. The remaining two brief chapters have an almost perfunctory air about them: as the narrator says, 'what more remains?' and the name White-Jacket appears no more.[107] Indeed, the chapter describing his fall and release from the coat begins with the narrator describing himself in the third person, as though already initiating a distance from the actual and the assumed self:

> Already has White-Jacket chronicled the mishaps and inconveniences, troubles and tribulations of all sorts brought upon him by that unfortunate but indispensable garment of his. But now it befalls him to record how this jacket, for the second and last time, came near proving his shroud.[108]

---

[105] Ibid., p. 394.
[106] As noted, White-Jacket's survival anticipates Ishmael's. The jacket's being mistaken for a shark is comically recalled during the making of film versions of *Moby-Dick*, for which various models of the whale were devised. George Cotkin details these in his enjoyable commentary *Dive Deeper* (New York and Oxford: Oxford University Press, 2012). John Huston had three costly models of the whale made for his 1956 version, with the screenplay by Ray Bradbury. These consisted of various inflatable rubber parts, with a 20-foot-high cylinder representing the midsection. This part was lost in a storm while filming in the Irish Sea and local legend maintains it prompted a warning from the Irish Coastguard Service, to 'be on the lookout for Moby-Dick'. See Oswald Morris, *Huston, We Have a Problem* (Lanham, MD: Scarecrow Press, 2006). Bradbury wrote a playful fictive memoir of his time in Ireland working on the screenplay with Huston; Ray Bradbury, *Green Shadows, White Whale: A Novel of Ray Bradbury's Adventures Making Moby Dick with John Huston in Ireland* (London: HarperCollins, 1992).
[107] Melville, *White-Jacket*, p. 394.
[108] Ibid., p. 391.

We seem to see birth and death juxtaposed – the rebirth of the man who had taken on the name of White-Jacket, by means of a kind of self-administered Caesarean section, and the death of the actual jacket, harpooned and drowned. But just as he will in *Moby-Dick*, Melville mixes up death and birth, so that in effect 'White-Jacket' as a name dies at the same time as the jacket itself. The coat has 'sunk to the bottom of the sea'; while White-Jacket has 'sunk into the bottom of the boat', and the ending of *White-Jacket* is less than six pages away.[109]

Redburn and *White-Jacket* may quite readily fit into the overall arc that literary scholars have described for them; narratives Melville wrote to redeem himself in the eyes of his publisher and to repair his reputation with his readership by recollecting his earlier mode of slanted autobiographical writing. But there are several dangers in this ready characterization. The main one is in overlooking the variety of styles within the texts, their compound natures, the figuration and troping that Melville uses, and in seeing how they form a self-referential network. Whatever else it is concerned with, *White-Jacket* is about *White-Jacket*, about its own birth, its own structuration and narrative, even about its authorship. While both novels are restrained in comparison with Carlyle's exuberance, they are equally inquisitive about the symbolic meanings of appearances and how appearance gives meaning, and of the relation between text and process. Thus, the pockets in the white coat are emblematic of the novel itself. Melville tells us that while it may appear to be revelatory this is a novel with its own hidden places, its reservations of identity, however precarious and transitory these turn out to be – after all, to tell someone that there are hidden pockets is to nullify their secrecy altogether. The very name provided for White-Jacket is part of this fictive fabric, Melville donning the dress of the author and assuming another self – exactly the same fictive contract with the reader that he will offer us in the first three words of the opening chapter of his next novel. When we agree to call that narrator Ishmael we are signing up to his fictional world, undertaking to voyage with him in it: to participate in his 'loomings'.

What Melville particularly captures in *Redburn* and *White-Jacket* is his deeply held ambivalence towards this assumed style of writing, and his representations of clothing indicate that his attitude towards these novels was considerably more complex than their speedy composition and his tendency to dismiss them imply. As noted earlier, his letter to Dana likened their writing to sawing wood; he had used the same imagery in his October

---

[109] Ibid., pp. 395, 394.

1849 letter to his father-in-law Lemuel Shaw, and this can readily be quoted in support of his dismissive attitude: '[N]o reputation that is gratifying to me, can possibly be achieved by either of these books. They are two *jobs*, which I have done for money – being forced to it, as other men are to sawing wood.'[110] But the letter goes on to complicate this attitude, and reinforces the ambivalence apparent in the clothes imagery used in both novels:

> [W]hile I have felt obliged to refrain from writing the kind of book I would wish to; yet, in writing these books, I have not repressed myself much – so far as *they* are concerned; but have spoken pretty much as I feel. – Being books, then, written in this way, my only desire for their 'success' (as it is called) springs from my pocket, & not from my heart.[111]

Clearly the letter touches on the Carlylean punning beloved by Melville; *White-Jacket* is a book with pockets written for his pocket. But it also touches on the very duality that both novels have exploited to the degree of ambivalence. That is, they are texts that both reveal and conceal. They conceal an inner self, or represent it only obliquely, yet simultaneously reveal that something is hidden. Like the white coat's pockets, we are being told that something is hidden, but the telling nullifies the concealment. It is the same with the clothes that Redburn wears to explore Liverpool – they defiantly reveal a self yet also conceal it.

Of course as Melville is keenly aware, this duality is the nature of fiction itself, and its capacity simultaneously to be revelatory and misleading. It is also the very essence of clothing in its twinned ambivalence. Like fashion it asserts belonging and kinship, here to a specific genre, yet also announces its individuality, its difference from others. Dress both hides a self and at the same time inevitably reveals one. Historically it developed for purposes of concealment (for modesty and comfort) yet simultaneously functions as display and as allure. It speaks of belonging and of not belonging. It was exactly this ambivalence that one of the first theorists of clothing, the English psychoanalyst John Carl Flügel placed at the forefront his influential study:

> [O]ur attitude towards clothes is ab initio 'ambivalent', to use the invaluable term that has been introduced into psychology by the

---

[110] Melville, *Correspondence*, p. 138.
[111] Ibid., pp. 138–9.

psychoanalysts; we are trying to satisfy two contradictory tendencies.... In this respect the discovery, or at any rate the use, of clothes, seems in its psychological aspects, to resemble the process whereby a neurotic symptom is developed.[112]

In these terms, Redburn and White-Jacket are neurotic characters, and *Redburn* and *White-Jacket* are neurotic books, their very titles invoking the affinities between character and text. The characters are obedient to the contradictory tendencies that Flügel identifies, using dress both as concealment and revelation, torn between a desire for visible individuation yet risking embarrassment and shame because of that excessive visibility. As Melville indicates in the letter to Shaw, this is the condition of the novels themselves, created from the contradictory desires of belonging (to a style, a genre, an accepted way of writing) and of original self-expression.[113] The two works, written over the summer that Melville turned 30 and only a few months after the birth of his first son, embody and express this contradiction because it arises from the circumstances of their composition, as Melville encodes an intense self-scrutiny of his motivation for writing and its potential to be misaligned with writing's practical effects. They embody his ambivalence towards authorship at this time; the question of whether to court originality and all of its risks, or to try and fit in, with the potential rewards this might bring. While critics generally tend to see the books as acts of conformity, the symbolism of the clothing indicates a 'neurotic symptom'.

Melville's imaginative representations of sartorial ambivalence and all that it signifies have a striking parallel with his own life around this time. Melville had completed *White-Jacket* by October 1849 and its American publication was swiftly arranged with Harper and Brothers. He took the novel's proofs to London to negotiate good terms for its publication there, simply by visiting various publishers and showing it to them (this was the trip for which he asked Shaw for a letter of introduction to Carlyle). The venture was successful. *White-Jacket* was sold to Richard Bentley for £200, and Melville extended his

---

[112] J. C. Flügel, 'The Fundamental Motives' from *The Psychology of Clothes* (London: Hogarth Press, 1930), in *The Fashion Reader*, ed. Linda Welters and Abby Lillethun (New York and Oxford: Berg, 2007), p. 171.

[113] David S. Reynolds finds ambivalence in the two texts, though argues that its source lies in the cultural conditions created by contemporary popular literature. The novels 'were indeed two *jobs* written for money' they were also 'quite sincere, since they give vent to powerful subversive forces surging upward from popular culture through Melville's unrepressed pen'. David S. Reynolds, *Beneath the American Renaissance* (New York: Knopf, 1988), p. 144.

trip to the continent, visiting Paris, Brussels and Cologne.[114] He kept a journal for this visit to Europe; it was published in 1948 and is a valuable resource for Melville scholars, not least because the trip provided raw material for subsequent fiction. But one thing the journal records is Melville's discomfort at his clothing. He frequently notes what others are wearing, especially when he attends a dinner hosted by the publisher John Murray. He also briefly mentions a practical joke on the voyage from New York, which involves what Elizabeth Bishop would have called a 'slight transvestite twist': 'Taylor played a rare joke upon McCurdy this evening, passing himself off as Miss Wilbur, having borrowed her cloak, &c. They walked together.'[115] While this is represented comically, there are moments in his fiction when Melville indicates the blurring of identity that cross-dressing implies – we saw it in Redburn's skirted jacket – and the subsequent discomfort of the spectator. This discomfort will form a key moment in *Israel Potter*, a future project very much on Melville's mind during this trip.

At times Melville reflects on his own inappropriate dress, characterizing himself on the continent in 'a villains [sic] garb'.[116] The discomfort arises from his choice of a green jacket to wear when he leaves New York. In the characteristically terse style Melville uses for the Journal, he refers to a remark made to him shortly before they arrive in Dover; 'Mysterious hint dropped me about my green coat.'[117] The coat 'attracted attention' when Melville walks through London a few days later, and he wore it for his meeting with Murray, noting the congruency of wearing 'my *green* jacket' while trying to sell *White-Jacket*, and although it is not mentioned, the coat is likely one reason for the 'vast deal of gazing' that he 'somehow' attracts a few days later (he is also possibly inebriated at this point).[118] Eventually Melville gives in and on his return to London from the continent he buys a new coat to replace the embarrassing jacket: 'Breakfasted at my old place. Then went & bought a Paletot in the Strand, so as to look decent – for I find my green coat plays the devel with my respectability here.'[119] The very next day Bentley offers

---

[114] This £200 for *White-Jacket* indicates the recovery of Melville's reputation that *Redburn* represented, and probably is also evidence of his personal charm in negotiation. Bentley had bought *Mardi* for 200 guineas, the most Melville ever received from a British publisher, but its poor sales clearly put them off *Redburn*, for which they were prepared to risk only £100. See Melville, *White-Jacket*, pp. 404–8.
[115] Melville, *Journals*, p. 11. See Bishop's poem 'Exchanging Hats', in Elizabeth Bishop, *The Complete Poems 1927–1979* (New York: Farrar Straus Giroux, 1984), pp. 200–1.
[116] Melville, *Journals*, p. 39.
[117] Ibid., p. 12.
[118] Ibid., pp. 13, 18, 21.
[119] Ibid., pp. 39–40.

the welcome sum for *White-Jacket* and Melville is able to start concluding his business and arranging for the voyage home. This is not the end of the green coat, however. It comes up once more, in a brief note Melville writes to Evert Duyckinck a few months after his return to New York. Presumably, Melville had already informed Duyckinck about the saga of the jacket, and he remarks that 'having been shut up all day' in the evening 'I mounted my *green* jacket & strolled down to the Battery to study the stars.'[120]

The green coat is an interesting emblem of the discomfort and sense of displacement that is apparent throughout this 1849 journal, which frequently records Melville's uncertainty. But wearing the coat is simultaneously an act of defiance, recalling the sartorial defiance of Redburn and White-Jacket. The duality is between clothing that at once signifies an individual identity and a willingness to conform. Certainly, Melville's green coat was an anomaly in Victorian London, when rules of gentlemen's daywear were hardening, and the black morning coat increasingly used for formal daywear would evolve into the business suit worn by professionals today. The green coat is an exact image of Melville's contradictory sense of authorship at this moment and of the intense introspection evident in the two novels and in the journal. Melville could not help reflect on the change in himself between his first and his second trip to England, between the first voyage in 1839, that he had so recently recollected for *Redburn*. As he puts it in the journal, '*then* a sailor, *now* Melville'.[121] The difference implies a good deal more; then just out of his teens, now a husband and a father; yet to go whaling and to the South Seas, yet to develop the capacity for translating experience into writing and to possess an identity in the mind of the reading public. There is also the question of who and what 'Melville' is to be in the future. This is a deeply searching query for a man whose predominant quality is a continual development, a recurrent unfolding, whose sense of the reality is that it is fluid. Identity must also become fluid, just as Redburn learns that 'This world . . . is a moving world . . . it never stands still; and its sands are forever shifting.'[122]

The autobiographical truth of *Redburn* and *White-Jacket* is not so much factual (critics have long demonstrated Melville's elaboration on various sources) as it is psychological, a deep uncertainty about identity and an anxious reluctance to be fixed in one role. As Melville realizes, a change of clothing may be a change of identity and thus an assertion of one's own multiple facets and fluidity; just as he may write two novels, his green jacket

---

[120] Melville, *Correspondence*, p. 159.
[121] Melville, *Journals*, p. 13.
[122] Melville, *Redburn*, p. 157.

simultaneously articulates conformity and flaunts difference. Indeed, the act of changing clothes in order to write recurs for Melville – it is the subject of a late untitled poem, probably written when he was working as a customs officer and writing *Clarel* in his free time:

> My jacket old, with narrow seam –
> When the dull day's work is done
> I dust it, and of Asia dream,
> Old Asia of the sun!
> There other garbs prevail;
> Yea, lingering there, free robe and vest
> Edenic Leisure's age attest
> Ere Work, alack, came in with Wail.[123]

It is as though writing requires a change of clothing, the assumption of an alternative identity, evident of course in White-Jacket making his white jacket as Melville is making *White-Jacket*. Notably, Melville paid attention to book covers and jackets, seeking alignment of the material of the book and its content. In one of his rare book reviews he whimsically commented on a reissue of Fenimore Cooper's *The Red Rover* in 1850:

> [W]e would have preferred for 'The Red Rover' a flaming suit of flame-colored morocco, as evanescently thin and gauze-like as possible, so that the binding might happily correspond with the sanguinary fugitive title of the book. Still better, perhaps, were it bound in jet black, with a red streak around its borders (pirate fashion) – or, upon third thoughts, omit the streak, and substitute a square of blood-colored bunting on the back, imprinted with the title.[124]

Although light-heartedly presented here, Melville consistently considered the connection between a book's abstracted theme and its actual materiality; this had of course already been evident in Redburn's realization that his father's guide with its 'old morocco cover' is no guide for him at all; as the

---

[123] Herman Melville, *Collected Poems*, ed. Howard P. Vincent (Chicago: Packard and Company, 1947), p. 391. In *The Cultural Roots of American Islamicism*, Timothy Marr examines Melville's fascination with the East and his repeated costuming of his characters in Eastern dress – and Melville's own wearing of a Turkish costume for a fancy-dress party in August 1850; see Hershel Parker, *Herman Melville: A Biography*, 1, pp. 760–1. Melville's liking for loose, flowing clothes was an occasional embarrassment for his family. His Turkish slippers are preserved at the Berkshire Athenaeum in Pittsfield.

[124] Melville, *The Piazza Tales*, p. 237.

dated binding should have told him. It reappears in *Pierre* as a satirical representation of the publishing industry, where Melville, with a nod to Carlyle, casts Pierre's editors as former tailors:

> [T]wo young men, recently abandoning the ignoble pursuit of tailoring for the more honorable trade of the publisher (probably with an economical view of working up in books, the linen and cotton shreds of the cutter's counter, after having been subjected to the action of the paper-mill), had on the daintiest scolloped-edged [sic] paper, and in the neatest possible, and fine-needle-work hand, addressed him a letter, couched in the following terms; the general style of which letter will sufficiently evince that, though – thanks to the manufacturer – their linen and cotton shreds may have been very completely transmuted into paper, yet the cutters themselves were not yet entirely out of the metamorphosing mill.[125]

A few years later in his nightmarish short story 'The Paradise of Bachelors and the Tartarus of Maids', the surreal account of paper manufacture will enforce the connection between the actuality of reading and the exploitation of the female mill-workers.

Melville engages deeply with the material actuality of things, of dress, of rooms and buildings, and of writing itself, with its pens and ink and paper; one critic has described his 'engagement with the written page' as 'violent'.[126] This engagement opens up a rich and important field of critical enquiry, but it should not obscure his development of Carlyle's insistence on symbolic meanings, and his use of clothing to confront and explore anxieties about writing, modernity and the self. While Carlyle provided for him an important articulation of this symbolism, he was, as we shall see, already keenly attentive to dress and its meanings, as is evident in his first two novels, *Typee* and *Omoo*.

---

[125] Herman Melville, *Pierre* (Evanston, IL: Northwestern University Press, 1971), p. 246.
[126] Elizabeth Renker, *Strike through the Mask* (Hampden Station, MD: Johns Hopkins University Press, 1996), p. xix.

3

He Was a European, and Had Clothes on: *Typee*

A few years before he absorbed Carlyle's *Sartor Resartus*, Melville showed a particular if not quite formulated interest in clothing in his first two books, *Typee* and *Omoo*. In these he both records and explores the meanings that clothes have – their actual meaning as commodities, objects of exchange, their suggestive and yet uncertain meanings in terms of power relations, and the relation between clothing and identity. These books also explore the ambivalences involved in clothing, and his narrators' shifting and unfixed attitudes. The imposition of clothing may represent the power of the colonizer to confer an identity on the colonized, and yet, through the natives' adoption and adaptation, may also represent an active resistance to that power. Melville's narrators, who respectively take the names Tommo and Typee, are in a state of flux about their own identities, their own place in the supposed binary civilized/savage. This uncertainty may be a source of terror and anxiety in the exposure to radically different cultures. In Paul Ricouer's terms, the very real attraction they feel towards the 'exotic' is far from being 'a harmless experience':

> However much we may be inclined toward foreign cultures – whether it is through a kind of scientific neutrality or through a curiosity and enthusiasm for the most remote civilizations, or whether it is caused by a nostalgia for the abolished past or even through a dream of innocence or youth – the discovery of the plurality of cultures is never a harmless experience.... When we discover that there are several cultures instead of just one and consequently at the time when we acknowledge the end of a sort of cultural monopoly, be it illusory or real, we are threatened with destruction by our own discovery. Suddenly it becomes possible that there are just *others*, that we ourselves are an 'other' among others.[1]

---

[1] Paul Ricoeur, 'Universal Civilization and National Cultures', in *History and Truth*, trans. Charles A. Kelbley (Evanston, IL: Northwestern University Press, 1973), pp. 277–8. Elizabeth Bishop's poem 'In the Waiting Room' is a celebrated record of this 'discovery of a plurality of culture' as a far from 'harmless experience' (*The Complete Poems 1927–1979*, pp. 159–61).

This sense of an endangered self is represented in several ways, notably in the attitudes towards tattooing. But *Typee* and *Omoo* are deeply ambivalent texts. This is not because ambivalence is carefully cultivated as an attitude, but because the ideas and attitudes shift and even contradict each other so much. In this respect, recent attempts to incorporate the composition process into our interpretative acts are highly significant, notably the work undertaken by John Bryant in his important consideration of *Typee*.[2] Bryant develops his idea of the 'fluid text' to challenge the concept of textual primacy and examines the manuscript and the revisions of *Typee*. 'Fluid text' is an appropriate designation not only because *Typee* is a shifting, unfolding text (or series of texts) but also because both the writing consciousness and the narrative consciousness are fluid, unfolding and developing. In fact, it seems at times Melville is not 'in control' of his text; if by that we mean deciding clearly in advance what to write and the attitudes to be conveyed. As will also be argued with respect to *Billy Budd*, *Typee* remains a work in progress, even in print. Tommo is 'harmed' by his experiences to some degree, in that the established sense of his own identity is challenged to the core; indeed, his sense of identity is suspended for parts of the text. But true to the text's ambivalences, part of him revels in this challenge as, like fiction itself, it opens up the possibilities of varied selves and identities: another of the ambivalences of *Typee* being generic.

Indeed, for a book that would to a large extent publicly define Melville as a writer for the rest of his career, the work we know as *Typee* had an uncertain birth. The uncertainty is not, as it would be for some of his other novels, in the difficulties and obstacles faced in the act of writing, but in the circumstances of its publication. In fact, *Typee* was written in almost ideal conditions for Melville, conditions that he often would long to have again. He had returned to the United States in autumn 1844 after almost four years of adventure that began with his signing on to the whaleship *Acushnet*, and continued when he absconded from her with a shipmate, Toby, while she was harboured in the Marquesas Islands. Back home in Lansingburgh, New York, he entertained his family with the stories of his adventures to the extent that they apparently encouraged him to write a book of his experiences. He began to write *Typee* in Manhattan in winter 1844, and by summer 1845 he had completed almost an entire manuscript; or at least, enough for his brother Gansevoort to take to London and meet with prospective publishers. The period of writing was one of the calmest in Melville's life. He was aged 25, with the prospect of a good marriage ahead

---

[2] John Bryant, *Melville Unfolding* (Ann Arbor: University of Michigan Press, 2008).

of him, confident in himself and with a story to tell: the story of leaving the ship and living among savages. Among *Typee*'s various literary precursors was Richard Henry Dana's best-selling *Two Years before the Mast*, published in 1840. Written expressly to make readers aware of the conditions of the common sailor, Dana's book told of American seafaring in a fresh way, and one that Melville could readily follow, and to which he was to return as an example for his later novels *Redburn* and *White-Jacket*. Its basis in fact was another part of its appeal, and Melville could certainly match this with his own authentic and exciting experiences.

In London, Gansevoort possibly showed his younger brother's manuscript to several publishers, but it was John Murray who showed interest.[3] Murray's was a distinguished publishing house. Founded in the mid-eighteenth century by John Murray's grandfather, it became the publisher for many leading writers, notably Jane Austen, Lord Byron and Sir Walter Scott. In 1843, Murray introduced the *Colonial and Home Library* imprint, hoping to take advantage of revisions made in 1842 to British copyright law that afforded better protection from overseas pirating. The series was mainly to be focused on travel writing, histories and biographies – that is, factual rather than fictional narratives, reflecting Murray's policy of moving away from poetry and fiction.[4] Despite including what are now important works, such as Darwin's *The Voyage of the Beagle* (1845) and Washington Irving's *Bracebridge Hall* (1845) the series was not particularly successful. The swift name change to *Home and Colonial Library* indicates disappointing overseas sales, and Murray was to discontinue the series altogether in 1849. While Murray clearly saw that *Typee* fitted perfectly into the series, there were two problems. First, there was the whole issue of authenticity. The series was for factual accounts, and *Typee* not only read like a novel, but it included details which could not possibly be verified. The second problem was a compound of the first one; it was that Melville's narrative read more like that of an experienced writer, rather than an

---

[3] It is not known for certain whether the manuscript was shown to other publishers in London, and the relevant letters that Gansevoort sent to Melville in September 1845 are unavailable. Melville apparently approached Harpers in New York as potential publishers in summer 1845, but while their reader thought highly of it, it was rejected on the grounds that it was too implausible to be true. See Parker, *Herman Melville: A Biography*, 1, p. 376, and Jay Leyda, *The Melville Log* (New York: Harcourt Brace and Co., 1951), 1, p. 196. After the success of *Typee* Harpers unhesitatingly accepted *Omoo* (Parker, *Herman Melville: A Biography*, 1, p. 470).

[4] The series grew from Murray's own interest in travel and exploration, and during his tenure of the firm, it started to publish what became the basis for the modern travel guidebook. *At John Murray's* by George Paston (London: Murray, 1932) has much useful information on the firm and on the publication of *Typee* and *Omoo*.

account by a common sailor with limited education attempting to write for the first time. Although Gansevoort apparently convinced Murray on this point, the issue of authenticity remained. It was resolved somewhat messily, with Melville providing further material designed to bulk up the factual elements, and Murray perhaps preferring to believe in it as factual rather than lose such an exciting narrative to another publisher. It is important not to overlook this aspect of *Typee*, that it was somehow always a work in progress. According to John Bryant, the manuscript evidence indicates Melville composed a short personal narrative and 'returned to it in discrete periods of revision'.[5]

Thus Melville's first book was published in February 1846, with the unwieldy and not especially engaging title *Narrative of a Four Month's Residence among the Natives of a Valley of the Marquesas Islands: or, A Peep at Polynesian Life*. A month or so later the American edition was published by Wiley & Putnam. There are textual variants from the British edition; some arise from adopting changing to American idiom, some are simply mistakes. Controversially, some reflect the publisher's attempt to make the text less critical of the Christian missionaries; John Wiley was a devout Methodist.[6] This American edition had a better title, though, and one that was closer to Melville's own preference – *Typee: A Peep at Polynesian Life. During a Four Months' Residence in a Valley of the Marquesas*. Subsequent British editions were almost unchanged from the first edition, although the title *Typee* was added, but the publication of the American editions is more complex.[7] Melville made further textual changes – and cut about a quarter of the text – for a revised edition that was published by Wiley & Putnam in August 1846.

The publication history of *Typee* is remarkable, then, in that three distinct versions of the book were published within seven months (there were also several pirated editions).[8] But the different editions in no way hampered its success. Although, just as Murray had feared, reviewers did challenge the authenticity of the narrative and queried whether Melville really had been a

---

[5] Bryant, *Melville Unfolding*, p. 31.
[6] See the Northwestern-Newberry edition, ed. Harrison Hayford, Hershel Parker and G. Thomas Tanselle (Evanston, IL: Northwestern University Press, 1968), pp. 308–9. The Murray first edition was used as the copy-text for this version, on the grounds that it was closest to Melville's manuscript and changes in subsequent editions were either not made by Melville or were made unwillingly. While it is the most authoritative edition that we have, the Northwestern-Newberry text needs to be updated to take into account the 1983 discovery of Melville's draft of three chapters.
[7] That is, apart from adding the appendix 'The Story of Toby' in 1847.
[8] The difficulties of determining an authoritative text for *Typee* are therefore complex. As noted, the Northwestern-Newberry editors chose the first English edition as copy-text (with, however, the American title and the Toby appendix), but the other texts cannot be readily dismissed.

common sailor, the overall assessment was positive and welcoming. In fact, the reviews for *Typee* were to be the best that Melville ever received, and the issue of authenticity was somewhat resolved, or at least receded, when the original of the text's 'Toby', Richard Tobias Greene, now a housepainter, turned up and verified as much as he could of Melville's narrative.[9] Not only were the reviews positive, but the sales were high. *Typee* was to be Melville's biggest selling work, the one that would be linked with his name for the rest of his life.

It is tempting to say that the questions of *Typee*'s authenticity are somewhat remote from us now. However, such concerns over the boundary between fact and fiction have certainly not gone away. They surfaced a few years ago in an astonishingly aggressive way over James Frey's *A Million Little Pieces*. Marketed as a memoir, the book became a best-seller in 2003, yet various investigations challenged its veracity and readers claimed to feel 'betrayed' when they discovered it was not a true memoir. Frey had broken what is called the 'autobiographical pact'; the understanding that when reading memoir the narrator and the author are identical, that the 'I' of the text is its author rather than a persona.[10] Readers invest in authenticity, in a literal way. Perhaps the authenticity issue regarding *Typee* means little to us because we know Melville as a novelist rather than as a travel writer, but this of course was how readers of *Typee* saw him, and expected *Typee* to be an accurate report on the Marquesas. This should remind us just how factual much of *Typee* is. Of course we have a good idea now of how much of *Typee* was invention. Thanks to the pioneering research of Charles Anderson we know that despite the titular claim to have had 'four months' residence' on the Marquesas Islands, Melville was there for about a month.[11] But there is a good deal of factual writing in *Typee*, and a wide range of references to

---

[9] This was, though, a rather limited verification, since Toby escaped from the natives after a short time, leaving Tommo with them for the bulk of the narrative.

[10] See Phillipe Lejeune, 'The Autobiographical Contract', in *French Literary Theory Today*, ed. Tsetavan Todorov, trans. R. Carter (Cambridge: Cambridge University Press, 1982). In fact, Random House, the parent company of the publishers, eventually offered to refund anyone who had bought the book in the belief it was a memoir.

[11] Charles Roberts Anderson, *Melville in the South Seas* (New York: Columbia University Press, 1939). Melville and Toby Greene deserted from the whaleship *Acushnet* while she was docked in Nukahiva Bay on 9 July 1842. Greene left in a ship called the *London Packet* on 28 and 29 July and Melville in the *Lucy Ann* on 9 August. See Parker, *Herman Melville: A Biography*, 1, pp. 214, 218, 220. Because he left Nukahiva before Melville, Greene was unable to confirm or to refute the claim of 'four months' residence'. It has also been pointed out that we have no evidence even for the four weeks of residence, and that Melville could have learned enough from conversation and already published sources on the Marquesas to fabricate his residence. See Mary K. Bercaw Edwards, 'Questioning *Typee*', *Leviathan: A Journal of Melville Studies*, 11:2 (2009), 24–42.

books on the South Pacific. Ironically, while these references were designed to add to the travel-book dimension of *Typee* they actually intensified the problems over the narrative's authenticity by making reviewers doubtful about a common sailor's ability to include them. The London *Times* reviewer commented 'His reading has been extensive... the voyages of Cook, Carteret, Byron, Kotzebue, and Vancouver are familiar to him; he can talk glibly of Count Bouffon and Baron Cuvier, and critically, when he likes, of Teniers.' Along with some detailing of inaccuracies this led the reviewer to conclude, 'The evidence against the authenticity of the book is more than sufficient to satisfy a court of justice.'[12] Melville may be absolved somewhat given that contemporary theories of autobiography often represent it as a way of reading rather than a kind of writing; it is about how we approach a text rather than a quality inherent in the text itself. Paul De Man wrote that autobiography 'is not a genre or a mode, but a figure of reading or of understanding that occurs, to some degree, in all texts', while H. Porter Abbott has written of the difference between autobiography and the novel being mostly about the 'different orientations toward the text' that the reader takes.[13]

What we actually get in *Typee* is a stunning mix of genres and of kinds of writing. It is a mixture of fiction, fact, guidebook, autobiography, romance, journal, history, essay, as well as being a captivity narrative, a critique of colonialism, an adventure story tinged with eroticism and a comic novel. While the literary model is *Robinson Crusoe*, *Typee* has both expansiveness and a sustained focus that Defoe's more picaresque novel lacks (readers tend to forget that Crusoe's adventures take him well beyond his Caribbean desert island). Critics now tend to emphasize *Typee* as a germinal text for Melville, in that the process of writing and revising it was a form of self-invention, an act of creating himself as a writer and as a new self. He expressed frustration at the reviewers' repeated association of him with *Typee* because this failed to acknowledge his astonishing development as a writer, yet he simultaneously asserted that the writing of his first book was the most important moment in his life. In fact, very late in his life, Melville was enthusiastic about a planned reprinting of his selected novels, including *Typee*.[14] The famous June 1851 letter to Hawthorne is typical of this duality. While working on *Moby-Dick* he complains of the persistence

---

[12] Branch, *Melville: The Critical Heritage*, pp. 78, 80.
[13] Paul De Man, 'Autobiography as De-facement', in *The Rhetoric of Romanticism*, ed. De Man (New York: Columbia University Press, 1984), p. 70; H. Porter Abbott, 'Autobiography, Autography, Fiction: Groundwork for a Taxonomy of Textual Categories', *New Literary History*, 19 (1988), 603.
[14] See Merton M. Sealts, Jr, *The Early Lives of Melville* (Madison: University of Wisconsin Press, 1974), pp. 52–5.

of reviewers who only want him to produce another *Typee*; 'To go down to posterity is bad enough, any way; but to go down as a "man who lived among the cannibals!"' But he continues: 'Until I was twenty-five, I had no development at all. From my twenty-fifth year I date my life. Three weeks have scarcely passed, at any time between then and now, that I have not unfolded within myself.'[15] One implication of this reflection on *Typee*'s composition is important, and readily overlooked. In a fundamental way, *Typee* records a process of learning, a process that Melville engages in but so too does his protagonist-narrator Tommo. As the narrative progresses, Tommo's apprehension of the world he has entered also changes; his is a fluid, shifting consciousness, indicative of Melville's own 'unfolding' during the composition.

Given this self-creation it was inevitable, even before *Typee* was published and became a popular success, that Melville should start writing a continuation of his experiences. *Omoo* appears to have been underway by April 1846, since a letter from Gansevoort refers to Melville's 'next book'.[16] *Omoo* was certainly progressing over the summer, as he was already in correspondence with Murray over publishing it, although he had to suspend work to attend to the revisions and the addition of the Toby material for *Typee*. The first draft of the sequel seems to have been ready by November 1846, and by mid-December Melville signed a contract with Harper & Brothers for *Omoo*.[17] He then agreed terms with Murray for publication in the Home and Colonial Library, with Melville telling Murray that it had 'a certain connection with "Typee"'.[18] Accordingly, *Omoo* was published by the end of March 1847 in Britain and about a month later in the United States.

Though there are clear differences between the two books, it is natural to pair *Omoo* and *Typee*, given their proximity in composition and publication, and the obvious continuity between them; Melville even revised a discarded chapter from *Typee* for inclusion in *Omoo*. The second novel begins by simply continuing the scene of Tommo's escape that had concluded *Typee*, and the full title of the British version asserts this continuity, *Omoo: A Narrative of Adventures in the South Seas; Being*

---

[15] Melville, *Correspondence*, p. 193.
[16] Parker, *Herman Melville: A Biography*, 1, p. 444.
[17] Having turned down *Typee*, Fletcher Harper appears to have accepted *Omoo* 'unseen' see Herman Melville, *Omoo* (Evanston, IL: Northwestern University Press, 1968), p. 329. Harpers were to publish Melville's next five novels, and formed his most sustained relationship with a publisher.
[18] Melville, *Correspondence*, p. 72.

a Sequel to the 'Residence in the Marquesas Islands. Harper's omitted the phrase after the semicolon, perhaps because they were not the publishers of *Typee*. Like *Typee*, *Omoo* was well-received and a popular success, and it turned out to be the most widely reviewed of all Melville's novels. The continuity between them does not mean there are no differences. 'Tommo' is now known as 'Typee'. The narrative is more free-ranging, closer to picaresque, reflecting his wandering through several locations, and since the captivity element of the earlier novel is absent, there is considerably less suspense and danger.[19] There is also more sustained consideration of the interaction between whites and the indigenous people of the South Seas; another result of the larger perspective and Typee's travels, but also of a broader historical perspective than was provided in *Typee*. Some of this has to do with Melville's different sources. For *Omoo* he drew more than for *Typee* on William Ellis's *Polynesian Researches during a Residence of Nearly Eight Years in the Society and Sandwich Islands* (1833) and Charles Wilkes's *Narrative of the United States Exploring Expedition* (1845). Ellis's book was of special importance. An ordained minister, Ellis went to Polynesia as a member of the London Missionary Society in 1816 and lived and travelled in the region for six years. He was interested in the economics of the area and was keenly observant of everyday features of Polynesian life.

Taken together, *Typee* and *Omoo* are very much concerned with modes of transition. Among them is Tommo's/Typee's sharp development, but the communities that he encounters are also in transition: because of the missionaries, because of colonization, because their way of life cannot be sustained in modernity. Conventional critical approaches to *Typee* tend to locate the relationship between primitive and modern, 'savage' and 'civilized' as the text's centre. That is, when Tommo runs away from the *Dolly* and joins the natives he enters a different form of reality, one that challenges his assumptions about primitivism. The natives in this regard come simultaneously to represent the familiar division of either the 'noble savage' of romantic primitivism, or the aggressive subhuman savage driven by lusts and appetites. The suspense in *Typee* is generated by two specific features; the uncertainty about whether Tommo is living with noble savages or with cannibals, and the tension between being tempted to stay and the increasing desire to escape. *Typee*'s popularity is, at least in retrospect, hardly surprising, because of its combination of adventure with its representation

---

[19] The suspense element in *Typee* is, however, mitigated by the first-person narration, and by Tommo's informing us early on of his return to the Marquesas after the adventures.

of the exotic and, notably, the eroticization of the natives and especially the figure of Fayaway; on one level, after Said, the text may readily fulfil all that we understand by orientalism.[20]

In fact it is worth pointing out that the basic elements of *Typee* – travel to a strange landscape, learning of the customs of the exotic natives, the erotic other, the question of the nobility or animalistic savage, and the need to return to familiar reality – are staples of adventure fiction. Indeed, they are almost exactly repeated by H. G. Wells in his 1895 best-selling novella *The Time Machine*. Like Tommo, the Time Traveller enters a different reality, encounters what he believes to be the pastoral romanticized natives (Happar/Eloi) and has a horror of the cannibalistic savages (Typee/Morlock), forms a relationship with the erotic other (Fayaway/Weena), panics over the loss of his means of escape (a boat/the Time Machine) before eventually making a getaway to his familiar world. Put alongside *The Time Machine*, the fantastic elements of *Typee* are magnified; the book is ostensibly representing a world of otherness that is seemingly as remote from nineteenth-century New York as the Eloi in the eightieth century are from Victorian London. *Typee* and *The Time Machine* in this regard share a common parent in *Gulliver's Travels*. But the most important difference is that Melville from the start foregrounds the relationship between the 'new world' and the visitor. That is, Gulliver and the Time Traveller are the first visitors to the places they tell of, but Tommo carefully frames his pioneering encounter with a consideration of previous interactions between the Marquesans and others. In so doing he not only insists on the relation between the civilized and the native, but he locates his own encounter within this framework.

As will so often be the case in Melville's writing, his sense of this relationship is troped by his detailing of clothing. A few pages into *Typee*, Tommo tells of his revisiting the Marquesas in a warship, between 'two and three years after the adventures recorded in this volume'.[21] This curious jump in time is anomalous in a mostly chronologically ordered account; and of course it connects with the first-person narration in incidentally assuring us from the start of Tommo's safe return. But it serves an important purpose in establishing a metaphor that will be repeated with variations throughout the text. Tommo relates his unintended return to Nukahiva, describing a formal visit to the US warship by King Moana and his wife, the

---

[20] Edward Said, *Orientalism* (London: Penguin, 2003). In *The Sign of the Cannibal* (Durham, NC: Duke University Press, 1998), Geoffrey Sanborn discusses *Typee* in these terms.
[21] Herman Melville, *Typee* (Evanston, IL: Northwestern University Press, 1968), p. 7.

'Island Queen'.[22] With the Marquesas by now under French rule, these are 'puppet' sovereigns, without any real power.[23] The ceremonial visit begins:

> They ascended the accommodation ladder, were greeted by the Commodore, hat in hand, and passing along the quarter-deck, the marine guard presented arms, while the band struck up 'The king of the Cannibal Islands'. So far all went well. The French officers grimaced and smiled in exceedingly high spirits, wonderfully pleased with the discreet manner in which these distinguished personages behaved themselves.
>
> Their appearance was certainly calculated to produce an effect. His majesty was arrayed in a magnificent military uniform, stiff with gold lace and embroidery, while his shaven crown was concealed by a huge chapeau bras, waving with ostrich plumes. There was one slight blemish, however, in his appearance. A broad patch of tattooing stretched completely across his face, in a line with his eyes, making him look as if he wore a huge pair of goggles; and royalty in goggles suggested some ludicrous ideas. But it was in the adornment of the fair person of his dark-complexioned spouse that the tailors of the fleet had evinced the gaiety of their national taste. She was habited in a gaudy tissue of scarlet cloth, trimmed with yellow silk, which, descending a little below the knees, exposed to view her bare legs, embellished with spiral tattooing, and somewhat resembling two miniature Trajan's columns. Upon her head was a fanciful turban of purple velvet, figured with silver sprigs, and surmounted by a tuft of variegated feathers.[24]

In keeping with *Typee*'s opening register, the various incongruities of this passage generate comedy, heightened considerably by the ship's band playing the wildly inappropriate tune 'The King of the Cannibal Islands'.[25]

[22] Mowanna's name is usually rendered as Moana, and his wife's name was Vaekehu (she was actually an adolescent when this visit took place).
[23] Although an attempt had been made to 'claim' the Marquesas for the United States, the French asserted ownership in 1842 as part of their expansionist policy in Polynesia. Moana's claim to be the chief of Nukahiva is very dubious.
[24] Melville, *Typee*, pp. 7–8. The frigate on which Melville was serving, the *United States*, did actually call at Nukahiva and was visited by the King and Queen on 7 October 1843. The author of the 'Abstract' log of the voyage records the visit rather laconically: 'During our visit the King & Queen visited the Ship, he being dressed in a French uniform given him by the French Admiral, and she in a red skirt which reached a few inches below the knee, about 15 years of age, with handsome features, and tattooed on all visible parts'. Parker, *Herman Melville: A Biography*, 1, p. 274.
[25] The song's lyrics rehearse a series of what are now deeply offensive stereotypes. It originated in the London music hall in the early nineteenth century and was popular

Yet this passage is of great significance for much that is to be examined in the novel. Clearly the King and Queen have been dressed by the French to embody French control; a simple but forceful illustration of political power expressed as the ability to determine another's identity, though their royal status has been acknowledged in the use of the colours red and yellow, of great significance to Polynesians.[26] Melville even represents the French annexation and intended colonization of the Marquesas in terms of dress. Describing the French soldiers drilling, he comments specifically on the effect of their uniforms:

> A regiment of the Old Guard, reviewed on a summer's day in the Champs Elysées, could not have made a more critically correct appearance. The officers' regimentals, resplendent with gold lace and embroidery, as if purposely calculated to dazzle the islanders, looked as if just unpacked from their Parisian cases.[27]

This is a classic synecdoche of the colonial, bringing one's values to another land and protecting oneself from contamination with the other. The regimentals looking as if they were just out of Parisian cases is an image echoed again by Melville in *Omoo* when Typee describes his accidental encounter with someone who turns out to be Mrs Bell, the wife of a sugar plantation owner:

> [A] beautiful young Englishwoman, charmingly dressed, and mounted upon a spirited little white pony. Switching a green branch, she came cantering toward me.
>
> I looked round to see whether I could possibly be in Polynesia. There were the palm-trees; but how to account for the lady?[28]

Her uncompromising dress means that she brings Englishness with her, so oblivious of her surroundings that they hardly exist at all. Hence Typee's sense of his own location is comically challenged, the signifiers of the South

---

throughout the century, with other topical words often being set to the tune. The sheet music was printed in London in 1830 and records A. W. Humphreys as the author of the words; no composer is listed. See Anthony Bennett, 'Rivals Unravelled: A Broadside Song and Dance', *Folk Music Journal*, 6 (1993), 420–5. Melville refers several times to the song in other novels; see Sanborn, *The Sign of the Cannibal*.

[26] The high value placed on these colours and their association with authority had been noted by Captain Cook in his encounters with Pacific islanders. See Douglas Oliver, *Polynesia in Early Historic Times* (Honolulu: Bess Press, 2002).

[27] Melville, *Typee*, p. 17.

[28] Melville, *Omoo*, p. 295.

Seas being incongruous with those of an English lady on a white pony. In *Heart of Darkness*, a text that shares a good deal with *Typee*, Conrad also uses clothes to characterize the insulated mentality of the colonizer, in this case, in the Belgian Congo. Marlow describes his meeting the company accountant, a man whose books are in 'apple-pie order' and who wears 'a high starched collar, white cuffs, a light alpaca jacket, snowy trousers, a clear necktie, and varnished boots. No hat'.[29] Marlow admires the accountant's determination to hold on to an appearance that is more appropriate to a Brussels summer than the Congo, just as Typee is attracted to someone he readily recognizes as an Englishwoman (he learns later she is from Sydney). But the accountant and Mrs Bell are simultaneously characterized as ghostly; he is described as 'a vision' and 'a miracle' – she is twice called an 'apparition' as well as 'a phantom'.[30] These are ultimately dematerialized figures, disengaged from the alien space around them, refusing to acknowledge a relation to it.[31] Mrs Bell is sharply contrasted with her husband, whose dress is both cosmopolitan and suited to the landscape and the climate. He is 'sun-burnt' and 'romantic-looking'; 'dressed in a loose suit of nankeen; his fine throat and chest were exposed, and he sported a Guayaquil hat with a brim like a Chinese umbrella'.[32] This adaptable openness to his immediate environment makes him a figure of solidity and, tellingly, of hospitality. What is absent but implied in Melville's text, and made explicit in Conrad's, is the fact of an agency that sustains the image of the accountant and of Mrs Bell. That is, while their European dress signifies a detachment from their locality, that dress itself can only be sustained by the labour of others, which is of course local native labour. Marlow is so taken with the elegance of the accountant that he simply asks him about the work, and is told 'I've been teaching one of the native women about the station. It was difficult. She had a distaste for the work.'[33]

Mrs Bell, the French soldiers and Conrad's accountant declare by their clothing their mental detachment from the locality. But of course the French have gone further, in enforcing a style of dress on the King and Queen, and Melville's use of the passive mood draws attention to this. While it is customary to use the phrase 'was dressed in', Melville's usage here clearly

[29] Joseph Conrad, *Heart of Darkness* (Harmondsworth: Penguin Books, 1981), p. 25.
[30] Ibid., p. 25; Melville, *Omoo*, pp. 295, 296.
[31] This idea is one element in Katherine Mansfield's multilayered 1922 short story 'The Garden Party', where only a brief mention of the endemic flora (the Karaka tree) indicates that the setting is colonized New Zealand, rather than an English provincial town with its designated hierarchies of class.
[32] Melville, *Omoo*, p. 296.
[33] Conrad, *Heart of Darkness*, p. 26.

indicates the imposition of dress: 'His majesty was arrayed'; 'She was habited'. Their passivity is emphasized by Melville's comment that it was in the Queen's dress 'that the tailors of the fleet had evinced the gaiety of their national taste'. The ability to determine another's dress is a fundamental sign of authority and power, since it is in effect a direction of their social identity. We tend to think of this authority as fundamentally parental; dressing a child is both a literal and an emblematic parental duty. It is literal in the simplest sense but emblematic in directing the child's social identity. Manuals on parenting always devote space to the topic of appropriate dressing, and the child's growing independence is typically signalled by self-dressing. Of course, conflicts arising from this assertion of right are common, and probably inevitable; parenting advice always anticipates and suggests means of tackling them.

In one respect, then, the King and Queen's being dressed by the French is a sign of their infantilized status as the colonized. But asserting the authority to dress another is far from restricted to a parental role; it is even encoded in mythology in the story of Pygmalion dressing Galatea. Again, dressing another is a sign of command, a determination of social identity, an exercising of absolute power. This is considerably compounded, as in the case of the King and Queen, when one is dressed in imitation of another. To dress another is an assertion of authority and also an attempt to make the other familiar rather than exotic. Melville will use this trope again, in 'Bartleby, the Scrivener', where the narrator's inability to accept (or comprehend) the otherness of his employees is signalled by his dressing one of them, nicknamed Turkey, in his own clothes: 'One winter day I presented Turkey with a highly-respectable looking coat of my own, a padded gray coat, of a most comfortable warmth, and which buttoned straight up from the knee to the neck.'[34] The narrator is astonished when wearing the smothering coat fails to make the ill-tempered Turkey imitate his own complacency; in fact it increases his restiveness and 'made him insolent'.[35]

It is easy to see the enforced clothing of Moana and Vaekehu according to the French 'national taste' as an attempt to elide or subordinate difference, an endeavour essential to the colonial enterprise. The gesture also appears in one of *Typee*'s model texts, *Robinson Crusoe*, when Robinson clothes Friday. Throughout Defoe's novel, the distinction between savage and civilized is maintained as a binary of nakedness versus clothing; 'he was an *European*, and had Cloaths on' Robinson says when he sees the savages with their

---

[34] Melville, *The Piazza Tales*, p. 17.
[35] Ibid., p. 18.

captive, who turns out to be a Spaniard.[36] After his rescue of the man he names Friday, Robinson receives Friday's voluntary 'Subjection, Servitude, and Submission'. He then clothes Friday: 'I beckon'd to him to come with me, and let him know, I would give him some Cloaths, at which he seem'd very glad, for he was stark naked.[37] Friday is, of course, subsequently dressed in the image of his new Master, rather than in individuating clothes:

> I gave him a pair of Linnen Drawers . . . which, with a little Alteration, fitted him very well; then I made him a Jerkin of Goat's-skin, as well as my Skill would allow . . . and I gave him a Cap, which I made of a Hare-skin, very convenient, and fashionable enough; and thus he was cloath'd, for the present, tollerably well; and was mighty well pleas'd to see himself almost as well cloath'd as his Master. It is true, he went awkwardly in these Things at first: wearing the Drawers was very awkard to him, and the Sleeves of the waistcoat gall'd his Shoulders, and the inside of his Arms; but a little easing them where he complain'd they hurt him, and using himself to them, at length he took to them very well.[38]

Friday's willing acceptance of the clothing is entirely to do with his voluntary submission; it is otherwise puzzling why he should be 'glad' and 'mighty well pleas'd' at being given something he has not hitherto needed in the heat of the Caribbean.[39] Robinson's need to dress Friday arises from his own missionary purpose in 'saving' the savage, but it is also a means of confirming his self-declared ownership of the island and his authority over others.

When compared with the clothing of Friday in *Robinson Crusoe*, the reclothing of Moana and Vaekehu becomes considerably more complex

---

[36] Defoe, *Robinson Crusoe*, p. 233. Shawn Thomson examines Melville's engagement with Defoe's novel in *The Fortress of American Solitude: Robinson Crusoe and Antebellum Culture* (Madison and Teaneck: Fairleigh Dickinson University Press, 2009).

[37] Ibid., p. 206.

[38] Ibid., p. 208. Clothing is of great significance in *Robinson Crusoe*. Robinson's making his own clothes while on the island is part of his self-making and is very much an expression of the book's Protestant ideology. The loss of his shipmates is poignantly represented by synecdoche: 'as for them, I never saw them afterwards, or any Sign of them, except three of their Hats, one Cap, and two shoes that were not Fellows' (p. 46). After much reflection he interprets his discovery of 'the Print of a Man's naked Foot' as providentially restorative, returning to him a form of the lost companionship (Defoe, *Robinson Crusoe*, p. 153).

[39] Defoe located Crusoe's island near Trinidad, whereas in his source Selkirk was a castaway on an island in the Pacific, off the coast of Chile.

than it might first appear. Both actions stem from the desire to colonize and claim the other, to suppress difference, to 'remake' the other in the likeness of the 'master'. But it is clear that, in absolute terms, this has failed in the case of the King and Queen. They come across as ludicrous because of the imposed incongruity of their dress, and because there is an underlying native identity that dress cannot erase or disguise. The comedy of the passage is developed not so much from the descriptions of the King and Queen as much as from the ridicule targeted at the French making-over of them. Even the imposition of the European titles 'King' and 'Queen' appears absurd – this is the force behind Melville's comment on the inappropriateness of Moana's tattooed face; 'royalty in goggles suggested some ludicrous ideas'. Moana's facial tattoos are far from incongruous, still less 'ludicrous', in a Polynesian chief, in fact they demonstrate courage and a willingness to endure pain. They only become ludicrous when juxtaposed with European 'royalty'. Instead of a golden crown, this 'king' has only a 'shaven crown'. Friday's grateful acceptance of the clothes given to him (he 'took to them very well') is an important element in what is after all his conversion narrative. But while they have accepted the French clothes, this 'King' and 'Queen' are innately defiant towards them. In asserting their individuality within the imposed costume, their difference from it, the cameo in effect is a narrative of resistance or, at the very least, of an accommodation between their native identity and that imposed by the Europeans.

Anthropologists and cultural historians have often traced native modifications of colonially imposed dress as a (sometimes ambiguous) mode of resistance to hegemony. Henrietta Harrison, for instance, in a study of indigenous Taiwan dress under both Chinese and Japanese rule, comments:

> [M]embers of indigenous elites appropriated elements of metropolitan clothing as symbols of status within their own communities, while at the same time consistently resisting styles, whether metropolitan or local, that would subordinate them within relationships fashioned by colonialism. The result of the tension between these two motivations has been a constantly shifting interplay between a rhetoric of the body drawn from the indigenous people's traditions and one drawn from the metropolitan centers.[40]

---

[40] Henrietta Harrison, 'Clothing and Power on the Periphery of Empire: The Costumes of the Indigenous People of Taiwan', *Positions: East Asia Cultures Critique*, 11:2 (2003), 333.

In *The Wretched of the Earth*, Fanon argued that the attempt to obliterate native forms of dress was part of the 'violence' of colonialism, to be countered only by the resurgence of native costume:

> The violence which has ruled over the ordering of the colonial world, which has ceaselessly drummed the rhythm for the destruction of native social forms and broken up without reserve the systems of reference of the economy, the customs of dress and external life, that same violence will be claimed and taken over by the native at the moment when, deciding to embody history in his own person, he surges into the forbidden quarters.[41]

Without this resurgence, the colonized would remain 'emaciated' and their indigenous dress becomes a relic: 'By the time a century or two of exploitation has passed there comes about a veritable emaciation of the stock of national culture. It becomes a set of automatic habits, some traditions of dress, and a few broken-down institutions.'[42] Indeed, a striking contemporary example of this tension and resurgence illustrates once again the symbolic power of dress. In June 2011 the artist Shuvaprasanna was denied entry to a gentlemen's club in Kolkata because he was wearing traditional Bengali clothes – a kurta and pyjama trousers, rather than the Western attire the club stipulates. The incident was seen as a throwback to colonial times, prompting a comment by the poet Joy Goswami: 'I believe a club which imposes such strict English dress code on visitors is actually feeding colonial culture in a free India and one must protest it.'[43]

However, it is wrong to think that a colonial imposition of clothing is straightforward or simple. Typically, the clothing that results is hybrid, showing interplay, modification and negotiation of styles. The issue is further complicated by the fact that the imposed clothing is an aspect of modernity, often factory-made rather than artisanal. That is, while the changes in native clothing form an essential part of colonial 'violence', it is also related to modernity, encounter and contest. Indeed, to assume otherwise – that the natives were naked savages who accepted European clothes – is in some measure to collude with the problematic representation of the submissive colonial. The natives had already developed their own complex systems

---

[41] Frantz Fanon, *The Wretched of the Earth*, trans. Constance Farrington (New York: Grove Press, 1963), p. 40.
[42] Ibid., p. 238.
[43] 'Kolkata luminaries protest western dress code', *India Blooms News Service* 13 June 2011. <http://news.webindia123.com/news/articles/India/20110614/1770996.html> [accessed 31 October 2013]

of clothing and self-decoration, and these did not simply disappear with the arrival of the missionaries and the colonists. As one commentator has observed: 'Colonialism was always a transformative encounter in which subject people were active participants rather than passive respondents to sartorial impositions from the outside. When dress served as a boundary-making mechanism, it did so in ways that were contested.'[44] This point is forcefully made by Chloë Colchester in her introduction to an important collection of essays, and is borne out by the detailed studies that follow. As she writes:

> [I]n the post-contact period, different cultural strands, including indigenous and introduced Christian religious practice, have given rise to a number of new composite clothing styles and practices, many of which have since become consolidated into established cultural forms. In some instances European style-clothing was made from indigenous cloth, in other instances . . . body-wraps made from matting, barkcloth or leaves were worn layered on top of Western-style garments. . . . Both the layering clothes and the overlay of distinctive clothing-related practices or imagery . . . suggest that European clothing was not subsumed within an overarching interpretive framework but that it was added to a pre-existing system of clothes, thereby making manifest a larger reality comprised of distinct levels or layers.[45]

This emphasis on the colonized people as active rather than passive is very much in opposition to the 'fatal impact' theory of colonial contact. This theory is derived mainly from Fanon's work and emphasizes the destruction of native culture through extinction or absorption; both of them 'violent' in Fanon's terms. The fatal impact argument is politically very powerful, perhaps necessary. But as history it may also be simplistic, overlooking the actualities of interaction and modification, and forms of native survival. Another problem with the fatal impact theory is that it may, unintentionally, reinforce the idea of white/settler culture as superior – an idea apparent in two celebrated book titles, James Fenimore Cooper's *The Last of the Mohicans* and Zane Grey's *The Vanishing American*. Acculturation theory is a more historically based and nuanced approach, emphasizing mutuality and an

---

[44] 'Colonialism and Imperialism' entry in *Clothing and Fashion Encyclopedia*, 2 April 2010. <http://angelasancartier.net/colonialism-and-imperialism> [accessed 31 October 2013]

[45] Chloë Colchester (ed.), *Clothing the Pacific* (Oxford and New York: Berg, 2003), pp. 10–11. The 'barkcloth' alluded to here is what in *Typee* is called tappa; Melville outlines the process of making it in chapter 19.

active ability to adapt. It is, however, equally open to direction by political positioning, since it risks understating the violence and the consequences of colonization. Henry Louis Gates, Jr, has outlined the dangers of both positions with admirable lucidity: 'You can empower discursively the native, and open yourself to charges of downplaying the epistemic (and literal) violence of colonialism; or play up the absolute nature of colonial domination, and be open to charges of negating the subjectivity and agency of the colonized, thus textually replicating the repressive operations of colonialism.'[46]

Read in this way, Melville's representation of Moana and Vaekehu is far more complex than its surface comedy suggests. While their French dress denotes allegiance to the colonizer, and hence their self-perceived superiority to the other islanders, their modifications of that clothing simultaneously declare resistance to it. While the conventions of clothing embody the power structure in a colonized society, they can also form the means of resistance to that structure, or its modification through synthesis, or at least alignment, with a prior order. As we shall see, the description of Moana and Vaekehu introduces what becomes an insistent proliferation of incidents regarding the mixing of clothing in *Typee*. While these vary in their overall intent and effect – and their emotional tenor – they consistently represent the native's body as a place of interplay, modification and negotiation of power structures.

It is important, though, to make a distinction between the work of the missionaries and the effects of French colonialism. In *Typee* and *Omoo*, Melville was mainly noting the effect of the missionaries on the indigenous peoples. As indicated earlier, the controversy that this aroused in the United States unnerved Wiley & Putnam, resulting in the publication of the revised *Typee* text in August 1846. Missionaries, usually Protestant evangelicals (though a Roman Catholic tradition also developed) had started their work in the Marquesas at the end of the eighteenth century. The most important early visit was that of William Pascoe Crook in 1797. Crook, an Englishman working for the London Missionary Society, wrote an account of the attempt, but after various difficulties he left after two years, and did not return until 1825.[47] By then, a series of other missions had been to the Marquesas, with

---

[46] Henry Louis Gates, Jr, 'Critical Fanonism', *Critical Inquiry*, 17:3 (1991), 462. Rod Edmond quotes this passage in his discussion of the issue in *Representing the South Pacific* (Cambridge: Cambridge University Press, 1997).

[47] William Pascoe Crook, *An Account of the Marquesas Islands 1797–1799*, ed. Greg Dening (Tahiti: Haere Po Editions, 2007). Crook was supposed to be accompanied by another missionary, John Harris, but Harris decided not to stay and Crook worked alone. Crook and the history of the Marquesas are explored in Greg Dening's *Islands and Beaches: Discourse on a Silent Land* (Carlton: Melbourne University Press, 1980), and his *Beach Crossings* (Philadelphia: University of Pennsylvania Press, 2004) is a meditative history of the islands.

Europeans often being accompanied by converted natives from Tahiti and Samoa. The work of missionaries was in most respects entirely different from the impulse to colonize; indeed, it is evident from their valuable records that missionaries like Crook and Ellis engaged with the natives in ways that now would mark them out as anthropologists or explorers rather than people single-mindedly aspiring to make converts. However, though from differing impulses, the missionaries were aligned with the colonialists in the matter of clothing. In fact the clothing of the natives and the introduction of modern European forms of dress was a major preoccupation of the missions. This was, broadly, for two reasons. First, the natives should be clothed as a matter of modesty, and especially for attending church services. Secondly, adoption of 'Christian' dress demonstrated the willingness of the natives to change lifestyle, to convert. They would no longer be the 'unbreeched heathen' that Tommo refers to prior to his experience of the islanders.[48] While these were the main reasons for the imposition of clothing, there were others, and these included the perceived benefits of creating a Christian communal identity through sewing-classes.

As with the colonizing of native dress, it is important not to cast the indigenous as simply the passive recipients of this new clothing. Indeed, rather than using the language of passive conversion, some historians and anthropologists speak of the 'appropriation' of Christianity by the Polynesians.[49] Several missionaries remarked on the eagerness of the natives to obtain the new dress, and, perhaps surprisingly, praised the resultant blending of styles. Here is Ellis:

> European cloths, cottons in particular, had long been favourite articles of barter with the natives, on account of their durability compared with native manufacture, their adaptation to the climate, variegated and showy colours, and the trifling injury they sustained from wet. They no longer traded for ardent spirits, muskets, powder, &c. and were consequently enabled to procure larger quantities of British woven cloth. Hitherto, however, they had generally worn the European cottons, &c. in the native manner, either as a light tehei, thrown over the shoulder, a pareu wound round the waist, or ahu buu, a kind of large scarf or shawl, loosely covering the greater part of the body. They were now desirous to assimilate their dresses in some degree to ours.[50]

---

[48] Melville, *Typee*, p. 35.
[49] For example, Part 2 of *Clothing the Pacific* is titled 'Clothing and the Appropriation of Christianity'.
[50] William Ellis, *Polynesian Researches* (New York: Harper, 1833), 2, p. 392.

Given the standard representation of missionary imposition of religion and of European culture on the indigenous people, the surprise is in Ellis's praise for hybridity, and in his recognition of the native's desire to assimilate European clothing 'in some degree'. He continues:

> When the loose European dress was white, the pareu, worn round the waist on the outside of it, was of dark blue; one end of it was sometimes thrown carelessly over the shoulder, or hung loosely on the arm, heightening the novel and not unpleasing effect produced by their blending, in the apparel of the same individual, the ancient native with the modern European costume. Their dress thus indicated, equally with their half-native and half-foreign dwellings, the peculiar plastic, forming state of the nation, and the advancement of that process which was then constantly imparting to it some fresh impression, and developing new traits of character with rapid and delightful progression.[51]

Dress is of great importance in Ellis's record of his visit. He observes the changing dress of the natives, accepts, learns and uses their language, and finds the emergence of a hybrid culture 'delightful'. Ellis's account is in some respects deeply ambivalent. The ultimate effects of his mission would be the transformation of the island cultures. That is, converting the islanders to Christianity involved much larger social changes, not always foreseen by the missionaries. As Nicholas Thomas puts it, there is 'an extensive literature on the ways evangelism was not limited to changing religious beliefs, but entailed at the same time a far wider conversion of "social habits" of work, residence, conjugality, and gender roles'.[52] At times Ellis is surprised at the pervasiveness of the changes Christianity initiates, perhaps because of his inability to realize that many of the activities of the islanders which did not seem to him to hold any religious significance were in fact, very much part of their spirituality and ritual. Here, for instance, he concludes

---

[51] Ibid., 2, pp. 392–3.
[52] Nicholas Thomas, 'The Case of the Misplaced Poncho: Speculations Concerning the History of Cloth in Polynesia', in Colchester (ed.), *Clothing the Pacific*, p. 84. Thomas cites four sources: Margaret Jolly and Martha Macintyre (eds), *Family and Gender in the Pacific* (Cambridge: Cambridge University Press, 1989); Margaret Jolly, '"To Save the Girls for Brighter and Better Lives": Presbyterian Missions and Women in the South of Vanuatu: 1848–1870', *The Journal of Pacific History*, 26:1 (1991), 27–48; Nicholas Thomas, 'Colonial Conversions: Difference, Hierarchy, and History in Early Twentieth-Century Evangelical Propaganda', *Comparative Studies in Society and History*, 34:2 (1992), 366–89, and Richard Eves, 'Colonialism, Corporeality and Character: Methodist Missions and the Refashioning of Bodies in the Pacific', *History and Anthropology*, 10 (1996), 85–138.

a description of recreational bow-use with the observation: 'In the Society and Sandwich Islands it is now altogether laid aside, in consequence of its connexion with their former idolatry. I do not think the missionaries ever inculcated its discontinuance, but the adults do not appear to have thought of following this, or any other game, since Christianity has been introduced among them.'[53]

Ellis is ambivalent because his urge (or duty) to describe native culture and practices is inevitably qualified by his responsibility to his missionary vocation and its transformational aspiration.

Shifts in clothing styles, then, are the most visible aspects of this transformation. As noted, the missionary duty of clothing the native was multifaceted. It derived partly from the New Testament duty of clothing the naked, as well as the need for modesty, demonstration of a commitment to conversion and to communal education as provided by sewing-classes. The most famous women's dress introduced to Polynesia was the 'Mother Hubbard', a long, flowing, rather shapeless tunic (rather like a nightgown) that was simple to make and which was wholly designed to cover as much flesh as possible.[54] It was worn only by the natives. However, as might be expected, the native adoption of this lifeless piece of Victoriana also changed it somewhat, to the extent that now we tend to think of it as indigenous. In Hawaii, it was transformed by colourful floral print designs and lighter cloth into the holokū and later into what we know as the mu'um'u or muumuu. Although he is today somewhat neglected by literary critics, many of W. Somerset Maugham's short stories set in Polynesia show his particular attention to conflicts over native and imposed forms of dress. His 1922 story 'Rain' set in Samoa, is especially well-focused on the missionary mindset at the end of the nineteenth century, embodied by the Davidsons. According to Mrs Davidson:

> In our islands . . . we've practically eradicated the lava-lava. A few old men still continue to wear it, but that's all. The women have all taken to the Mother Hubbard, and the men wear trousers and singlets. At the very beginning of our stay Mr. Davidson said in one of his reports: the inhabitants of these islands will never be thoroughly Christianized till every boy of more than ten years is made to wear a pair of trousers.[55]

---

[53] Ellis, *Polynesian Researches*, 1, p. 176.
[54] The *OED* cites Simon Winchester, writing in 1992: 'There are many obese ladies, wearing the all-enveloping Mother Hubbard smocks forced upon them by Western missionaries.'
[55] W. Somerset Maugham, *Collected Stories* (New York and London: Knopf, 2004), p. 11.

After Melville, Robert Louis Stevenson was another famous literary visitor to the Marquesas. For health reasons he travelled there in 1888, the first of three extended voyages to the South Seas which culminated in his settling in 1890 on Upolu, one of the Samoan Islands, where he died in 1894; he is buried there. Stevenson and his family were much beloved by the Samoans, whose various causes he eloquently championed in letters, essays and short stories. In the *South Seas* (1890) is an account of his voyages, and he wrote many short stories set in Polynesia. His novella *The Ebb-Tide* (1894) is particularly interesting for its attack on conventional missions and imperialism in the South Seas. Like Melville, Stevenson specified the obsession of the missionaries with the provision of clothes; one of his characters, Attwater, anticipates a D. H. Lawrence-like view of religion, and condemns the Victorian missionaries accordingly:

> They go the wrong way to work; they are too parsonish, too much of the old wife. . . . Clothes, clothes, are their idea; but clothes are not Christianity, any more than they are the sun in heaven, or could take the place of it! They think a parsonage with roses and church bells, and nice old women bobbing in the lanes, are part and parcel of religion. But religion is a savage thing, like the universe it illuminates; savage, cold, bare, but infinitely strong.[56]

As we have seen, the association of clothing with Europeans and nakedness with savagery is a crucial binary, to the extent that clothing the native is one step towards Christianity and civilized behaviour. But there are two problems with the representation of the naked savage. First, they were in fact scarcely ever completely naked and, secondly, they would not have thought of themselves as naked, since tattooing, body-painting and the wearing of body ornaments were forms of clothing. Indeed, it is thought that these actually preceded human development of clothes, certainly in climates where little or no protection was needed from the weather. Remembering that decorations and tattooing were forms of dress further complicates Melville's representation of Moana and Vaekehu. Comical as Tommo finds them, Moana's goggles are just as much 'clothing' as his military uniform and chapeau bras.

The supposed nakedness of the natives is an important aspect of travel narrative; perhaps, a significant source of its attraction for the reader, since there can be an erotic 'charge' presented under the guise

[56] Robert Louis Stevenson, *Dr Jekyll and Mr Hyde and Other Stories* (Harmondsworth: Penguin, 1979), pp. 252–3.

of knowledge or science. As Mary Louise Pratt suggests, with respect to eighteenth-century travel writing, there is an 'eroticized vocabulary of nakedness, embellishment, dress, and undress' which 'introduced the desires of readers into the discussion'.[57] That is, the travel writer had licence to write of the nakedness of the native and this was an expectation of the reader.[58] In this respect, Tommo's excited anticipation of seeing 'naked houris' in the Marquesas is entirely consistent with the construction of an Orientalist narrative.[59] Perhaps, though, the nakedness of the supposed savages, and the representation of them as happy in their nakedness, also has to do with European uneasiness and shame over nakedness. Adam and Eve are naked until their disobedience and the Fall makes them ashamed of it. But while there are certainly representations of nakedness as primal innocence, it is more usually associated with guilt and shame. To be naked is to be degraded in some way; perhaps involving an unwelcome and distasteful reminder of our animal state. The disintegrating King Lear tears off his clothes in sympathy with naked Poor Tom; 'thou art the thing itself: un-accommodated man is no more but such a poor, bare, forked animal as thou art'.[60] There are also Swift's degraded humans, the Yahoos whose nakedness is so offensive that Gulliver marks his difference from them by not taking off his clothes in the sight of the Houyhnhnms.

Furthermore, to be stripped of clothing is to lose identity. In the West, the forcible stripping of someone is a common feature of degradation rituals (such as hazing), and may even be systematic, and compulsory in certain regimes or institutions. Erving Goffman famously described stripping procedures in his 1961 study *Asylums* as one of the 'processes by which a person's self is mortified'.[61] That is, some institutions (Goffman has prisons in mind) require a surrender of identity that is ritually enacted by loss of one's own clothing, nakedness and reclothing. Or think of Sylvia Plath's lines, from someone in a hospital bed 'I am nobody . . . / I have given my name and my day-clothes up to the nurses.'[62] The opening pages

---

[57] Mary Louise Pratt, *Imperial Eyes* (London: Routledge, 1992), p. 87.
[58] Later, this would be extended to photographing naked or near-naked native women, ostensibly for anthropological purposes. Raymond Corbey and others have queried this motivation through an analysis of pose, reminding us that 'Sexual pleasure begins with the privilege of sight'. Raymond Corbey, 'Alterity: The Colonial Nude', *Critique of Anthropology*, 8:3 (1988), 79.
[59] Melville, *Typee*, p. 5. See Sanborn, *The Sign of the Cannibal*, p. 79.
[60] William Shakespeare, *King Lear*, III, 4, 104–6.
[61] Erving Goffman, *The Goffman Reader*, ed. Charles Lemert and Ann Branaman (Oxford: Blackwell, 1997), p. 55.
[62] Sylvia Plath, 'Tulips', *Collected Poems* (London: Faber and Faber, 1988), p. 160.

of *Typee* introduce this idea of nakedness as mortification for the civilized, as Tommo tells of a visit made by a missionary couple. This is the first white woman that the natives have seen and, fascinated by her clothing, they are inclined to regard her as a kind of goddess. However, their curiosity impels them to look beneath her clothes:

> But after a short time, becoming familiar with its charming aspect, and jealous of the folds which encircled its form, they sought to pierce the sacred veil of calico in which it was enshrined, and in the gratification of their curiosity so far overstepped the limits of good breeding, as deeply to offend the lady's sense of decorum. Her sex once ascertained, their idolatry was changed into contempt; and there was no end to the contumely showered upon her by the savages, who were exasperated at the deception which they conceived had been practised upon them. To the horror of her affectionate spouse, she was stripped of her garments, and given to understand that she could no longer carry on her deceits with impunity. The gentle dame was not sufficiently evangelised to endure this, and, fearful of further improprieties, she forced her husband to relinquish his undertaking, and together they returned to Tahiti.[63]

Nakedness as a source of degradation and shame derives, as Joanne Finkelstein puts it, from the fact that 'when naked we continue to perceive the body as if it should be clothed'.[64] This sense of nakedness as lack, privation is emphasized by Kenneth Clark in his classic study *The Nude*: 'To be naked is to be deprived of our clothes, and the word implies some of the embarrassment most of us feel in that condition.'[65]

Yet from its opening paragraphs Melville introduces a dialectic between nakedness as shame and nakedness as romantic freedom. The nakedness of the primitive other attracts because it appears to offer an appealing and liberating alternative to this shame; the cliché of the savage happy in his

---

[63] Melville, *Typee*, p. 7.
[64] Joanne Finkelstein, *The Fashioned Self* (Cambridge: Polity Press, 1991), p. 112. Finkelstein is here elaborating on the observations made by Anne Hollander in *Seeing through Clothes* (New York: Avon, 1980).
[65] Clark is making a distinction between 'naked' and 'nude'; 'The word '"nude" . . . carries, in educated usage, no uncomfortable overtone. The vague image it projects into the mind is not of a huddled and defenseless body, but of a balanced, prosperous, and confident body: the body re-formed'. Kenneth Clark, *The Nude: A Study in Ideal Form* (London: Folio Society, 2010), p. 1. The classic fine art distinction between nude and naked was, however, very much challenged by Lucian Freud, whose intensely realist depictions were, defiantly, of naked people, not nudes.

nakedness, a reminder of Eden before the Fall. This is exactly what Tommo promises us from the opening pages of his narrative, when he conjures up the connotations of the name 'Marquesas' just before he tells the story of the missionary woman stripped of her calico:

> 'Hurra, my lads! It's a settled thing; next week we shape our course to the Marquesas!' The Marquesas! What strange visions of outlandish things does the very name spirit up! Naked houris – cannibal banquets – groves of cocoa-nut – coral reefs – tattooed chiefs – and bamboo temples; sunny valleys planted with bread-fruit-trees – carved canoes dancing on the flashing blue waters – savage woodlands guarded by horrible idols – *heathenish rites and human sacrifices*.[66]

Melville continually qualifies nakedness in *Typee*. The natives appear naked, but this is not the case: they are 'otherwise naked'; naked 'with the exception of a slight cincture about his loins'; completely naked 'with the exception of a slight girdle of bark'; naked 'to the waist' and so on.[67] Melville raises the suggestive possibilities of nakedness, and invokes it when speaking in the abstract of the natives, but he carefully qualifies it when relaying the actuality of the people that he comes to know.

In part this replicates the ambivalence towards nakedness. There is attraction yet also embarrassment, and a consequent impulse to cover up the nakedness of the other. But it is also an acknowledgement that in spite of the clichéd expectations of the islands ('naked houris'), the people are simply not naked. Not only this, but there is the gradual realization that even if they were without clothes, the natives are still not naked. As noted earlier, this is in part because of the realization that body ornaments are a mode of dress, perhaps preceding the development of clothing. Carlyle's observations in *Sartor Resartus* have parallels in Tommo's narrative. In a chapter titled 'The World in Clothes', Carlyle writes:

> among wild people, we find tattooing and painting even prior to Clothes. The first spiritual want of a barbarous man is Decoration, as indeed we still see among the barbarous classes in civilized countries.[68]

---

[66] Melville, *Typee*, p. 5, italics in original. Melville certainly knew of the Marquesas before he visited them; his cousin Thomas was there in 1829 while serving in the US navy. See Geoffrey Sanborn, *Whipscars and Tattoos* (New York and Oxford: Oxford University Press, 2011), pp. 96–9.
[67] Melville, *Typee*, pp. 14, 29, 68, 90.
[68] McSweeney and Sabor (eds), *Sartor Resartus*, p. 31.

Both Carlyle and Melville appear to maintain the distinction between savage and civilized, while actually challenging it. Carlyle asserts that the 'spiritual want' of self-decoration is shared by all, and serves as a point of commonality between all humans; hence the comically oxymoronic 'barbarous classes in civilised countries'. Melville makes the same point when in his description of Rear-Admiral Du Petit Thouars. The Marquesas have been annexed in the name of France, and Thouars receives tribute from the indigenous king of Tior, who

> advanced slowly and with evident pain, assisting his tottering steps with the heavy war-spear he held in his hand, and attended by a group of grey-bearded chiefs, on one of whom he occasionally leaned for support. The admiral came forward with head uncovered and extended hand, while the old king saluted him by a stately flourish of his weapon. The next moment they stood side by side, these two extremes of the social scale, – the polished, splendid Frenchman, and the poor tattooed savage. They were both tall and noble-looking men; but in other respects how strikingly contrasted! Du Petit Thouars exhibited upon his person all the paraphernalia of his naval rank. He wore a richly decorated admiral's frock-coat, a laced chapeau bras, and upon his breast were a variety of ribbons and orders; while the simple islander, with the exception of a slight cincture about his loins, appeared in all the nakedness of nature.[69]

Although Tommo insists on the incongruity of the pair as they stand together, the details of the clothing actually invite us to reflect on their congruence. Both sets of clothes are highly symbolic. The Rear-Admiral's formal frock-coat and hat are rich in symbolism, as naval and military uniform continues to be, conforming as it must to a rigid set of conventions for different occasions, as well as incorporating specific allusions which can appear ludicrous to the outsider (think of the British army's rules over which regiments are allowed to wear bearskin hats). Similarly, his ribbons and orders are highly allusive. While Tommo contrasts this with the 'slight cincture' worn by Tior's sovereign, he is to learn that dress for the native too is symbolic. In fact, given the climate of the islands, it is in some regards more symbolic than functional, a fact that leads inevitably to the understanding that all clothing has symbolic import. The use of 'cincture' is

---

[69] Melville, *Typee*, p. 29. I have followed the names of indigenous peoples and places as they appear in *Typee* rather than attempt to render these as they actually were. For example, 'Tior' would have been 'Taio'a'.

also interesting. In all his writing Melville uses it only twice, here in *Typee*, and both times early on in the work.[70] It is rather a literary word for the native waist girdle or belt; the three *OED* citations before 1853 are from Milton (*Paradise Lost* IX, 1117; where it refers to the first clothes made by Adam and Eve in their shame), William Cowper's translation of the *Iliad*, and Wordsworth's *White Doe of Rylstone* (VII, 114).[71] It is a typical word for Tommo to use in the early part of his narrative, a poetic and imaginative representation of the other, rather than a term that is earned by living among the islanders. As his experiences unfold and Tommo learns, *Typee* being very much about his education, the congruence of the apparently ill-matched pair will be more apparent to him. That is, one of the things that Tommo comes to understand is that the supposed binary of civilized and savage is far from clear and far from absolute, even though his prior assumption is of their polarization.

There is a further element of the passage that Tommo will reconsider as his experiences with and reflections on the islanders grow. Only the cincture, Tommo says, prevents Tior's chief from being in 'all the nakedness of nature'. But Tommo has already drawn attention to the tattoos that this man wears. At this stage, Tommo does not think of the tattoos as dress; that is, in Carlyle's terms, as equally symbolic for the islander as clothes are for the European. Again the difference between the islander and Thouars is stated, but also contradicted by a subtle sense of their similarities. Here Melville's punning brings together 'polished' admiral and the 'tattooed savage' because in a sense both are 'polished; the tattoos as eloquent as the frock-coat.

As Tommo learns more about the islanders, he comes to recognize the significance of tattooing, and will elaborate, like Carlyle, that 'tattooing and painting' are not only a form of clothing but are likely antecedent to it. He also changes his representation of mixed clothing, with a developing sense that clothing is far more complex than he had initially understood. The dress of the natives, especially when mixed, alerts him to the complex ambiguities of their current cultural situation: it cannot be lightly dismissed in a comic tone. As Claire Sponsler has reminded us, the signs that clothing give us may seem straightforward, since they appear to be all about surface, but they may be deeply ambivalent about the meaning and substance beneath. As she comments, 'clothing is a complex sign, one that is open

[70] Ibid., pp. 15, 29.
[71] Wallace Stevens uses 'ceintures', a rather archaic version of the same word in 'Disillusionment of Ten O'Clock'. There, it connotes the exotic tropics to contrast with the Puritan 'white night-gowns' (*The Collected Poems* (New York: Knopf, 1981), p. 66).

to multiple and conflicting interpretations. . . . Although clothing might seem to promise instant recognition of others, their social condition, and their relation to the viewer's self, it often leads to confusion, deception and misrecognition as well.'[72] Her elaboration on this is especially useful for considering dress in *Typee*:

> [A]s a commodity clothing is entangled with mechanisms of production and consumption that complicate its social meanings. If clothing's signifying gestures are in many cases hard to restrict, so too are its paths of acquisition. A T-shirt imprinted with the logo of a college in the United States can find its way to a rice farmer in Indonesia, while huaraches handmade in Central America wind up on the feet of a banker in London. Easy to acquire and readily traded from one person to another, clothing has social uses and cultural values that are flexible and shifting. What clothing means is thus nearly endlessly open to revision as it shifts from owner to owner and context to context.[73]

While her study is concerned with late medieval drama, Sponsler does consider the challenges made to the sumptuary laws due to the increased commodification of clothing. This is highly relevant for *Typee* because the communities that Tommo observes are undergoing a profound shift. This is not only because of the missionaries and the attempts of colonizers, but because modernity's production of clothing, the new availability of different modes of dress, is inevitably transformative, both in what they wear and in their modes of production. This was in fact a key point made by Ellis when reflected on the eagerness of the islanders to acquire modern clothes. One chapter of *Polynesian Researches* focuses on the impact of European clothing on the natives and their economy:

> The desire to obtain foreign clothing was now very great, equal to that with which they sought iron tools; and whenever they procured one article of it, it was worn forthwith, without waiting till the suit was completed. This often rendered their appearance to a European eye exceedingly ludicrous. There was a degree of propriety usually manifested by all classes of the females in their dress: they either paid more attention to their appearance than the other sex, or were better informed; and the only inconsistency we ever observed was that of a

---

[72] Claire Sponsler, *Drama and Resistance* (Minneapolis: University of Minnesota Press, 1997), p. 2.
[73] Ibid.

woman's sometimes wearing a coat or jacket belonging to her husband or brother. The men, however, were less scrupulous: and whether it resulted from their fondness of variety, or a supposition that the same clothes, worn in different ways, would appear like distinct articles of dress, I am not able to say; but I have seen a stocking sometimes on the leg, and sometimes on the arm, and a pair of pantaloons worn one part of the day in a proper manner, and during another part thrown over the shoulders, the arms of the wearer stretched through the legs, and the waistband buttoned round the chest.[74]

He also remarks that the characteristic response of the islanders on seeing European clothes was to 'wonder when and how they were made'.[75] In recording native enthusiasm for European hats and bonnets, he notes a significant consequence of this: they begin to make their own versions of these, indicating a shift in the island economy and an adaptation of their traditional skills to modernity.

While critical accounts of *Typee* tend to emphasize Tommo's Edenic representation of the isolated people with whom he will live, and his acceptance of a binary between primitive and civilized, it should be recalled that he is largely describing a community prior to sustained contact with the Europeans. Certainly his description of the young couple who will lead him and Toby to their community calls to mind Adam and Eve:

> They were a boy and a girl, slender and graceful, and completely naked, with the exception of a slight girdle of bark, from which depended at opposite points two of the russet leaves of the bread-fruit tree. An arm of the boy, half screened from sight by her wild tresses, was thrown about the neck of the girl, while with the other he held one of her hands in his.[76]

Strictly speaking, this is Adam and Eve after the Fall, wearing girdles to hide their nakedness, even though Melville manages to make the girdles resemble the conventional fig-leaves placed in portraits of Adam and Eve in the garden before the Fall. The sense of the Edenic is developed, though, by Tommo's representation of them in traditional clothing, unmixed by contact with the clothes of modernity. This is especially notable in the descriptions of Mehevi, Kory-Kory, Fayaway and Marheyo, the four natives

---

[74] Ellis, *Polynesian Researches* 1, pp. 393–4.
[75] Ibid., p. 397.
[76] Melville, *Typee*, p. 68.

with whom Tommo spends most time. Tommo's own entry into the Edenic is represented by his leaving behind the clothes of the civilized and taking on, however uncomfortably and unsuitably, a form of native dress.

> [S]hortly after Toby's disappearance, perceiving the uncertainty of the time I might be obliged to remain in the valley – if, indeed, I ever should escape from it – and considering that my whole wardrobe consisted of a shirt and a pair of trousers, I resolved to doff these garments at once, in order to preserve them in a suitable condition for wear should I again appear among civilized beings. I was consequently obliged to assume the Typee costume, a little altered, however, to suit my own views of propriety, and in which I have no doubt I appeared to as much advantage as a senator of Rome enveloped in the folds of his toga. A few folds of yellow tappa tucked about my waist, descended to my feet in the style of a lady's petticoat, only I did not have recourse to those voluminous paddings in the rear with which our gentle dames are in the habit of augmenting the sublime rotundity of their figures.[77]

This is partly an essential convention of romance – the exchanging or relinquishing of one's clothes to play the part of another, leaving behind everyday reality. This is also the problem with the missionary wife who was degraded by being stripped. Her strong sense of decorum and appropriateness was inflexible, and could not be accommodated to circumstance – she cannot exchange her clothes; fixed in her identity she is, ironically, bereft of her defining calico and left degraded. Tommo recognizes the need temporarily to change his clothes, in effect suspending his civilized identity for a time, and even wearing what can be seen as non-masculine attire. This suspension is key to the narrative and eventually to Tommo's developing anxieties. It is notable that he exchanges his shirt and trousers to what is in effect a dress, however much he attempts to mitigate this by reference to the toga. As elsewhere in Melville, changing to the clothing associated with the other gender generates uneasiness. But here he changes willingly in order to begin his adventure, a typical feature of romance. Indeed, this flexible exchange was the starting-point for the popular 1970s BBC children's animation *Mr Benn*. Each episode began with Mr Benn walking along a street (Festive Road) wearing his everyday office clothes (dark suit and bowler hat), and entering a mysterious shop. There he was shown to a dressing-room and emerged in entirely different clothes, appropriate for the adventure he was about to have (as a cowboy or a pirate, for example).

[77] Ibid., p. 121.

After the adventure he returned to the shop and left it dressed in his usual clothes. While light-hearted, the series was disturbing on one level, since it invited the question of whether Mr Benn's usual clothes were also a kind of costume: where was the 'real' Mr Benn – in his adventure or in the framed reality?[78] In this respect, *Typee* is a romantic adventure, a kind of holiday, a carefully framed interlude in Tommo's life, with a 'peep' at another reality; and from the start we have been reassured that this is just a visit.

But what is evident here is Tommo's reluctance to take on the new clothes. His only reason, he says, for doing so is to preserve his 'civilized' clothes for his intended return, even though the return is now jeopardized after Toby has left the valley, and the true nature of the Typee, that they are in fact cannibals, has been revealed. It is important that Tommo declare his unsuitability for the native dress, thereby pre-empting any suspicion of his becoming a 'renegado', voluntarily joining the Typee. Thus the depiction of native life as paradisal and potentially superior to the civilized in chapter 17 has an inbuilt safeguard: this is an observer's outside account. He must wear the new dress with reluctance, being 'obliged' to do so, and he must emphasize its personal unsuitability to him. In part this is because he fears the transforming power of dress, its potential for changing identity. Indeed, the transvestite nature of the costume he assumes raises the possibility of transgressing the most fundamental of all binaries, between male and female.

Tommo witnesses the transformative power of clothing when he fails to recognize the utterly changed Mehevi when he is dressed in formal costume with a range of ornaments and with his body painted (or tattooed).[79] Melville does maintain the idyllic sense of the Typee through reference to their unmixed clothing. This is particularly evident in Marnoo, an Apollo-like figure who visits Typee and is welcomed as a hero and a prophet. Marnoo is the archetype of primitive beauty; he was

> twenty-five years of age, and was a little above the ordinary height; had he been a single hair's breadth taller, the matchless symmetry of his form would have been destroyed. His unclad limbs were beautifully formed; whilst the elegant outline of his figure, together with his beardless cheeks, might have entitled him to the distinction of standing

---

[78] The series developed from several books by David McKee. In truth Mr Benn's adventures were not terribly exciting; the series' interest is in the transformation the clothes make from ordinary life of Festive Road to the recreational world. The games of the children in the street usually provided a clue to the costume Mr Benn will wear, and episodes always included the phrase 'as if by magic the shopkeeper appeared'.
[79] Melville, *Typee*, p. 78.

for the statue of the Polynesian Apollo.... But the marble repose of art was supplied by a warmth and liveliness of expression only to be seen in the South Sea Islander under the most favorable developments of nature. The hair of Marnoo was a rich curling brown, and twined about his temples and neck in little close curling ringlets, which danced up and down continually, when he was animated in conversation.[80]

Unusually, Tommo even admires Marnoo's tattoos, and presents him wearing traditional native dress, a 'slight girdle of white tappa, scarcely two inches in width, but hanging before and behind in spreading tassels'.[81] Marnoo is the idealized native, yet it turns out that he can speak English, having been taken off to sea in a trading vessel for three years, and that he had lived for a while in Australia. Although he crosses the boundaries between civilized and primitive, he is apparently enriched rather than impoverished by this, and has chosen to return to native life, respected by all, and free to roam among the different tribes on the island. He is in some respects the mirror image of Tommo, in that after a (prolonged) 'peep' at civilized life he has returned to his origin. Tommo sees in Marnoo the uncontaminated native, who has done what Tommo hopes to do, that is, to return unscathed to his former state after his 'peep'. Indeed, Marnoo is instrumental in Tommo's escape from the Typee. He tells an islander, Karakoee, of Tommo's situation, who in turn informs the captain of a whaleship who had put into Nukahiva in search of fresh crew.

Marnoo and Karakoee are sharply contrasted characters, and the differences between them are instructive regarding the unfolding nature of *Typee*, and the challenge that Melville provides for his readers. Particularly, the contrast problematizes critical summaries of the book. Several critics have commented on Melville's obedience to the cultural binary of civilized and savage, suggesting that even while he is sympathetic to the natives and abhors the political and religious forces that will destroy their way of life, he does not question the existence of the gulf between the two states. While he fiercely attacks the 'unprovoked atrocities' wrought by the Europeans, he cannot break out of the fundamental dichotomy on which his account, and even his rage, depends.[82] One of *Typee*'s most thoughtful critics, Rod Edmond, takes this approach. He argues that Melville's idealizing of the primitive is ultimately a limited and conservative gesture, and one which upholds the binary assumption that is at the basis of the colonial enterprise. Thus, he is in the

[80] Ibid., pp. 135–6.
[81] Ibid., p. 136.
[82] Ibid., p. 26.

'fatal impact' camp, foreseeing only loss and degradation: 'Melville's inversion of one set of commonplaces of colonial discourse in the Pacific means that he is unable, finally, to conceive the possibility of a hybrid culture.'[83]

There is of course much in Tommo's observations and comments to support this view, and one of the most significant strands of both *Typee* and *Omoo* is that of a paradise in the process of despoliation, a process recorded with anger and despair by its observer. 'Ill-fated people!' Tommo exclaims, 'I shudder when I think of the change a few years will produce in the paradisiacal abode; and probably when the most destructive vices, and the worst attendances on civilization, shall have driven all peace and happiness from the valley.'[84] He even has his own tableau of fatal impact, the imagined moment when the islanders in their canoes go out to welcome the incoming ship:

> When the inhabitants of some sequestered island first descry the 'big canoe' of the European . . . they rush down to the beach in crowds, and with open arms stand ready to embrace the strangers. Fatal embrace! They fold to their bosoms the vipers whose sting is destined to poison all their joys; and the instinctive feeling of love within their breast is soon converted into the bitterest hate.[85]

But there is a competing, contradictory narrative in *Typee* and *Omoo*, where Melville questions the binary of civilized and savage and provides some sense of survival and adaptation through accommodation. To recognize these contradictions means in part responding to the hybridity of the text itself, and to acknowledge a composition process which includes Melville's ongoing and shifting reflections on his experiences during the act of writing. We have seen already that the hybrid appearance of Moana and Vaekehu can be read both as comic and as an act of maintaining their native identity even while acceding to European power. Similarly, the character of Marnoo indicates that the hospitable embrace need not be fatal. In spite of these examples (and, indeed, within them), Melville's complex attitude towards extinction and adaptation is evident. These conflicting views coexist in the text and are unresolved within it, and are actually intensified by Tommo's representation of Karakoee, especially when contrasted with the figure of Marnoo.

[83] Rod Edmond, *Representing the South Pacific* (Cambridge: Cambridge University Press, 1997), p. 97.
[84] Melville, *Typee*, p. 195.
[85] Ibid., p. 26.

Even though Tommo tells us that he had been familiar with Karakoee since the *Dolly* first landed in Nukuheva, he does not appear until the last few pages of the text, functioning as a sort of *deus ex machina*. Guessing that a ship has entered the bay, and that Toby is on her, Tommo becomes desperate to escape, although simultaneously realizing the determination of the Typee to force him to stay. Along with about 'some fifty of the natives' and after a variety of obstructions, Tommo arrives at the beach.[86] There he sees the 'English whale-boat' in the bay, and he also sees Karakoee:

> I perceived, to my indescribable joy, the tall figure of Karakoee, an Oahu Kanaka, who had often been aboard the 'Dolly', while she lay in Nukuheva. He wore the green shooting-jacket with gilt buttons, which had been given to him by an officer of the Reine Blanche – the French flag-ship – and in which I had always seen him dressed. I now remembered the Kanaka had frequently told me that his person was tabooed in all the valleys of the island.... Karakoee stood near the edge of the water with a large roll of cotton-cloth thrown over one arm, and holding two or three canvass bags of powder; while with the other hand he grasped a musket, which he appeared to be proffering to several of the chiefs around him. But they turned with disgust from his offers, and seemed to be impatient at his presence, with vehement gestures waving him off to his boat, and commanding him to depart.[87]

As someone visibly representing commerce between the islanders and the visiting ships, Karakoee is appropriately dressed in this hybrid clothing. Although he is a mixed metaphor, this does not make him appear at all ludicrous in Tommo's eyes. He is, as it turns out, at this moment trading for Tommo's release and, his hybrid clothing is an emblem of Tommo himself at this point, caught between competing modes of identity. Unlike Tommo, though, Karakoee's identity is expressed as an achieved balance. For Tommo it is an intolerable moment of unsettlement, and if it is a balance at all it is one that he cannot sustain. Tellingly, one of the items Karakoee offers for exchange is the 'large roll of cotton-cloth', since this functions emblematically as to what is at stake for Tommo. That is, whether he will be reclothed in his accustomed civilized former dress, or be forced to stay and adopt the dress of the native; this is the crisis point of his narrative.

The fact that Karakoee is taboo strengthens his association with Tommo, who was made taboo by Mehevi, and also with Marnoo.[88] Marnoo's taboo

---

[86] Ibid., p. 246.
[87] Ibid., p. 249.
[88] Ibid., p. 222.

means that he is free to go anywhere on the island and will be hospitably received. Tommo elaborates on this at their first meeting:

> Though the country is possessed by various tribes, whose mutual hostilities almost wholly prelude any intercourse between them; yet there are instances where a person having ratified friendly relations with some individual belonging to the valley, whose inmates are at war with his own, may, under particular restrictions, venture with impunity into the country of his friend, where, under other circumstances, he would have been treated as an enemy. In this light are personal friendships regarded among them, and the individual so protected is said to be 'taboo', and his person, to a certain extent, is held as sacred.[89]

But here the contrast is evident between Marnoo on the one hand and Tommo and Karakoee on the other. Although all are tabooed, Marnoo's taboo gives him freedom, whereas the taboo placed on the others restricts their movements. Tommo cannot come to terms with this apparent contradiction in the meaning of taboo, and admits it, referring to 'the perplexing arcana of the taboo', saying it 'always appeared inexplicable' to him, and he introduces his most concentrated examination of it by stating that it is so 'strange and complex' that 'I have in several cases met with individuals who, after residing for years among the islands in the Pacific, and acquiring a considerable knowledge of the language, have nevertheless been altogether unable to give any satisfactory account of its operations.'[90] The problem for Europeans, apparent from the moment that Captain Cook introduced the word into English, is that taboo means both 'sacred' and 'forbidden', 'holy' and 'unclean'. Because these concepts are a polarized in the European mind but not in the Polynesian, Tommo can only see contradiction between the treatment of Karakoee, himself and Marnoo.[91] As with other aspects of Marquesan cultural practices, Tommo willingly admits his ignorance, his status as outsider; indeed, this is repeated so often that it becomes a kind of essential guarantor of his own

---

[89] Ibid., pp. 139–40.
[90] Ibid., pp. 160, 221.
[91] See Franz Steiner, *Taboo* (London: Routledge, 2004). On the problem of translating *tapu* from Polynesian into English, Steiner explains: 'with few exceptions there are no Polynesian words meaning approximately what the word "holy" means in contemporary usage without concomitantly meaning "forbidden". The distinction between prohibition and sacredness cannot be expressed in Polynesian terms. Modern European languages on the other hand lack a word with the Polynesian range of meaning; hence Europeans discovered that taboo means both prohibition *and* sacredness' (pp. 33–4). See also Alex Calder, '"The Thrice Mysterious Taboo": Melville's *Typee* and the Perception of Culture', *Representations*, 67 (1999), 27–43.

identity; to understand would be to take a step towards his assimilation.[92] Karakoee's status is essential to Tommo's escape. His French jacket represents his status as a go-between, a figure of exchange between the natives and the Europeans. He is in this sense a figure of hybridity, like Marnoo, but, unlike Marnoo who is at home anywhere, Karakoee belongs fully to neither culture. His importance to Tommo lies exactly in this status, as Tommo is effectively traded from one culture to another.

It is here worth remembering that while *Typee* utilizes a variety of literary genres, it is in some measure a captivity narrative. While we know of course that Tommo escapes from his ambivalent confinement (we know this of all first-hand captivity narratives), the theme of being taken prisoner by 'savages' was a long-established one in American writing. It has certainly been popular since the end of the seventeenth century, when the Puritan Mary Rowlandson published her account of being held hostage by the Wampanoag during King Philip's War in 1676. While she inevitably interprets her experiences according to her religion and to scripture, finding biblical parallels for her captivity, Rowlandson's narrative establishes the essential components for subsequent narratives. Prominent among these are the development of a relationship with the captors, exposure to their way of life and customs, and an overwhelming fear that the captivity will be permanent. Rowlandson's strategy for maintaining her identity as a civilized Puritan is to deny any notion of kinship or shared humanity with the Wampanoag, whom she characterizes as savage, devilish, and lacking in the traits of the human. Such characterization is essential for her identity maintenance, since any sense of affiliation or connection with them would damage the core elements of her sense of self, and imply some kind of equivalence between them and her. This lack of empathy includes her reluctance to eat the food that they provide for her ('filthy trash', she calls it), a lack of curiosity about their rituals, and she expresses a complete lack of sympathy over the death of one of the Wampanoag children.[93]

---

[92] Melville's Preface initiates this recurring trope: 'There are some things related in the narrative which will be sure to appear strange, or perhaps entirely incomprehensible, to the reader; but they cannot appear more so to him than they did to the author at the time' (*Typee*, p. xiv).

[93] Mary Rowlandson, *Narrative of the Captivity and Restoration of Mrs. Mary Rowlandson* (Minneapolis: Filiquarian Publishing, 2008), p. 16. The narrative is structured by a series of 20 'Removes'. In Remove 13, Rowlandson records the death of the Indian child: 'My mistress's papoose was sick, and it died that night, and there was one benefit in it – that there was more room' (ibid., p. 32). She then goes on to complain of the 'howling' of the natives after the death, refusing to acknowledge their mourning practices. Rowlandson records the death of her own child in the Third Remove.

Clearly Melville's narrative is entirely different, showing curiosity about and sympathy with the Typee and gladly accepting their hospitality.[94] But, like Rowlandson, his deepest fear is loss of his own identity, of what he likes to think of his 'visit' to the island becoming permanent, never to return to his own clothes. For Rowlandson, the attempt at ransom eventually worked, and after about 12 weeks in captivity she was released on payment of £20. Rather more dramatically, Karakoee's attempt to exchange goods for Tommo's freedom fails, and an adventurous escape concludes his narrative. But the attempted exchange is important, primarily because the high value of the refused articles makes Tommo realize the determination of the Typee to keep him, and making plain at last his status among them:

> When I remembered the extravagant value placed by these people upon the articles which were offered to them in exchange for me, and which were so indignantly rejected, I saw a new proof of the same fixed determination of purpose they had all along manifested with regard to me, and in despair, and reckless of consequences, I exerted all my strength, and shaking myself free from the grasp of those who held me, I sprung upon my feet and rushed towards Karakoee.[95]

As we have seen, Tommo's fluid narrative incorporates his varying, developing and even contradictory attitudes towards his circumstances. There is in effect a fear of being fixed, and this fear is clearly manifested in his dread of being a permanent fixture in Typee life. This fear extends into *Omoo*, where the narrator wants to maintain the detached involvement of a beachcomber and does not want to be defined as a long-term inhabitant. In both narratives this fear is expressed in a horror of tattooing. It is of course inevitable that Melville should discuss tattooing in these books. His source material, including Ellis's *Polynesian Researches* and Georg H. Langsdorff's *Voyages and Travels in Various Parts of the World* described it, and European visitors to Polynesia almost always commented on the practice. The word 'tattoo' was introduced into English in 1771 by Captain Cook as a rendering of the Tahitian word 'tatau'. 'Tatau' means to strike or mark, and should remind us that tattooing was an extremely painful process; before the 1880s, which saw the development of electrical tattoo

---

[94] Sympathy and understanding of the captors can of course lead to an empathy which ultimately involves a rupture from one's former identity; this is evident in one of the twentieth century's most famous captivity narratives, *Every Secret Thing* by Patricia Hearst (Garden City, NY: Doubleday, 1982).
[95] Melville, *Typee*, p. 250.

machinery, the ink was hammered into the skin, and an elaborate tattoo might take several days to complete.⁹⁶ The Marquesans in particular were, and still are, renowned for their tattooing, even though there is much uncertainty over the meaning of particular designs. From very early on, European contact with tattooed Polynesians led to sailors wanting to be tattooed, for a variety of possible reasons. Tattooing might show solidarity with one's shipmates or messmates, could be a means of identification in case of shipwreck, might generally be a signifier of the travelled sailor, or could even indicate willingness to join a Polynesian community.⁹⁷ While forms of body decoration had been long established in Europe, contact with Polynesia introduced a vogue for tattooing, with the extensively tattooed body becoming an object of display at dime-museums and fairgrounds: around the time Melville is writing *Typee* and *Omoo*, P. T. Barnum is displaying his first 'illustrated man' at the American Museum in New York, and much later would show the famous Captain Costentenus, whose whole body was tattooed.

As noted earlier, in *Sartor Resartus* Carlyle claimed that tattooing and body-painting were analogous to dress, yet preceded clothing in human development: 'The first spiritual want of a barbarous man is Decoration.'⁹⁸ But this ignores exactly what Tommo and Typee insist on, and which drives their fears – the fact that tattooing is permanent. In this respect tattooing is the exact opposite of clothing. Dress can be changed, and in wearing different clothing one can proclaim or explore a different identity. Hence Tommo can with some security take off his sailor's clothes and wear a modified version of native dress for a time. But to be tattooed is to be

---

⁹⁶ Melville emphasizes the pain: 'I beheld a man extended flat upon his back on the ground, and, despite the forced composure of his countenance, it was evident that he was suffering agony. His tormentor bent over him, working away for all the world like a stone-cutter with mallet and chisel. In one hand he held a short slender stick, pointed with a shark's tooth, on the upright end of which he tapped with a small hammer-like piece of wood, thus puncturing the skin, and charging it with the colouring matter in which the instrument was dipped' (*Typee*, p. 217). Frederick Douglass reprinted this passage in his anti-slavery *North Star* newspaper in June 1848. See Robert K. Wallace, *Douglass and Melville: Anchored Together in Neighborly Style* (New Bedford: Spinner Publications, 2005), pp. 56–7.

⁹⁷ See Joanna White, 'Marks of Transgression: The Tattooing of Europeans in the Pacific Islands', in *Tattoo: Bodies, Art and Exchange in the Pacific and the West*, ed. Nicholas Thomas, Anna Cole and Bronwen Douglas (London: Reaktion, 2005), pp. 72–89. Although Melville is mentioned only briefly, this important collection of essays includes much that is of interest in reflecting on *Typee* and *Omoo*. *Wrapping in Images: Tattooing in Polynesia* by Alfred Gell (Oxford: Clarendon Press, 1993) is an essential study of the practice; see also Samuel Otter, *Melville's Anatomies* (Berkeley: University of California Press, 1999).

⁹⁸ McSweeney and Sabor (eds), *Sartor Resartus*, p. 31.

fixed for the rest of one's life, to be always marked, stuck in the same role. In the remarkable Western resurgence of tattooing since the 1980s, there are always accompanying warnings about its permanence. This resurgence for the first time resulted in the spread of tattooing to the middle classes, becoming a practice no longer associated only with seafarers or criminals; tattooing became part of American visual culture.[99] In 1992 even the Barbie doll was available with a tattoo. Although the controversy this caused at the time led to the doll being withdrawn, Mattell introduced a tattooed Barbie once again in 2009, and parents appeared far more complacent about this 'Totally Stylin' Tattoos Barbie, with 40 fun tattoo stickers'. Although some parents objected to the tattooing on grounds of Barbie's exemplarity, it should be pointed out that the 1992 doll fundamentally changed the most important feature of Barbie and why the doll encourages active play with her children owners. That is, you can easily change Barbie's clothing and effect a change in her character and identity. But the tattoo created permanence, hence effacing the very flexibility that was crucial to her as a means of encouraging a child's role-playing. It is the permanence of tattoos that generates anxiety; and which means that most states in the United States have restrictions on them, and in several, it is illegal to have one's face tattooed.[100]

The dread of tattooing apparent in *Typee* and *Omoo* is not merely because of the considerable pain involved. A tattoo is 'a suit to be worn for life', as Typee reflects.[101] *Omoo* includes a more extended analysis of tattooing than *Typee* does, mainly because Melville's focus has shifted towards the effects of tattooing on the whites, and the identity of the beachcombers, of whom he is one. He particularly describes one character:

> [A] renegado from Christendom and humanity – a white man, in the South Sea girdle, and tattooed in the face. A broad blue band stretched across his face from ear to ear, and on his forehead was the taper figure of a blue shark, nothing but fins from head to tail.

---

[99] See Mindy Fenske, *Tattoos in American Visual Culture* (New York and Houndmills: Palgrave Macmillan, 2007). Partly an analysis of her own tattooing practices, Fenske's book usefully traces the growing acceptance of the tattoo, and its presence on iconic American figures such as the Marlboro Man.

[100] Restrictions are typically to do with age, sobriety and sometimes enforcing a time period between 'ordering' a tattoo and its being executed. The practice is forbidden by some religions, notably Judaism, following the stipulation in Leviticus 19.28: 'You shall not etch a tattoo on yourselves.'

[101] Melville, *Omoo*, p. 31.

> Some of us gazed upon this man with a feeling akin to horror, no ways abated when informed that he had voluntarily submitted to this embellishment of his countenance. What an impress! Far worse than Cain's – *his* was perhaps a wrinkle, or a freckle, which some of our modern cosmetics might have effaced; but the blue shark was a mark indelible, which all the waters of Abana and Pharpar, rivers of Damascus, could never wash out. He was an Englishman, Lem Hardy he called himself, who had deserted from a trading brig touching at the island for wood and water some ten years previous.[102]

Hardy is an extreme example of the beachcomber's ambiguous status, an existence balanced between two worlds. He is also a figure of horror to Typee and the other beachcombers, since his tattoos make a return to 'civilization' impossible. Thus an important tension in both *Typee* and *Omoo* is between the desire to remain a visitor to the islands, and the temptation – or possible coercion – of staying. Tommo believes he can sustain his status as a visitor, and the existence and availability of his sailor's clothes is reassurance of an identity awaiting resumption. Tattooing, or at least, the extensive tattooing practised by the Marquesans, would make return impossible.

Hardy is in fact a precursor of Melville's most tattooed character: not, as one might think, Queequeg, or John Paul Jones in *Israel Potter*, but the self-styled Ishmael who narrates *Moby-Dick*. In the somewhat whimsical chapter 'A Bower in the Arsacides', Ishmael is shown the skeleton of a huge Sperm Whale, which is being used as a place of worship. Before providing us with the measurements of the skeleton, he tells us how he recorded them:

> The skeleton dimensions I shall now proceed to set down are copied verbatim from my right arm, where I had them tattooed; as in my wild wanderings at that period, there was no other secure way of preserving such valuable statistics. But as I was crowded for space, and wished the other parts of my body to remain a blank page for a poem I was then composing – at least, what untattooed parts might remain – I did not trouble myself with the odd inches; nor, indeed, should inches at all enter into a congenial admeasurement of the whale.[103]

---

[102] Ibid., p. 27. Notably, Hardy's tattooing is voluntary; Joanna White uses archival materials to describe the pressures the islanders placed on beachcombers to be tattooed, and cites examples of forcible tattooing. See White, 'Marks of Transgression', 82–8.
[103] Melville, *Moby-Dick*, p. 451.

This is one of the few chapters which allude to Ishmael's life after the sinking of the *Pequod*. The tattoos mark him of course as a 'wild' wanderer and an outcast, like Hardy, unable to return to civilized life, and a further confirmation of the reason he had for inviting us to call him Ishmael.[104] They also indicate his obsession with the whale; he is as obsessed as Ahab had been, and the tattooing may also represent his loss of the beloved and much-tattooed harpooner Queequeg.[105]

It is important here to reiterate Tommo's insistence on himself as a visitor to this world, that he has no intention of belonging here and must resist tattooing. In this respect he is comparable to Dana in being a 'social explorer'. Dana did not belong to the class of sailor that he temporarily joins and subsequently reports on in *Two Years before the Mast*. In this regard he anticipates the experiences of Jack London choosing to live in London's impoverished East End in order to write *People of the Abyss* (1903) and a generation later of George Orwell living as a tramp to authenticate the second narrative of (the anonymously published) *Down and Out in Paris and London* (1933). In all of these narratives there is a specific moment when the 'explorer' changes clothing. As noted in the previous chapter, the opening page of *Two Years before the Mast* is very much about this exchange of clothing, from Harvard student to common sailor: 'The change from the tight dress coat, silk cap and kid gloves of an undergraduate at Cambridge, to the loose duck trowsers, checked shirt and tarpaulin hat of a sailor, though somewhat of a transformation, was soon made, and I supposed that I should pass very well for a jack tar.'[106] Dana's transformation is not at this moment entirely complete, lacking as he does the sailor's gait and sun-browned face and hands, but it is the moment when an alternative identity is being temporarily assumed. London and Orwell write of the transformative moment in almost identical terms. London visits an old-clothes shop to fit himself out for the journey:

> [T]he chief difficulty was in making the shopman understand that I really and truly wanted old clothes. But after fruitless attempts to

---

[104] Ishmael is the son of Abraham and his wife Sara, born to a surrogate mother, Hagar. When Abraham and Sara subsequently have a son, Isaac, born of Sara, Isaac is declared their true heir, and Ishmael and Hagar are cast out. Before Ishmael's birth, an angel told Hagar 'And he will be a wild man; his hand will be against every man, and every man's hand against him' (Genesis 16.12).

[105] Geoffrey Sanborn argues that Melville's understanding of and interest in tattoos deepened during the composition of *Moby-Dick*, and that the contradictory representations of Queequeg's tattoos indicate that Melville first thought of him as being from an unspecified island, but reconceived of him as a Maori. See Sanborn, *Whipscars and Tattoos*, pp. 103–6.

[106] Dana, *Two Years before the Mast and Other Voyages*, p. 5.

press upon me new and impossible coats and trousers, he began to bring to light heaps of old ones. . . . I selected a pair of stout though well-worn trousers, a frayed jacket with one remaining button, a pair of brogans which had plainly seen service where coal was shovelled, a thin leather belt, and a very dirty cloth cap. My underclothing and socks, however, were new and warm, but of the sort that any American waif, down in his luck, could acquire in the ordinary course of events. . . . No sooner was I out on the streets than I was impressed by the difference in status effected by my clothes. All servility vanished from the demeanor of the common people with whom I came in contact. Presto! in the twinkling of an eye, so to say, I had become one of them. My frayed and out-at-elbows jacket was the badge and advertisement of my class, which was their class. It made me of like kind, and in place of the fawning and too-respectful attention I had hitherto received, I now shared with them a comradeship. The man in corduroy and dirty neckerchief no longer addressed me as 'sir' or 'governor'. It was 'mate', now.[107]

Orwell knew London's account well, and blatantly echoes it at the same narrative moment. Leaving the old-clothes shop (an ironic Mr Benn, similarly bound for an adventurous episode) Orwell writes: 'The clothes were a coat, once dark brown, a pair of black dungaree trousers, a scarf and a cloth cap; I had kept my own shirt, socks and boots, and I had a comb and razor in my pocket. It gives one a very strange feeling to be wearing such clothes.'[108] As in London's account, the clothes immediately effect a change in attitude, putting him 'instantly into a new world':

Everyone's demeanour seemed to have changed abruptly. I helped a hawker pick up a barrow that he had upset. 'Thanks, mate', he said with a grin. No one had called me mate before in my life – it was the clothes that had done it. . . . Clothes are powerful things.[109]

---

[107] Jack London, *Novels and Social Writings* (New York: Library of America, 1982), pp. 11, 12–13.
[108] George Orwell, *Down and Out in Paris and London* (London: Secker and Warburg, 1986), p. 129.
[109] Ibid., p. 130. In his biography of Orwell, Bernard Crick notes the 'borrowing' of the passage from London; see *George Orwell: A Life* (Harmondsworth: Penguin, 1992), pp. 184–5). There is more than borrowing here though; while he is keen to provide his readers with authenticated experiences, Orwell is also declaring the literary tradition to which his work belongs, and is writing himself into it.

These are all transformation scenes, where the protagonist enters a new world by wearing the right clothing. But they are also scenes in which a core identity is being reserved, to ensure that the stay in the other world will be a visit. Dana claims that the clothes give him entry into another world, but knows all along that the costume of his other identity is hanging up ready for him to wear again. By keeping his own new underwear and socks, London maintains a core identity to which he always has access. He also provides himself with a pragmatic secret talisman, a kind of return ticket: 'Inside my stoker's singlet, in the armpit, I sewed a gold sovereign . . . and inside my stoker's singlet I put myself.'[110] Orwell not only keeps his own shirt and footwear, but during the three- or four-year period in which he occasionally played the role of a tramp, he left clothes with friends so that he could return to Old Etonian respectability at any time he chose. Certainly, as Peter Keating has pointed out in a study of British 'exploration narratives' the disguise has a dual function, serving both as entry into one world and escape from another, but the social explorers desperately need the assurance of return.[111]

It is because of this intended return that Melville insists on the word 'peep' in the title of *Typee* – 'a peep at Polynesian life' being the phrase common to both the British and the American editions. 'Peep' is in some ways a word suggesting what readers ought not to expect – this is not going to be a sustained, scholarly account of a prolonged period of residence. But 'peep' carries connotations of secrecy, of something shameful, covert; as in the phrase 'peeping Tom'; indeed one critic argues the word 'implies the salacious re-seeing of already-seen image'.[112] The *OED* indicates that voyeuristic furtiveness is bound up with the meaning of peep: 'An act of peeping; a quick look or glance, esp. through a narrow opening or out of a place of concealment; a surreptitious or furtive glance.'[113] As well as Tommo peeping at other people, he has had a 'peep' at another possibility for his own life. But although this is a 'peep' enlarging his sense of reality, it simultaneously generates deep discomfort as well as pleasure. In Ricouer's terms, his discovery that there is a plurality of cultures has not been a 'harmless experience'; it has lead to the realization that 'we ourselves are an *other* among others'.[114] This is why *Typee* is

[110] London, *Novels and Social Writings*, p. 12.
[111] He writes 'attempted disguise is as much an attempt to break from one form of status as it is to adopt the trappings of another'. Peter Keating, *Into Unknown England, 1866–1913* (Manchester: Manchester University Press, 1976), p. 18.
[112] Sanborn, *The Sign of the Cannibal*, p. 79.
[113] Harriet Beecher Stowe's usage in *Uncle Tom's Cabin* (1852) is cited, referring to the 'glimpse' at slavery: 'You've only seen a peep through the curtain.'
[114] Ricoeur, 'Universal Civilization and National Cultures', p. 278.

such a disturbing text, and confusing when we try to reduce Tommo's complex attitudes into a single point of view. *Typee* records a kind of interlude in a life, a visit, but a dangerous one. Tommo lays aside his usual clothing and embarks on his adventure, and he must be reclothed to signal its conclusion. Ending the story is one attempt to close off the threat offered by his restless self-understanding, but an ending cannot adequately perform this. Tommo cannot stay, but his sense of belonging to any community has been compromised; Tommo 'returns to what he knows and dislikes, having run away from a world he has enjoyed but failed to know and accept'.[115]

Tommo's escape and taking refuge on the Australian whaleship *Julia* is the opening narrative of *Omoo*; a quite remarkable beginning to a novel, since it relies entirely on the reader's knowledge of *Typee*. Welcome though this rescue is for Tommo, it is striking that the immediate action of *Julia*'s crew is to re-dress him. That is, they literally divest him of the marks of the savage and reclaim him for the civilized. Indeed, when Tommo goes on board he characterizes the sailors entirely by their clothing; Scotch caps and faded blue frocks, the chief mate sporting a Panama hat.[116] Tommo is quickly re-dressed, having been hauled onto the ship with uncut hair and beard, wearing a 'robe of the native cloth'.[117] Having met with the captain, Tommo is divested of his tappa cloak and given a blue frock instead, and his hair is cut. In effect, he undergoes a ritual of reclamation, during which he is strikingly passive: 'some one removing my tappa cloak slipped on a blue frock in its place; and another, actuated by the same desire to make a civilized mortal out of me, flourished about my head a great pair of sheep-shears, to the imminent jeopardy of both ears, and the certain destruction of hair and beard'.[118] The detail about being shaved is especially telling; Tommo is being reclaimed from a condition of barbarism, and is to be renamed; he is in effect being baptized. His uncivilized appearance threatens the crew's sense of themselves and he needs to be reformulated in their own image.

In 'The Open Boat' Stephen Crane has a similar moment of reclamation. When the men who have survived the shipwreck and the ordeal of their time in the boat are swept onto the shore, they are quickly restored to community after their ordeal: 'It seems that instantly the beach was populated with men with blankets, clothes and flasks, and women with coffee-pots and all the remedies sacred to their minds.'[119] This hospitable and generous

[115] Edmond, *Representing the South Pacific*, p. 93.
[116] Melville, *Omoo*, p. 5.
[117] Ibid., pp. 5–6.
[118] Ibid., pp. 6–7.
[119] Stephen Crane, *Prose and Poetry* (New York: Library of America, 1984), p. 909.

ritual of reclothing is a form of restoration and salvation, of 're-dress'. It is also a means of stabilizing what has been threatened in the narrative: the very identities of the men as they revaluate their sense of themselves during the experiences. In the story's last words, Crane emphasizes the transformed identity of the three survivors: 'they felt that they could then be interpreters'.[120] But he implies that the existential nakedness of the men is somehow threatening to the community that saves them. Their changed attitude threatens to 'reinterpret' and may well challenge the premises of stable communal identity. Thus the act of reclothing the men is generous but not merely altruistic because it is a means of asserting communal identity and enveloping them within it. Similarly, the shaving and reclothing of Tommo is a generous gesture of acceptance while it is an act of reclamation, a ritual of return to civilization and a rite of membership of the crew. Melville balances the willed reclothing of Tommo by the Typee with his actual reclothing by the white sailors; it is not, then, so much about whether Tommo will choose the primitive or the civilized, but which will claim him.

Typee and *Omoo* are very much about re-dress, adventure, peeping and return, just as Tommo is re-dressed having being temporarily clothed in the non-masculine folds of yellow tappa. At the same time, these books record Melville's re-dress, his own unfolding, the intense consideration of the costumes he wears and will wear in the future. His metaphor of 'unfolding' during the act of writing is a telling one, and it should make us pause when we seek to make generalizations about so fluid a text as *Typee*. Certainly, critical approaches to *Typee* and *Omoo* frequently result in important insights and summaries, but often at the cost of engaging with their specific textual dynamics. In sharp contrast with Dana, and with social explorers such as London and Orwell, Melville did not have the experiences in the South Seas, and then write a record of them on his return. For Melville the act of writing is a dynamic, extended reflection on his experiences, a reflection by no means static, but growing in complexity as he learnt more about the South Sea islands, as he reflected more and more deeply on the meaning of his experiences, and as he unfolded. The two books are 're-dressing' in

---

[120] Ibid.

that Melville is assuming the writer's costume in order to formulate and make available his experiences, but he also knows that it is a costume, a pose, a protean identity of possibilities rather than permanence. Hence his mixing of genres and styles, the trying-out of ideas, the shifting attitudes, the textual hybridity and, above all, the relish in the freedom that writing, like costume, allows one to adopt a variety of temporary identities.

4

The Dress Befitted the Fate: Israel Potter's Lives

It is likely that *Israel Potter*, published in book form in 1855, is Melville's least read and least critically studied novel. Many well-informed people have never heard of it, and although it has been the subject of some thoughtful criticism, and a book-length study, Melville scholars tend to pay it far less attention than they do to his other writings. Some have dismissed it altogether; one of Melville's biographers described it as 'hardly more than a heap of sketches' and a book without 'serious inner coherence'.[1] *Israel Potter* is overlooked not, like *Mardi* or *Pierre* because of some perception of intrinsic artistic failure, nor, as with *Clarel*, the sheer difficulty of intellectual access. *Israel Potter* is an intriguing and appealing story, has a realized historical setting, and is written with exceptional clarity and ease of tone. Yet it remains largely unread.

Several reasons can be suggested for this neglect. It was written at a moment in Melville's career when his sense of readership was strongest, and, like (the also unjustly neglected) *Redburn*, there is a damaging perception that the impulse to write it came from the need to satisfy this audience and make money rather than from some sort of urging of the imagination. *Israel Potter* has several claims to being unique in Melville's career. It is his only novel to have appeared serially prior to book publication; it was published, anonymously, in nine instalments in *Putnam's Monthly Magazine*, starting in July 1854.[2] Although such serial publication was far from uncommon in the mid-nineteenth century, this was Melville's only attempt at it,

---

[1] Newton Arvin, *Herman Melville* (New York: William Sloane Associates, 1950), p. 245. See Arnold Rampersad, *Melville's Israel Potter: A Pilgrimage and Progress* (Bowling Green, OH: Bowling Green University Popular Press, 1969). There is also a long essay published as a pamphlet: Alexander Keyssar, *Melville's* Israel Potter: *Reflections on the American Dream* (Cambridge: Harvard University Press, 1969).

[2] *Putnam's* had a policy of publishing work anonymously, although it was fairly well-known that in this case Melville was the author. The anonymity explains a remark by one of the reviewers, that Melville was now 'revealed' as the author of the serial. Branch, *Melville: The Critical Heritage*, p. 338.

although he was later to collect in book form some of the shorter pieces of fiction, including 'Bartleby the Scrivener' and *Benito Cereno* that he had published earlier in *Putnam's*.[3] *Israel Potter* was also a new kind of fiction for Melville, being the only historical novel he completed and published; the other, *Billy Budd*, was left unfinished at his death. Furthermore, it was historical in including actual characters from Colonial and Revolutionary history. These include Israel himself, Benjamin Franklin, John Paul Jones, Ethan Allen, and there is a cameo appearance by George III. It is also a new departure in that Melville followed very closely, at least in its early chapters, one sourcebook; the *Life and Remarkable Adventures of Israel R. Potter*, published in 1824.[4] While Melville often used source material, he generally followed several sources, and he never used any as closely as this. The nearest, and contemporaneous, analogy is with his use of Amasa Delano's memoirs for *Benito Cereno*. Although he uses three or four more sources as *Israel Potter* progresses, he was significantly reliant on the *Life and Remarkable Adventures*, especially in the first six chapters. For some, this close use of a source lends weight to the idea that *Israel Potter* was a kind of quickly written pot-boiler in which very little of Melville's imagination was invested. Indeed, in June 1854 when he sent 60 pages of the manuscript to George Putnam with the proposal that the work should appear in the magazine, Melville assured him that 'There will be very little reflective writing in it; nothing weighty. It is adventure.'[5] In his influential biography Leon Howard commented that Melville had 'found nothing in his sources to inspire him'.[6] This view can also be coupled with the fact that *Putnam's* paid Melville by the page – he received $5 for every page of *Israel Potter* – to imply that his use of existing material was somewhat shrewd.[7]

[3] *Bartleby* was published in two instalments (November and December 1853); *Benito Cereno* in three (October–December, 1855); both were collected in *The Piazza Tales*, published in 1856.
[4] The short book is helpfully reprinted in the Northwestern-Newberry edition of *Israel Potter*. The book's author and publisher was Henry Trumbull, even though his authorship is not evident from the title page. Trumbull's use of a first-person narration is intended to give the impression this is Potter's own autobiography. Little is known of Trumbull's life and circumstances, though there is some useful information on him (and identification of errors in his life of Potter) in *Beggarman, Spy: The Secret Life and Times of Israel Potter* by David Chacko and Alexander Kulcsar (Cedarburg, WI: Foremost Press, 2010). Chacko and Kulcsar have also depicted Potter's adventures and the Colonial and Revolutionary period in two novels, *Gone Over: Israel Potter's War* (Cedarburg, WI: Foremost Press, 2009) and *The Brimstone Papers* (Cedarburg, WI: Foremost Press, 2010).
[5] Melville, *Correspondence*, p. 265.
[6] Leon Howard, *Herman Melville: A Biography* (Berkeley: University of California Press, 1958), p. 214.
[7] A total of $421.50; Parker, *Herman Melville: A Biography*, 2, p. 232.

When it appeared in book form, *Israel Potter* had a relatively small print-run of 1,400. But it received some good reviews, and proved to be a popular work, at least by the standards set by Melville's recent novels. An English edition and a second American printing followed very quickly, and by early October of 1855, only 7 months after the first edition, a third was in print and over 2,500 copies had been sold.[8] There was even a pirated edition, published in London by George Routledge in 1855.[9] While these were not huge sales, they were very good ones for Melville, given that his most recent novel, the poorly received *Pierre*, had sold fewer than 300 copies.[10] Moreover, Melville at this point in his career was quite unused to seeing more than one edition of his books, still less pirated ones. Several of the reviews of *Israel Potter* claimed that this was a genuine return to form, by which was generally meant that he had reverted to the style of *Typee* and *Omoo*, the works still most associated with Melville's name. As one commented, he was a writer 'whose earlier productions placed him high among our writers of fiction, but whose late works have been unsatisfactory, not to say ridiculous'.[11] Some reviewers even claimed it was Melville's finest work: 'in some respects the best thing he has ever done'; 'not excelled by anything which Herman Melville has ever written before' and 'equal to anything Mr Melville's pen has produced'.[12] There was even an essay review of more than 50 pages devoted to it in the prestigious French periodical *Revue de deux mondes*.[13]

However, the contemporary success of *Israel Potter* seems to have worked against its garnering much positive critical reception later on; as though Melville had withheld his imaginative powers in the attempt to secure his readership. This approach often arises from a critical mindset that is suspicious of popularity or contemporary success, believing that these must be the results of an author's debasing a talent. Yet Melville had always sought popularity and readership, trying to emulate Hawthorne in finding a way of writing both what he desired and what would please the public, and was genuinely surprised that the sales of *Moby-Dick* and *Pierre* had been so disappointing. That *Israel Potter* was well-received should not make it aberrational in our critical evaluation. It is a text that very directly addresses

[8] Leyda, *The Melville Log*, 2, p. 509.
[9] See Herman Melville, *Israel Potter* (Evanston, IL: Northwestern University Press, 1982), pp. 243–4. It was also pirated a decade later, under the title *The Refugee*, by T. B. Peterson and Brothers (ibid., pp. 238–9, 242, n. 14).
[10] Parker, *Herman Melville*, 2, p. 150.
[11] Branch, *Melville: The Critical Heritage*, p. 338.
[12] Higgins and Parker, *Herman Melville*, pp. 456, 456, 458.
[13] Parker, *Herman Melville*, 2, p. 249.

Melville's abiding concerns about the self in modernity. Nor is it a work of fiction that Melville undertook quickly or offhandedly. There is evidence that he had long thought about the possibility of writing a narrative based on Potter's story and that it was the opportunity unexpectedly provided by Putnam's that resulted in this being actualized. Melville had almost certainly owned a copy of the *Life and Remarkable Adventures* before 1849. During his visit to London in December that year, trying to find a publisher for *White-Jacket* (and dismissing as laughable the positive reviews of *Redburn*), he recorded in his journal that he had browsed 'among the old book stores': 'Looked over a lot of ancient maps of London. Bought one (A.D. 1776) for 3 & 6 pence. I want to use it in case I serve up the Revolutionary narrative of the beggar.'[14] This indicates not only the long gestation period that *Israel Potter* was to have, but also, when taken with other contemporary journal entries, suggests that he thought of this projected work as radically different from something like *Redburn*, which he claimed he had written 'to buy some tobacco with'.[15] Melville also bought *A History of the County of Berkshire* in 1850 and made notes on enlistment before the battle of Lexington, again probably with Israel Potter in mind; he departed from his source in having Potter's childhood home in Massachusetts rather than Rhode Island.[16]

Israel Potter may seem something of an aberration in Melville's work, when juxtaposed with the ambitious epic romance of *Moby-Dick* and with the particular writing style, allusive, dense, wrought by a sometimes outrageous imagination which defies the artistic demands of realism (although it could equally be said that *Moby-Dick* is aberrational). *Israel Potter* is muted, with its plain style and its third-person narrative, a sharp departure from the involved first-person narratives typical of the preceding fiction. But if we think of Melville's development as a writer and his turn away from romance after the publication of *Pierre*, then, for all of the uniqueness of its scene of writing, *Israel Potter* seems less of an aberration. Israel's story is of relentless displacement, dislocation from family and nation, passivity and alienation and the loss of upward trajectory in his circumstances. These align him closely with other characters Melville develops in the work he prepares for *Harpers* and for *Putnam's* between 1853 and 1856. It is an extended visit to the world inhabited by Bartleby. *Israel Potter* is a post-romance novel, part of a new departure for Melville, his most sustained consideration of the self in modernity.

[14] Melville, *Journals*, p. 43.
[15] Ibid., p. 13. For those inclined to denigrate *Israel Potter*, Melville's use of the phrase 'serve up' here suggests something opportunistically aligned with popular taste.
[16] Leyda, *The Melville Log*, 1, pp. 378–9.

As so often with Melville, the fiction is something of an analogue to his own circumstances. This is a period in which he reflects, even broods, on failure, on aftermath, on the thwarting of ambition and the failure of aspiration, and on the failure of the nation, the state and the society.[17] Potter's story, of leaving the American colony in 1775 and returning to the United States from what he calls his exile, in 1823, has echoes of Washington Irving's 'Rip Van Winkle'. The story of Rip falling asleep in a colony and awakening in a republic fascinated Melville, and he used it for his poem that bears the same title. As well as the opportunities this echo suggested, there was also a simple coincidence which almost certainly gave, or intensified, a perception of personal analogy between Melville and Israel: their having the same birthday, 1 August. There were other obvious correspondences which no doubt caught Melville's attention, notably Israel's serving in a whaleship, and it is worth recalling that Melville knew of Israel Potter's story before he used the name Ishmael for *Moby-Dick*. While it is important not to overstress the possible meanings of the birthday coincidence, the possibility of writing about Israel long occupied Melville, and he realizes it at a particular moment in his life, and a quite different moment from that of 1849. He may have even felt a particular affinity with Potter, who was writing up (via Trumbull) his life and adventures with the aim of generating an income he could live on; as one critic has put it, 'Potter must have appealed to Melville as a figure who... tried to escape poverty through authorship.'[18] Another has commented that Israel is an image of Melville's own soul.[19]

While Trumbull's book is a crucial starting-point for Melville's novel, it needs to be emphasized that it was primarily a starting-point. He follows the narrative of Israel's life fairly closely for about the first six chapters of the novel, which deal with Israel's flight from the family home, his varied adventures, participation in the battle of Bunker Hill, capture by the British, imprisonment in England, his escape, consequent pursuit, his employment as a gardener and his being recruited by 'friends of America' for an undercover mission to Paris. Melville is selective in the details he uses, and makes some changes to Israel's story. As noted, he relocates Israel's family home to the area around Berkshire, Massachusetts. Although the shift

---

[17] Critics of the novel have often argued that it is very much concerned with the United States in the 1850s, with the loss of the aspiration and idealism that led to the revolution. See John Samson, *White Lies* (Ithaca, NY: Cornell University Press, 1989).
[18] Ann Fabian, *The Unvarnished Truth* (Berkeley and London: University of California Press, 2000), p. 1.
[19] William Ellery Sedgwick, *Herman Melville: The Tragedy of Mind* (Cambridge: Harvard University Press, 1944), p. 181.

intensifies the correspondence between Melville and Potter, it was probably made simply because this was the area around Melville's home, the place where he actually wrote *Israel Potter*. A more significant change is Melville's shifting from Potter's first-person narrative (or, Trumbull's assumption of Potter's voice) to a third-person narration. Although Israel's consciousness and perception remain at the narrative centre, the change allows Melville to comment on Israel's circumstances from a broader perspective, and to be more selective in his representation. It also allows him to complete the story with the death of Israel being recorded in the final sentence: 'He dictated a little book, the record of his fortunes. But long ago it faded out of print – himself out of being – his name out of memory. He died the same day that the oldest oak on his native hills was blown down.'[20] While there are good reasons for it, this use of third-person narration increases a sense that *Israel Potter* is aberrational. Typically, Melville used first-person narrators: Tommo, Typee, White-Jacket, Harry Redburn, Ishmael. The exceptions to this are *Mardi*, a first-person narration by an unnamed American sailor, and the third-person narrative of *Pierre*.[21] Given that *Mardi* and, more immediately, *Pierre*, were critical disasters, it is interesting that Melville maintained third-person narration, and altered his source to do so.

While the early parts of *Israel Potter* are close to Trumbull, Melville then makes considerable changes. In the whimsical dedication to the Bunker Hill Monument, he notes the 'change in the grammatical person' from the original, and makes light of the other changes: 'From a tattered copy, rescued by the merest chance from the rag-pickers, the present account has been drawn, which, with the exception of some expansions, and additions of historic and personal details, and one or two shiftings of scene, may, perhaps, be not unfitly regarded something in the light of a dilapidated old tombstone retouched.'[22] The figurative language here creates an intimate and significant association between Israel's life and his narrative. Like the book, Israel is to be clothed in tatters, and he is figuratively and literally being 'rescued' by Melville in the act of writing *Israel Potter*. Melville also completely alters the pacing of Trumbull's narrative and reshapes it to provide dramatic tension, condensing 45 years of Israel's life in London into one brief penultimate chapter. The two most significant 'expansions' and 'additions' were in the characters of Benjamin Franklin and John Paul Jones. In Potter's account, the meeting with Franklin is very brief. He delivers a

---

[20] Melville, *Israel Potter*, p. 169.
[21] *Mardi*'s narrator is generally referred to as Taji, because of the identity he craftily assumes, though this is not his name.
[22] Melville, *Israel Potter*, p. vii.

letter to him in Paris, converses with him for an hour or so, then, having been in Paris for two days, returns to England with some letters. John Paul Jones does not appear in Trumbull's narrative at all; Potter never met him. But in *Israel Potter*, Franklin and Jones play important roles. Melville's imaginative investment in the tale is chiefly evident in the contrasts that he sets up between the two men and Israel, and these expansions and additions are central to the novel's themes.

The analysis that follows is very much tied to Melville's narrative progression. This is not to try and retell the story, but to attempt to emphasize and explore the particular stages of Israel's journey from selfhood to what, it is argued, is loss of self, a passage very much delineated in terms of changing dress. In starting his novel by following Trumbull's narrative, Melville sets up a story of adventure, exactly as promised to Putnam. It begins in a familiar way, with a young man leaving his home and family to seek fulfilment elsewhere. But from very early on, both narratives depart from the anticipated story of fulfilment. For one thing, the 18-year-old Israel is a reluctant adventurer, leaving home in secret because his father has thwarted his courtship of their neighbour's daughter. His intention is always to return. This is represented symbolically by his taking his clothes with him; this is of course practical, but it also indicates that he has no intention of divesting himself of his existing identity. One Sunday he bundles as much of his clothing as he can into a large handkerchief and then hides this in the woods. That night he sneaks out of the house, collects the clothes, and is off on his travels. Melville follows Potter's account very closely, at times changing only the narrative voice from 'I' to 'he'. In both narratives, Israel is represented from the start as someone pursued, rather than as someone who has left home because of ambition. He feels driven out, especially by his tyrannical father, and fears pursuit. In Trumbull's narrative, Israel needs to 'to evade the pursuit of my friends by whom I knew I should be early missed and diligently sought for'.[23] Melville also draws attention to this, citing Israel's need to 'elude all search'.[24] Israel does evade capture, and over the next three years takes up a variety of occupations; farm labourer, part of a team of surveyors, hunter, trapper and farmer. Having become wealthy through shrewd trading with Native Americans, he returns home, and presents the money to his parents. However, finding them still opposed to his marrying, he leaves home again after a month, this time going to sea, eventually working on a whaleship. After a particularly difficult voyage

---

[23] Trumbull's narrative in Melville, *Israel Potter*, p. 292.
[24] Melville, *Israel Potter*, p. 8.

when he is a harpooner, Israel once more returns home, and, for the third and now last time, leaves.[25]

Melville's representation of Israel's varied occupations in the opening two chapters is oddly ambivalent. On the one hand, he emphasizes that Israel's enterprise, independence and the range of skills he developed were typical of a class of American, and would be crucial in the coming battles for the new republic: 'In this way was bred that fearless self-reliance and independence which conducted our forefathers to national freedom.'[26] However, the actual character of Israel is made vacant by these very activities. As he plays a variety of roles, his character seems to diminish. A void seems to develop; rather than being active and independent, he seems curiously passive, lacking individual motivation, shaped by circumstances and lacking any clear goal. This vacancy is intensified as the plot develops; Israel becomes a soldier, fights and is wounded at Bunker Hill, volunteers for naval service, is taken prisoner and transported to England on a frigate after his brig encounters a British ship, is thwarted in leading a revolt of the prisoners, manages to avoid the smallpox that kills a third of his fellow-prisoners, and is imprisoned for a month in a ship at Spithead. The swiftly paced account of these events continues, and intensifies, the paradoxical aspect of Israel's story. He is represented as a decisive leader, but his passivity and indirection accompany this characterization, so that we are again left with an absence of subjectivity and the sense that Israel is entirely shaped by circumstance, lacking consistency and direction.

Melville's embellishments to Trumbull's text draw attention to this. 'From the field of the farmer', Melville writes, 'he rushed to that of the soldier, mingling his blood with his sweat. While we revel in broadcloth, let us not forget what we owe to linsey-woolsey'.[27] The gentleman's fine broadcloth is a sharp contrast to the coarse inferior wool of a soldier (and to the eventual 'tatters' worn by Israel), but it can only exist because of the work and sacrifice of others. This is of course a key motivation behind Trumbull's narrative; to remind readers of the debt owed to those who fought in the revolutionary war, and the shameful neglect of Israel, the pensionless veteran. While Melville's text matches this motivation, and will in fact enlarge the theme of indebtedness, he is also continuing the representation of Israel as an undeveloped character, 'rushed' suggesting a thoughtless and impulsive change of direction. While the literal meaning of 'linsey-woolsey'

---

[25] Melville deviates from Trumbull's narrative in having Israel's 'sweetheart' now married to someone else.
[26] Melville, *Israel Potter*, p. 9.
[27] Ibid., p. 13.

is invoked by the contrast with broadcloth, it is a notable metonym for the servant or soldier, and as such it is reductive: Israel being identified entirely by the clothing. Linsey-woolsey also has another connotation, of someone who is confused. The *OED* has the figurative definitions, 'a strange medley in talk or action; confusion, nonsense' and 'giving the appearance of a strange medley', 'being neither one thing nor the other'. This is the contradictory, confused Israel. In a further aside Melville introduces what he will develop further in the next few chapters, Israel as a fugitive.

After a literal description of the effects of the smallpox on the American prisoners in the marine hospital, Melville asks 'Why talk of Jaffa?'[28] In the Old Testament book of Jonah, Jaffa is the port from which Jonah departs for Tarshish, disobeying God's command to go to Nineveh. On that voyage he is swallowed by the whale; this is of course the subject of the sermon given by Fr Mapple that Ishmael hears in chapter 9 of *Moby-Dick*. Melville immediately picks up the Jonah/Israel analogy a few sentences later, when he compares Israel's month-long confinement 'in the black bowels' of the floating prison to 'Jonah in the belly of the whale'.[29] While some of the themes of Jonah's story – disobedience, transgression, flight, ordeal – are aspects of Israel's, Melville omits the other elements – Jonah's acceptance of God's will, and his eventual submission. At this point, from midway through chapter 3, Melville markedly changes the narrative pace of the novel, with a more detailed account of the imprisonment and escape in England and the subsequent pursuit of Israel by the authorities. This phase culminates in Israel's finding a secure position as gardener to Sir John Millet, then to Princess Amelia and finally at the King's own garden at Kew.[30] After this period of stability the narrative changes pace again, as Israel becomes secretly involved with the American cause and Melville interweaves more fictive material into the text. But this section (chapters 3–6) is the book's most sustained examination of the transformations in Israel's character. It is also the part where the variety of Israel's clothing is most detailed, where almost bewildering changes in clothing proliferate to the point that we are left with no certainty of identity at all.

Melville's foregrounding of clothing begins when Israel is able to escape from his two guards after they get drunk. At this point he is handcuffed and wearing the clothes assigned to him, those of an English sailor, that is, a pea-jacket, a blue shirt and duck trousers. Having rid himself of the handcuffs, Israel encounters two workers in a field: 'They had rosy cheeks,

[28] Ibid., p. 15.
[29] Ibid.
[30] Amelia was the daughter of George II, and the aunt of George III.

short sturdy legs, showing the blue stocking nearly to the knee, and were clad in long, coarse, white frocks, and had on coarse, broad-brimmed straw hats. Their faces were partly averted. "Please, ladies," half roguishly says Israel, taking off his hat, "does this road go to London?"[31] The 'ladies' turn out to be men, astonished by Israel's assumption, and in his confusion he comically compounds his error by addressing them as 'gentlemen'.

This invented episode has several effects. Primarily it emphasizes Israel's naivety and his foreignness. As a stranger in a strange land he had earlier mistaken the neat English countryside for a park. But it also marks him out as someone whose reading of clothes is uncertain, insecure. If he cannot read the identity of others by looking at their clothes, then it is obvious that he is at a grave disadvantage, and is in danger; in fact, that he is dislocated from this reality. He also realizes that he can be read by his clothes, revealed as an outsider. Clothes are fundamentally signifiers of gender and, though this is less obvious today than in the eighteenth century, of class and social status. What Israel has not grasped is the power of clothes to deceive, of the way that one may use clothes to dress as another. Of course he is quick to learn the need for disguise, but he is unable to imitate those who confidently utilize clothing as an expression of their freedom of identity; when he wears costume his self is diminished, not enlarged. Indeed, it is often argued that men who choose to dress in garments intended for women are attempting to gain something of the freedom that women have to change their image through clothing, and thereby to express different aspects of their identity. That is, the sartorial vocabulary available to women as self-expression is considerably larger than that of men, and for a man to dress as a woman is to try and appropriate something of that freedom, to express a larger and more varied sense of one's self. In the Introduction to her book of photographs portraying male transvestites, Sara Davidmann draws attention exactly to this: 'for most [men] wearing women's clothing enables them to be more their real selves'. She goes on: 'As a woman I can recreate my image as often as I like, and change the way the world reads that image and therefore sees me. The process of creating a visual image to present to the world is a core element in the lives of the subjects of the photographs.'[32] As we shall see, this is true also of the dandy. Israel's unease at this point is provoked by the sudden uncertainty about what had seemed to him fixed, and it sets the tone for much of his experience in England.

Of course in any pursuit narrative, which *Israel Potter* is at this point, clothes come to have the utmost significance, since to evade capture, one

---

[31] Melville, *Israel Potter*, p. 18.
[32] Sara Davidmann, *Crossing the Line* (Stockport: Dewi Lewis, 2003), n.p.

must have both the ability to assess others by their appearance and the opportunity to change one's own clothes. This idea is fundamental to one of the finest of all fictional pursuit narratives, John Buchan's *The Thirty-Nine Steps* (1915), sometimes considered 'the greatest manhunt of all time'.[33] On the run from both the police and a gang of conspirators, Richard Hannay in a short space of time changes into a variety of clothes which he gains by trading and bartering. But more than that, he must convincingly fulfil the role that each set of clothes prompts. The change of clothes alone will not guarantee safety; the successful playing of each role is essential. Hannay is encouraged by recalling the counsel of his old friend, the scout Peter Pienaar: 'the secret of playing a part was to think yourself into it. You could never keep it up . . . unless you could manage to convince yourself that you were *it*.'[34] This is more than a kind of method acting – it is about how one's own identity is predicated upon how one performs before others. But, as in Sartre's consideration of the waiter, whose acting as a waiter demonstrates that this is what he is not, however much his performance convinces others, the performance results from, in fact requires, a reservation of identity, identity temporarily being withdrawn, made covert by performance.[35] Israel's problem is that he lacks the confident self-awareness that derives from a stable identity such as Hannay's, which would allow him to make the crucial distinction between who he is and the role he needs to assume at a given moment. As such he cannot play a part successfully, since fully to occupy a role requires a complete awareness that it is a role. Once he had left home he is used to being passive, to being scripted, and thus can never take a lead and convince.

Like Hannay, Israel perceives that his first task is to exchange clothes.

> Well knowing that his peculiar dress exposed him to peril, he hurried on . . . resolving at the first opportunity to change his garments. Ere long . . . he saw an old ditcher tottering beneath the weight of a pick-axe,

---

[33] John Buchan, *The Complete Richard Hannay* (London: Penguin, 1992), cover blurb. Geoffrey Household's *Rogue Male* (1939) is another classic pursuit narrative.
[34] Buchan, *The Complete Richard Hannay*, p. 47.
[35] 'But . . . there is no common measure between his being and mine. It is a "representation" for others and for myself, which means that I can be he only in *representation*. But if I represent myself as him, I am not he; I am separated from him as the object from the subject, separated *by nothing*, but this nothing isolates me from him. I can not be he, I can only play *at being* him; that is, imagine to myself that I am he. . . . I am a waiter in the mode of *being what I am not*'. Jean-Paul Sartre, *Being and Nothingness*, trans. Hazel E. Barnes (London: Routledge, 2000), p. 60.

hoe and shovel, going to his work; the very picture of poverty, toil and distress. His clothes were tatters.[36]

Israel proposes an exchange of clothes with the ditcher, who readily agrees, having much to gain from the transaction, considering that Israel's outfit is comparatively 'prince-like'. Israel's new outfit is prophetic of his future, effectively a transformation to pauper:

> Little did he ween that these wretched rags he now wore, were but suitable to that long career of destitution before him; one brief career of adventurous wanderings: and then, forty torpid years of pauperism. The coat was all patches. And no two patches were alike, and no one patch was the color of the original cloth. The stringless breeches gaped wide open at the knee; the long woollen stockings looked as if they had been set up at some time for a target. Israel looked suddenly metamorphosed from youth to old age; just like an old man of eighty he looked. But, indeed dull dreary adversity was now in store for him; and adversity, come it at eighteen or eighty, is the true old age of man. The dress befitted the fate.[37]

Being transformed by a change of clothing almost always signifies an improvement in circumstance, an upward move evident in the cliché 'rags to riches'. It represents the opportunity to rise in the world, enter a different class. Indeed, it more than signifies or represents the change – it is that change. Clothing is an inescapable aspect of aspiration, while it is also the actuality of aspiration, and is especially associated with women's power to transform oneself through dress. As Carolyn Steedman has remarked, by way of correcting male-centred representations of working-class women in 1950s Britain, 'Women are . . . without class, because the cut and the fall of the skirt and good leather shoes can take you across the river and to the other side: the fairy-tales tell you that goose-girls may marry kings.'[38] But while Melville uses the signifiers of mythic metamorphosis, he reverses the effect of the spell: Israel is now aged, in rags and patches.[39] Nor, as might have been expected, does the ditcher's appearance improve; although they

---

[36] Melville, *Israel Potter*, p. 19.
[37] Ibid.
[38] Carolyn Steedman, *Landscape for a Good Woman* (London: Virago, 1996), pp. 15–16.
[39] Melville makes some key changes to Trumbull's account. There, Israel meets the old man and proposes an exchange of clothes; he agrees, and they got to his home and Israel receives the man's best suit, heavily patched and old though it is.

are of better quality, Israel's sailor clothes are far too large for him, and he becomes a ludicrous figure.

As well as indicating his diminishing identity, its patchwork nature, the state of Israel's clothing in some measure reflects his uncertain sense of his immediate social and economic environment. Rural England is contradictory. It appears wealthy to him, yet appalling poverty is also evident. Parts of the countryside are so well-kept to appear like a park, with labourers so costumed that they can be mistaken for ladies or gentleman, whereas other parts are kept by characters such as the ditcher. This confusion and the puzzle – whether England is wealthy or not, how these states coexist – is sustained in this section of the novel, and is to be intensified as Israel finds himself in the Royal estates, first that of Princess Amelia, and then that of the King himself, at Kew.

Furthermore, Israel is coming to England at a very particular time, just as the industrial revolution and early forms of mass production in modernity are initiating radical changes in society, and at the beginning of what has been called 'the great reclothing of rural England'.[40] This is actually represented in the novel. Melville's invention of the two labourers, whom Israel mistakes for ladies, is intended to represent a considerably older style of rural dress. What he takes to be their dresses, 'frocks', would have been smock-frocks, a mode of dress becoming increasingly rare from the mid-eighteenth century, but, like the bonnet-wearing woman worker, still associated with the supposed idyll of pre-modern rural life. This was particularly true of nineteenth-century idealized representations of English agricultural labour, in literature and pre-Raphaelite paintings. A good example, almost contemporaneous with Melville's writing of *Israel Potter*, is the feminized shepherd depicted in Dante Gabriel Rossetti's 1854 painting, 'Found'. It is worth recalling that, uniquely in Melville's works, *Israel Potter* is set largely in late eighteenth-century England, the place and period that involved the profound social changes initiated by the industrial revolution. This is the century that sees the advent of modernity, the loosening of tradition and radical alterations in the relation between self and society. At its deepest level, this is the theme of Melville's novel: Israel's inability to be an actor in modernity. To use Marshall Berman's terms, Israel is struggling to become a 'subject', 'to get a grip on the modern world and make [himself] at home in it'.[41] This contrasts sharply with Franklin and Jones, who, to echo

---

[40] Margaret Spufford, *The Great Reclothing of Rural England* (London: Palgrave Macmillan, 2003).
[41] Berman, *All That Is Solid Melts into Air*, p. 5.

Berman again, possess the ability to seize the 'adventure, power, joy, growth and transformation' of themselves that modernity offers.[42] With this detail of the frocked workers, Melville is reminding us of the swiftly changing social environment around Israel. The smock-frock will be replaced, first by manufactured clothing and then by mass-produced clothing. A Royal Commission report on the Agricultural Labourer published in 1894 includes the comment that 'The old smock-frock is very nearly extinct.'[43] A decade earlier Thomas Hardy, always a close observer of clothing and its relation to social transition, had lamented the end of the smock, and its being replaced by the practice of wearing old clothes, or cast-offs in which to work.[44] His 1886 novel *The Mayor of Casterbridge* shows exactly this transition. It opens with Hardy describing Michael Henchard walking with his wife and daughter, and his status as a 'skilled countryman' (a hay-trusser) and his identifiable place in the rural community are immediately evident from his dress. He is wearing 'a short jacket of brown corduroy . . . a fustian waistcoat with white horn buttons, breeches of the same, tanned leggings, and a straw hat overlaid with black glazed canvas'.[45] Twenty-five years later, after his rise to wealth and authority and his calamitous fall with all its losses, he is back working in the fields as a general rather than a skilled labourer. Now he wears the suit of clothes he had worn as mayor, despite its being threadbare: 'the remains of an old blue cloth suit of his gentlemanly times, a rusty silk hat, and a once black satin stock, soiled and shabby. Clad thus, he went to and fro.'[46] Although Henchard does eventually work and dress once more as a hay-trusser, Hardy signals a social transition as well as a personal one in Henchard's clothing, as modernity loosens the identification of self with occupation.[47] Melville does the same with Israel in this section. When he sees the men in smocks he encounters an archaic idyllic representation of English society, but his own actual transition is to wearing the cast-offs of the ditcher, once a Sunday best suit. It is in effect a move to modernity, confirmed also by the fact that he is heading to London, becoming part of the industrial revolution's population shift from countryside to urban centre.

[42] Ibid., p. 15.
[43] Quoted in Rachel Worth, 'Rural Working-Class Dress, 1850–1900: A Peculiarly English Tradition?' in *The Englishness of English Dress*, ed. Christopher Breward, Becky Conekin and Caroline Cox (New York and Oxford: Berg, 2002), p. 98.
[44] Thomas Hardy, 'The Dorsetshire Labourer', *Longman's Magazine*, July 1883, quoted in Worth, 'Rural Working-Class Dress', p. 99.
[45] Thomas Hardy, *The Mayor of Casterbridge* (London: Macmillan, 1963), p. 1.
[46] Ibid., p. 262.
[47] Ibid., p. 357.

As Israel the ironic harlequin continues his weary journey to London, he is briefly recaptured by some soldiers, who take him to be a deserting British sailor, identified by the blue collar of his British Navy bargeman's shirt. This was a piece of clothing that had been issued to him while a prisoner and which he was unwilling to relinquish. Again, Melville is drawing attention to the contradictory (and even almost comic) aspects of Israel's situation. The collar that he kept as a touchstone of his identity was not even his own, and it results in his being incarcerated for being something that he is not. Having escaped once more, he continues what Melville calls, in the title to chapter 4, the 'wanderings' of 'the refugee' until, having received a hint that a prominent landowner, Sir John Millet, is looking for labourers, he presents himself to him. This is another key moment in the text, when we see Israel through the eyes of others, and all they see is clothes.

> [S]crewing up his courage, he advanced; while seeing him coming all rags and tatters, the group of gentlemen stood in some wonder awaiting what so singular a phantom might want.
> 'Mr. Millet', said Israel, bowing towards the bare-headed gentleman.
> 'Ha, – who are you, pray?'
> 'A poor fellow, sir, in want of work.'
> 'A wardrobe too, I should say', smiled one of the guests, of a very youthful, prosperous, and dandified air.[48]

Ironically, the 'rags and tatters' are at this moment the 'right' clothes for Israel to be wearing, since they communicate both his need and display his social inferiority to this 'group of gentlemen', thereby declaring his eligibility for manual work. In this period dress in English society is becoming increasingly politicized; as one historian of dress has put it, 'throughout the eighteenth century (with sumptuary legislation long abandoned) the English pioneered the "political" concept of dress, exploring notions of class in clothing'.[49] Israel's inadequate clothing is read as a sign of deference, the acknowledgement of his inferior status. Notably, it is the 'dandified' gentleman (another addition to Trumbull's narrative), who comments on the lack of 'wardrobe'. This introduces the contrast between Israel and the figure of the dandy which will be developed later in the novel. The dandy reminds us that clothes are a costume, saying something about us, indicating

---

[48] Melville, *Israel Potter*, p. 24.
[49] Aileen Ribiero, 'On Englishness in Dress' in Breward, Conekin and Cox (eds), *The Englishness of English Dress*, pp. 19–20.

the role that we are playing at any particular time. To quote Aileen Ribiero again, 'Clothes have the chameleon ability to create character, status and mood. Using dress in all its forms is a kind of role-playing.'[50] While his clothes make the case for him as a fit labourer, Israel lacks the ability to play the part that the clothes script for him. That is, he cannot readily make an adjustment of identity to circumstance, to the requirements of the moment. Again embellishing Trumbull's story, Melville has Israel say that he is unable to buy a hoe, as he possesses only 'four English pennies'. *'English pennies. What other sort would you have[?]'* is the response.[51] Similarly, he is unable to address Sir John by his title, calling him 'Mr. Millet'.

These mistakes may be seen as Israel's stubborn defiance of the English, his firm commitment to being an American and a republican. It reappears in his accidental encounter with George III, when he does not remove his hat and even declares 'I have no king'.[52] But they actually indicate that he is unable to take on a role appropriate to the occasion, that he cannot 'fit into' his circumstances, into his costume, he lacks the agency and ability to control circumstance. In spite, then, of the disguise provided by the language of his dress, and his desperate need to conceal what he actually is, he is exposed so quickly it is almost comic. 'I perceive that you are an American; and, if I am not mistaken, you are an escaped prisoner of war' says Sir John, while the moment he keeps his hat on in the royal presence, the king immediately exclaims 'You aint an Englishman, – no Englishman – no, no.'[53]

Israel regains his health and strength under the protective care of Sir John, and, tellingly, there is another change of clothing, when he exchanges his 'rags and tatters' for some cast-offs given to him by Sir John.[54] Melville now changes the pace of the narrative once again, compressing into less than a page the six months spent with Sir John, almost two months in the service of Princess Amelia, and three weeks working for a farmer. Then Melville briefly resumes once more the flight and pursuit narrative, when Israel has been betrayed and only narrowly escapes capture by the soldiers. He finds employment as a gardener once again, in the royal garden at Kew. Seasonally laid off, he then starts work for a farmer once more, but in less than a week he is exposed and again takes flight.

Melville carefully weaves the pursuit narrative into this narrative of intermittent employment, reminding us of the danger facing Israel, and adding drama to the text. But he is also using the signifiers of the slave

---

[50] Ibid., p. 22.
[51] Melville, *Israel Potter*, p. 24.
[52] Ibid., pp. 30, 31.
[53] Ibid., pp. 26, 30.
[54] Ibid., p. 27.

narrative, a widely distributed form at the time he is composing *Israel Potter*. As noted, Israel is represented as a fugitive from the start, initiating the motif of his entire life. While Israel is in England, Melville makes explicit parallels between him and the runaway slave in the United States, '[h]arassed day and night, hunted from food and sleep, driven from hole to hole like a fox in the woods'.[55] These parallels include a fierce pursuit by soldiers who are compared to bloodhounds, Israel's being concealed in a garret, and Sir John's characterization of the men hunting Israel, making them sound like the patrols of slave-catchers: 'The soldiers you meet prowling on the roads, are not fair specimens of the army. They are a set of mean, dastardly banditti, who, to obtain their fee, would betray their best friends.'[56] Even Israel's sporadic employment is represented as a kind of slavery, specifically because its conditions are dictated entirely by the character of the employer. Thus Sir John is like a paternalistic slaveholder, concerned for Israel's welfare and providing him with food and clothing, whereas the superintendent of Princess Amelia's garden is like a slave overseer, 'harsh' and 'overbearing' who has cowed the other employees into 'tame servility'.[57] Melville makes specific reference to American slavery when he has Jones describe how he intends to treat his enemy the Earl of Selkirk, whom he plans to take to America as a hostage; 'For the earl's to be on sale, mind; so much ransom; that is, the nobleman, Lord Selkirk, shall have a bodily price pinned on his coat-tail, like any slave up at auction in Charleston.'[58]

These allusions are hardly surprising. As Melville is writing *Israel Potter*, slavery and abolition are among the most urgently discussed topics in the United States, and the debate had been considerably exacerbated in New England with the passing of the Fugitive Slave Act of 1850. This deeply controversial appeasement of the South was intended to ensure the return of slaves who had fled slaveholding states. Whereas earlier runaway slaves were considered free, or could petition for freedom, if they entered a free state or territory, now not only would they be returned to slavery, but the act declared that it was the legal duty of all citizens to assist in their returning, and there were heavy penalties for helping slaves.[59] Inevitably, slavery is very much on Melville's mind at this time, and is both intensified

---

[55] Ibid., p. 29.
[56] Ibid., p. 27.
[57] Ibid.
[58] Ibid., p. 93.
[59] The Act caused outrage in New England and many leading figures spoke out against it. In an 1851 address 'to the citizens of Concord' Emerson declared that 'it must be disobeyed'; Thoreau delivered a speech in 1851 titled 'Slavery in Massachusetts'. Harriet Beecher Stowe said the Act was the main stimulus for her writing *Uncle Tom's Cabin*.

and complicated by the fact that his father-in-law, Lemuel Shaw, was Chief Justice of the Massachusetts Supreme Court, and was dedicated to upholding the laws, in spite of the controversy this inevitably aroused. As Melville is completing *Israel Potter* he is turning his attention to an account of a slave revolt on a Spanish ship, which he will develop into *Benito Cereno*. It should also be noted that *Israel Potter* is written when the slave narrative is a popular genre. Frederick Douglass's 1845 *Narrative of the Life of Frederick Douglass*, had been a best-seller, and was much reprinted.[60] Indeed it was often bound together with *Uncle Tom's Cabin*; one of the biggest selling novels of the nineteenth century, and one that included several thrilling scenes of pursuit.

The affinities between Melville and Douglass, who were almost exact contemporaries, have come to be explored recently. They formed the subject for the Fifth International Conference sponsored by the Melville Society, held in New Bedford in 2005, and one book, a collection of essays and a special issue of the Melville Society Journal *Leviathan: A Journal of Melville Studies* have been devoted to it.[61] Although they seem not to have met, they had friends in common, notably R. H. Dana, and Douglass had reprinted extracts from *Typee* in his anti-slavery newspaper *North Star*.[62] Melville's use of elements of the slave narrative in *Israel Potter*, especially the pursuit and the question of ownership and identity, has attracted some critical attention.[63] But the connection between *Israel Potter* and the slave narrative actually involves the much larger issue of genre because, like the slave narrative, *Israel Potter* is in large measure an anti-narrative or a counter-narrative. That is, like the slave narrators, Melville challenges an existing genre exposing some of the assumptions behind it. For example, two of the most famous slave narratives are Douglass's 1845 *Narrative of the Life* and Harriet Jacobs's *Incidents in the Life of a Slave Girl* (1861) and as a literary tactic, both play off conventional genres; the autobiography in Douglass's case, and for Jacobs the domestic romance.[64] Thus Douglass

---

[60] It is estimated that over 30,000 copies had been sold by 1850; see Henry Louis Gates, Jr, and Nellie McKay (eds), *The Norton Anthology of African American Literature* (New York and London: Norton, 1997), p. 301.

[61] Respectively, Wallace, *Douglas and Melville*; *Frederick Douglass and Herman Melville: Essays in Relation*, ed. Robert S. Levine and Samuel Otter (Chapel Hill: University of North Carolina Press, 2008); special issue of *Leviathan: A Journal of Melville Studies*, 10:2 (2008).

[62] See Wallace, *Douglass and Melville*, pp. 56–7.

[63] See Anne Baker, 'What to Israel Potter Is the Fourth of July? Melville, Douglass, and the Agency of Words', *Leviathan: A Journal of Melville Studies*, 10:2 (2008), 9–22.

[64] Although *Incidents in the Life of a Slave Girl* was, after long delays, published in book form in 1861, parts of it had been published earlier, notably in *The New York Tribune*

famously begins his narrative by stating that he is unable to say when he was born. While he starts with the three words that form the classic opening to an autobiography, after that his emphasis is on what he lacks, what he cannot say:

> I was born in Tuckahoe, near Hillsborough. . . . I have no accurate knowledge of my age, never having seen any authentic record containing it. By far the larger part of the slaves know as little of their ages as horses know of theirs, and it is the wish of most masters within my knowledge to keep their slaves thus ignorant.[65]

Autobiography requires a capacity for sustaining a narrative frame to one's life, to make connections between past and present; it is also a means of aligning the self with others and creating or locating contexts for one's identity. But as Douglass asserts, one of the dehumanizing strategies of the slavery system is the deprivation of a personal and a historical past, and of the contexts for personal identity that the free take for granted. Similarly in her narrative, Jacobs uses the signifiers and convention of a romance narrative: pursuit, virtue and purity endangered, but she inverts these. Slavery has systematically and personally deprived her of any chance of a conventional family and any hope of living up to the contemporary white ideals of womanhood, marriage and domesticity. In the South, the mute acceptance of appalling sexual abuse has concealed the moral destruction of the family. So she challenges the fundamental and unspoken premise of the romance; that it is for free white middle-class women and provides a model of womanhood which is unattainable for a slave. As she comments, 'the condition of a slave confuses all principles of morality, and, in fact, renders the practice of them impossible'.[66] Shrewdly using romance plots, she even plays with the famous line from *Jane Eyre*, where 'Reader, I married him' is turned into 'Reader, my story ends with freedom; not in the usual way, with marriage.'[67]

Israel Potter resembles the slave narratives that are its contemporaries in that it too is a kind of counter-genre, an ironic *bildungsroman* centred on someone who does not become, a counter-success narrative about

in 1855. The book was published without its author's name on the title page, and in the narrative Jacobs used the name Linda Brent to conceal her own identity.

[65] Frederick Douglass, *Narrative of the Life of Frederick Douglass* (Harmondsworth: Penguin, 1986), p. 47.
[66] Harriet Jacobs, *Incidents in the Life of a Slave Girl* (New York and Oxford: Oxford University Press, 1988), p. 85.
[67] Ibid., p. 302.

someone who does not succeed. Like the slave narratives, it is concerned with lack, about someone for whom an identity framework and contexts for self-understanding are disrupted – not systematically as in the case of slavery, but by a set of accidents. But unlike slave narratives such as those by Douglass and Jacobs, Melville does not provide a synthesizing narrative. For Douglass and Jacobs, writing is the activity that leads to self-definition. While the act of writing can operate only within freedom, its essential premise, their narratives are both a record and a representation of freedom. As Sidonie Smith has claimed, through writing, the slave 'could again liberate himself from slavery – in this case the spiritual slavery of the past rather than the physical slavery of the South. He achieved this ... by giving distance to the pain of the past through the imposition of artistic form on the matter of experience.'[68] Thus although the slave narrative may be counter-generic it is on another level a form of success narrative, since it ends in freedom and ends, as do all autobiographies, with the act of writing. In fact, Douglass's narrative is a determinedly American one of success.

But Israel's life never comes into focus in such a way, and this is one of the consequences of Melville's decision to shift from the first-person narrative of his source. When Israel wrote up his own story (or, at least, told it to Trumbull who did), it became a particular kind of narrative, in that, exactly like the slave narrative, the very articulation of an identity is also the making, or remaking of one. As Raymond Williams observed:

> It is, in the first instance, to every man, a matter of urgent personal importance to 'describe' his experience, because this is literally a remaking of himself, a creative change in his personal organization, to include and control the experience. This struggle to remake ourselves – to change our personal organization so that we may live in a proper relation to our environment – is in fact often painful.[69]

Through his chosen mode of narration, Melville does not register Israel as the agent of his own 'remaking' and indicates that there is no change in his personal economy, no control at all over experience. *Israel Potter* is thus far

---

[68] Sidonie Smith, *Where I'm Bound* (Westport, CT and London: Greenwood Press, 1974), p. 10.
[69] Raymond Williams, *The Long Revolution* (Harmondsworth: Penguin Books, 1975), p. 42. In her study of nineteenth-century personal narratives, including that of Israel Potter, Ann Fabian quotes part of this passage, but wonders whether it can apply so readily to writers 'assuming the pose of poor and humble narrators' and whether their narratives reinforce humility and deference; Fabian, *The Unvarnished Truth*, p. 7.

more radical than the fugitive slave narratives, which of necessity chart the movement from slavery to freedom and self-definition. *Israel Potter* is a novel whose trajectory is one of increasing estrangement, from one's family, native land, and eventually from oneself. In articulating the ironies of Israel's life, Melville echoes a formulation common in slave narrations; the gulf between the national ideology of liberty and the presence of slavery, the theme, for instance, of Douglass's renowned 1852 speech, 'What to the Slave is the Fourth of July?' In Israel's case the irony is in his inability to benefit from the American nation and its freedoms for which he fought. But the deeper irony is of the personal dislocations that are the consequences of his service in the American cause, his intense self-estrangement.

This is why Melville records Israel's numerous changes of clothing, especially in the first third of the novel. They represent a disappearing self, a set of costumes with no identity within. Thus in chapter 6, Israel takes up his role as messenger for those who secretly support the American cause when, 'disguised in strange clothes' provided for him by a farmer, he meets with Horne Tooke, James Bridges and John Woodcock at Woodcock's home.[70] While these three are secretly 'friends to America', Melville emphasizes the duplicity of the clothing worn by Tooke and Bridges; 'attired, in the manner of that age, in long laced coats, with smallclothes, and shoes with silver buckles'.[71] ('Smallclothes', more usually, 'small-clothes', are knee-breeches.) Tooke, an actual historical character, and Bridges are wearing these clothes as part of a masquerade, their outward conformity concealing their treasonous affinities. In Trumbull's narrative no mention at all is made of what Tooke and Bridges are wearing; again, Melville enriches his source material and draws attention to the discrepancy between appearance and true identity. These are two characters who know very well that they are playing roles, and that these roles require disguise. Having agreed to take a message to Franklin in Paris, Israel is then dressed for the mission, a costume that includes boots with hollowed heels to conceal a message.

While in some respects the chapters that involve Franklin maintain a lightness of tone, with an almost comic element, they are complex in the developing contexts of Israel's identity. Although Franklin scarcely appears in Potter's own account, Melville's expansion is crucial to his narrative. Specifically, Melville contrasts Franklin's rational pragmatism, his inherently flexible, shifting, self-created identity, a self that changes according to context, with Israel's inability to manage and sustain a self. Franklin, the great and universally popular representative of the Enlightenment, was

---

[70] Melville, *Israel Potter*, p. 34.
[71] Ibid.

well-known for affecting an unostentatious simplicity of dress and manner, and for not following the custom of wearing a wig. Indeed, he was often taken to be a Quaker, and was represented pictorially in this way, given his emulation of the modesty of clothing associated with the Society of Friends. Franklin's style of dress is so well-known to be instantly recognizable, and forms an enduringly popular choice for costume parties.[72] His pragmatism was expressed in his dress, and while working for the American cause in Paris, the period represented in *Israel Potter*, he was renowned for wearing an American fur cap, not only to keep warm, but to advertise the supposed simple virtues of the Americans.

Melville alludes directly (if clumsily) to Franklin's mode of dress, and to the idea that his dress is consistent with his thought: 'the economic envoy's plain coat and hose, who has not heard of?' he asks, and comments, 'Franklin all over is of a piece. He dressed his person as his periods; neat, trim, nothing superfluous, nothing deficient.'[73] He also alludes indirectly to some of Franklin's sayings: 'sublime thoughts and tattered wardrobe'; '[b]e a plain man, and stick to plain things'.[74] But his description of Franklin's dress at his first meeting with Israel considerably complicates this 'plain' representation. He is '[w]rapped in a rich dressing-gown – a fanciful present from an admiring Marchesa – curiously embroidered with algebraic figures like a conjuror's robe, and with a skull-cap of black satin on his hive of a head ... seated at a huge claw-footed old table, round as the zodiac'.[75] This is an immediate and comprehensive undoing of Franklin's self-representation. The implied association with aristocracy, the luxuriant orientalist embroidery, and the connotations of conjuror, alchemist, necromancer and astrologist all contradict the sustained image of plainness and of democratic rational enlightenment.

In the next chapters, Melville elaborates on the gap between Franklin's image, teachings and actual behaviour. The effect is mostly comic, as Melville satirizes Franklin's Polonius-like tendency to discourse and to offer advice on any subject, and while he advises Israel against the poisonous luxuries of brandy, cologne and the attractive chambermaid, he deprives him of each of them. But the effect is not merely comic, and Melville's motivations are far more complex than simply exposing Franklin as a hypocrite. Franklin comes across as contradictory rather than insincere or hypocritical; he is

---

[72] Generally based on the 1785 portrait attributed to Joseph-Siffred Duplessis. Franklin, seated and unwigged, wears a plain grey frock-coat and no personal ornamentation whatever.
[73] Melville, *Israel Potter*, p. 46.
[74] Ibid., pp. 47, 45.
[75] Ibid., p. 38.

contradictory precisely because he has cultivated a multiplicity of selves. Melville calls him 'labyrinth-minded', but he is also the master of that labyrinth.[76] While the different selves may lay Franklin open to a charge of insincerity, it is perhaps 'insincerity' that needs to be interrogated; as Oscar Wilde puts it, '[i]s insincerity such a terrible thing? I think not. It is merely a method by which we can multiply our personalities.'[77]

Franklin's occupying multiple selves is most evident in his *Autobiography*, and, indeed, this act of claiming identity is one of the functions of modern autobiography. While Melville refers to Franklin's sayings of Poor Richard and his *Way to Wealth*, he does not mention the *Autobiography* (which has a complicated history of both composition and publication), however his representation of Franklin derives from the autobiography and from what the writing of autobiography represents.[78] The *Autobiography* is not only a key American text, but is usually regarded as a foundational text for modern autobiography. This is primarily because rather than recording his life, relaying it to us factually, Franklin is finding (or creating) a pattern for it. His objective is not to provide a chronicle of his life but to demonstrate how his character developed. Hence his informing metaphor in the autobiography is the making of the book itself; his life is a text that needs to be edited, presented and fashioned in order to demonstrate coherence, order and plan. Franklin's aim in the autobiography is not so much to reveal facts or truth but to give shape and meaning to his experience, and the making of that shape actually requires the suppression of facts that may not fit in with it.[79] Franklin's modernity is in this self-shaping; in fact, autobiography itself is a mode of writing almost exclusively associated with modernity,

[76] Ibid., p. 47.
[77] Oscar Wilde, *The Picture of Dorian Gray* (London: Penguin Classics, 2003), p. 137. This view is actually expressed by the narrator, although it is a belief shared by Gray.
[78] Franklin started to write the work that we know as his *Autobiography* in 1771, when he was 65. He suspended work on it in the same year, though, and did not resume writing until 1785, and although he continued working on it until his death in 1790, it is unfinished, and records his life only up to 1757. Numerous editions of the autobiography, then titled 'The Life of Benjamin Franklin, written by himself' appeared from the 1790s onwards. The title *Autobiography of Benjamin Franklin* was first used for an edition probably published around 1818 (the word 'autobiography' was then new; the *OED* records the neologism being proposed in 1797, but not in usage until 1809). Modern versions of Franklin's *Autobiography* mostly derive from the edition published in 1869.
[79] Franklin's suppressions and evasions have long preoccupied critics, but to emphasize these is to miss the actuality of the autobiography and to read it as if it were something else entirely. In this respect, H. Porter Abbot has urged us to read autobiography 'fictively': 'to ask of the text before all else: How is this complete? . . . to align oneself with the author in a joint project of rendering the text an artful whole' ('Autobiography, Autography, Fiction', 613).

with being 'modern', about being a subject in modernity. Franklin's shaping is also apparent in the transitions that his text records. It is a personal trajectory from Puritanism, represented by his growing up in Boston, towards enlightened rationality, represented by Philadelphia. It is a personal movement from poverty to wealth, and a national trajectory, as the United States is fashioned from a colony into an independent republic. Melville's invocation of Franklin involves the sharp contrast between someone who has the ability to master and organize his multiple (and conflicting) experiences and varied identities into coherence and order, that is, to fashion oneself in modernity, and Israel, who lacks exactly this capacity. Melville acknowledges Franklin's success in performing modernity to highlight the nature of Israel's failure, his inability to adapt the self to the circumstances of the modern, to make and sustain identity. 'Having carefully weighed the world', Melville writes, 'Franklin could act any part in it.'[80]

Israel's failure is made even more poignant by Franklin's insistence on the capacity of all for success. Melville has given Israel a copy of his book *The Way to Wealth*, and he has a copy of *Poor Richard's Almanack*, but their possibilities, and the opportunities they represent, are lost on him. The claim that success and self-making are achievable is of course one of the key reasons for Franklin's enduring popularity and influence. In effect he creates a cultural template which is an articulation of the nation's creed, its belief in the possibilities of self-realization. His story in the *Autobiography* is really the story of a nation's ideology; as Sacvan Bercovitch has put it, Franklin is one of the almost mythical American figures who 'confirm American selfhood as an identity in progress, advancing from prophecies performed towards paradise to be regained'.[81] This model of progress requires a point of departure, and Franklin's famous account of his arrival in Philadelphia has been widely imitated (and parodied) – a version of it is a standard and essential feature of any success narrative. He comes to Philadelphia hungry, exhausted, knowing no-one and with scarcely any money, just 'a Dutch Dollar and about a Shilling in Copper'. He uses the money to buy some bread, though to his surprise the baker gives him 'three great Puffy Rolls'. 'I was surpriz'd at the Quantity', Franklin writes, but takes them, 'and having no Room in my Pockets, walk'd off, with a Roll under each Arm, & eating the other'.[82] The image establishes the starting-point for the success journey, and Franklin's story of self-realization is the originating model for

---

[80] Melville, *Israel Potter*, p. 48.
[81] *The Puritan Origins of the American Self* (New Haven: Yale University Press, 1975), p. 143.
[82] Benjamin Franklin, *Writings* (New York: Library of America, 1987), p. 1329.

an entire genre. The success narrative was most influential in the hands of Horatio Alger, probably the most widely read of all American authors, with his novels selling a combined total of over 20 million copies. In them, Ragged Dick and his avatars gain upward social mobility and a measure of independence through a combination of hard work, dedication to an ideal and the ability to recognize a lucky opportunity.

In part, then, Melville's development of Franklin in *Israel Potter* functions straightforwardly as a counter to Israel's story of failure and invisibility, challenging the illusion that one can emulate the extraordinary achievement of Franklin, and making his novel, as one critic has described it, an 'ironic parody of the American myth of self-making'.[83] But it is more than that, and the contrast between Franklin and Israel functions also on a deeper level. One aspect of Franklin's success is his ability to present a consistency of surface, apparent in the choice of plain dress, while maintaining a multifaceted inner self, one made up of so many characteristics as to seem almost contradictory. Melville reminds us of Franklin's 'multifariousness': 'Printer, postmaster, almanac maker, essayist, chemist, orator, tinker, statesman, humorist, philosopher, parlor-man, political economist, professor of housewifery, ambassador, projector, maxim-monger, herb-doctor, wit: – Jack of all trades, master of each and mastered by none – the type and genius of his land. Franklin was everything but a poet.'[84] The fact that Franklin is not 'a poet' is especially telling. While Franklin composed a good deal of verse and verse epigrams for the various editions of *Poor Richard's Almanack*, Melville is here invoking the Romantic sense of the poet. Especially relevant is Coleridge's celebrated reflection on the poet in chapter 14 of his *Biographia Literaria*:

> The poet, described in ideal perfection, brings the whole soul of man into activity, with the subordination of its faculties to each other, according to their relative worth and dignity. He diffuses a tone and spirit of unity that blends, and (as it were) *fuses* each into each by that synthetic and magical power to which I would exclusively appropriate the name of Imagination. This power . . . reveals itself in the balance or reconcilement of opposite or discordant qualities.[85]

[83] Gale Temple, 'Fluid Identity in *Israel Potter* and *The Confidence-Man*', in *A Companion to Herman Melville*, ed. Wyn Kelley (Malden, MA: Blackwell, 2006), p. 454. Outdoing Franklin's poor beginnings and the three rolls of bread, Melville has Israel going 'three days without food, except one two-penny loaf' (Melville, *Israel Potter*, p. 23).
[84] Ibid., p. 48.
[85] Quoted in Duncan Wu (ed.), *Romanticism: An Anthology* (Oxford: Blackwell, 1994), p. 177. Melville had owned a copy of the *Biographia Literaria* since 1848; Parker, *Herman Melville*, 1, p. 577.

Melville represents Franklin as someone whose multiple identities are not synthesized into a singular unity, they are allowed, rather, to coexist, with all of their contradictions and imbalances. As a representative of modernity his success comes from a cultivation of his separate selves, from his ability to adapt his identity to changing circumstances, and to act in the world, to master rather than be mastered. As Melville puts it, his 'totality' can be seen only by seeing him in contact with 'many different men'.[86]

Franklin's changing of identity to fit and become the master of various situations is an aspect of his modern pragmatism; it also marks him out as a precursor to the Confidence-Man who will be the subject of Melville's next novel. Such a representation of Franklin is not exclusive to Melville. In his essay on Franklin in *Studies in Classic American Literature*, Lawrence comments on the multiplicity of roles and asks his reader 'How many selves have you?'[87] But there is a darker side to this pragmatism and the cultivation of multiple selves, which involves a moral judgement on character. That is, the cultivation of appearance may easily slip into a form of disguise, and can be used to conceal inner reality. There are two particular moments in Franklin's *Autobiography* where this flexible pragmatism threatens to become a kind of manipulation. One is when Franklin discusses his rationale for abandoning vegetarianism:

> [I]n my first Voyage from Boston . . . our People set about catching Cod & hawl'd up a great many. Hitherto I had stuck to my Resolution of not eating animal Food; and on this Occasion, I consider'd . . . the taking every Fish as a kind of unprovok'd Murder. . . . All this seem'd very reasonable. – But I had formerly been a great Lover of Fish, & when this came hot out of the Frying Pan, it smelt admirably well. I balanc'd some time between Principle & Inclination: till I recollected, that when the Fish were opened, I saw smaller Fish taken out of their Stomachs: – Then, thought I, if you eat one another, I don't see why we mayn't eat you. So I din'd upon Cod very heartily . . . returning only now & then occasionally to a vegetable Diet. So convenient a thing it is to be a *reasonable Creature*, since it enables one to find or make a Reason for everything one has a mind to do.[88]

Reason here is applied retrospectively in order to justify an action. While this is pragmatic, it runs entirely counter to the spirit of the Enlightenment,

---

[86] Melville, *Israel Potter*, p. 48.
[87] Lawrence, *Studies in Classic American Literature*, p. 15.
[88] Franklin, *Writings*, p. 1339.

where reason is to be used to determine a course of action.[89] The second moment where pragmatism courts deception comes when Franklin discusses the relation between appearance and success. It is not enough, he writes, to be industrious; you must also make this conspicuous in your appearance, your dress and manner. He has at this point opened a stationery shop in Philadelphia:

> In order to secure my Credit and Character as a Tradesmen, I took care to be not only in *Reality* Industrious & frugal, but to avoid all *Appearances* of the Contrary. I drest plainly; I was seen at no Places of idle Diversion . . . a Book, indeed, sometimes debauch'd me from my Work; but that was seldom, snug, & gave me no Scandal: and to show that I was not above my Business, I sometimes brought home the Paper I purchas'd at the Stores, thro' the Streets on a Wheelbarrow. Thus being esteem'd an industrious thriving young Man, and paying duly for what I bought, the Merchants who imported Stationary solicited my Custom, others propos'd supplying me with Books, & I went on swimmingly.[90]

Today, self-help manuals call this 'impression management' and it is a cornerstone for success. Franklin provides the counter-example in his rival David Harry, who 'was very proud' and 'dressed like a gentleman', and whose business fails where Franklin's prospers. The point here is that Franklin is always aware of being on display, always presenting a self in the attempt to master and to control. It is however only one short step from this self-commodification to actual duplicity (again a precursor to the Confidence-Man), and this is how Melville presents Franklin. He confidently plays so many roles because there is no single, synthetic self; in the modern world Franklin succeeds because he can 'act any part in it'. This is again in contrast to Israel, whose faltering occupation of diverse roles is forced upon him and increasingly suggests that there is no inner self at all.

---

[89] The rationale for eating the fish is consistent with Franklin's admiration of the Quaker members of the administration in colonial Pennsylvania for their ability to find ways of acting in the modern world yet remaining obedient to their principles. For instance, he recalls the problem that arose when the crown needed money for military purposes. 'They were unwilling to offend Government, on the one hand, by a direct Refusal; and their Friends, the Body of Quakers, on the other, by a Compliance contrary to their Principles. Hence a Variety of Evasions to avoid Complying, and Modes of disguising the Compliance when it became unavoidable. The common Mode at last was to grant Money under the Phrase of its being "*for the King's use*", and never to inquire how it was applied' (ibid., p. 1415).

[90] Ibid., p. 1369.

While several critics have claimed that Israel is in search of a coherent self, it is more the case that he is increasingly unable to hold together any self at all.[91] Furthermore, Israel is easily taken in by appearance, trusting it as substance. For example, he cannot 'read' the flirtatious chambermaid the way the worldly Franklin can, 'a young French lass, bloom on her cheek, pink ribbons in her cap, liveliness in all her air, grace in the very tips of her elbows'.[92] This not only marks him out as the comic innocent in Paris but it also suggests he is ill-equipped for urban modernity. To trust in appearance is to be continually open to being deceived. It also suggests Israel's overall failure to see beneath surfaces, to consider substance and nuance.

The contrast between Israel and Franklin is matched by the contrast with John Paul Jones. Although Jones is entirely absent from Trumbull's narrative of Potter, he plays a substantial role in Melville's novel. In fact, for Melville one of the attractions of using Trumbull's narrative may have been the opportunity it provided (or was made to provide) for narrating some of Jones's naval adventures around the British Isles at the time that Israel is in England and France.[93] Certainly, the accounts of the raid on Whitehaven, the attempt to capture the Earl of Selkirk and the engagement with the *Serapis* lend pace and excitement to the novel, and were almost certainly a major reason for the popularity of *Israel Potter*, given that the 'adventure' element of the tale was part of Melville's pitch to Putnam's. Several of the reviewers explicitly praised these episodes, and in the twentieth century they stimulated one major critic, Yvor Winters, to praise *Israel Potter* as 'one of the few great novels of pure adventure in English'.[94] The adventures recounted from chapter 11 up to chapter 22 and the strong characters of Jones and Ethan Allen overshadow Israel altogether, and this is especially striking as the book then concludes by covering the remaining 45 years of Israel's life in four short chapters. As one reviewer pointed out, *Israel Potter*'s subtitle 'His Fifty Years of Exile' is misleading; 'A downright good book, though *five* years, in place of *fifty*, would have been a more appropriate title, seeing that forty-five of them are shuffled off in a few pages at the close.'[95]

[91] See Temple, 'Fluid Identity in *Israel Potter*', pp. 453, 456.
[92] Melville, *Israel Potter*, p. 52.
[93] Melville turned to James Fenimore Cooper's two-volume *History of the Navy of the United States* (1839) for source material at this point. Cooper published a pamphlet on Jones in 1846, in a series called *Lives of Distinguished American Naval Officers*, published by Carey and Hart in Philadelphia, and the title character of his fourth novel, *The Pilot* (1823) is based on Jones.
[94] Yvor Winters, *In Defense of Reason* (Chicago: Swallow Press, 1943), p. 233. The somewhat idiosyncratic essay is titled 'Herman Melville and the Problems of Moral Navigation'.
[95] William Young, in Branch, *Melville: Critical Heritage*, p. 339.

On a simple level, the contrast between Israel and Jones is straightforward enough – the bold, decisive man of action, a true leader, contrasted with the passive Israel, in no way the agent of his own destiny. As with Franklin, the contrast intensifies the poignancy of Israel's fate; while he has participated in Jones's heroic actions, he is forgotten while others are praised and remembered.[96] While this contrast is significant, it is complicated by several factors. In particular, some of Jones's qualities do influence Israel in a positive way, and he briefly achieves a measure of self-assertion and enterprise, and one of his deeds proves decisive when he performs heroically, if destructively, during the battle between the *Serapis* and the *Richard*.[97] His temporary cunning is evident in chapter 20 when, ending up (yet again) on an English ship, he becomes a respected member of the crew, under the name of Peter Perkins.

However, the comparison with Jones works also at a more complex level, evident from Melville's detailing his clothing. From very early on in his days in the merchant navy, Jones was known for his flamboyant dress, earning him the nickname 'the dandy skipper'.[98] One aspect of Melville's ambiguous representation of Jones draws attention to this dandyism, with a rather exaggerated emphasis. The initial description stresses the exotic elements of his character:

> He was a rather small, elastic, swarthy man, with an aspect as of a disinherited Indian Chief in European clothes. An unvanquishable enthusiasm, intensified to perfect sobriety, couched in his savage, self-possessed eye. He was elegantly and somewhat extravagantly dressed as a civilian; he carried himself with a rustic, barbaric jauntiness, strangely dashed with a superinduced touch of the Parisian *salon*. . . . He looked like one who never had been, and never would be, a subordinate.
>
> Israel thought to himself that seldom before had he seen such a being. Though dressed à-la-mode, he did not seem to be altogether civilized.[99]

---

[96] Although Jones was a celebrated figure, after his death in Paris in 1792 his body was buried in what became a neglected and obscure graveyard. Following a concerted campaign his grave was located and his remains were brought to the United States in 1906. In 1913 they were installed in a sarcophagus (modelled on Napoleon's coffin) in the Naval Academy Chapel in Annapolis.
[97] He kills more than 20 men and wounds many more by hurling a grenade; Melville took this entirely from Cooper's *History of the Navy*.
[98] William P. Leeman, *The Long Road to Annapolis* (Chapel Hill: University of North Carolina Press, 2010), p. 12.
[99] Melville, *Israel Potter*, p. 56.

Jones is marked out here as one of Melville's Anacharsis Cloots figures, a tattooed cosmopolitan whose dress emphasizes a confident transgression of boundaries. This is of course embodied in Jones's life. He was born in Scotland, captained a merchant ship in the tropics, fought for the American cause and died in France. The performative element of his identity that Melville emphasizes is also embodied in his life. Even the name John Paul Jones is an act of self-invention; his name was simply John Paul, and he added 'Jones' in or around 1773.[100] More explicitly Jones is a dandy, although a slightly anachronistic one, since dandyism supposedly began in the 1790s.[101] Even while serving in the navy, he adapted the uniform to his own ends: 'Jones wore his own variation of the prescribed Continental navy officer's uniform – a dark blue coat with white lapels, gold epaulets, gold buttons, a white waistcoat, white breeches and stockings, and a sword.'[102] Melville refers to Jones's 'dandified air' and his 'dandyish look of sentimental conceit'.[103] He certainly knew of Thomas Carlyle's comments in the chapter of *Sartor Resartus* titled 'The Dandiacal Body':

> A Dandy is a Clothes-wearing Man, a Man whose trade, office and existence consists in the wearing of Clothes. Every faculty of his soul, spirit, purse, and person is heroically consecrated to this one object, the wearing of Clothes wisely and well: so that the others dress to live, he lives to dress. . . . And now, for all this perennial Martyrdom, and Poesy, and even Prophecy, what is it that the Dandy asks in return? Solely, we may say, that you would recognise his existence; would admit him to be a living object; or even failing this, a visual object, or thing that will reflect rays of light.[104]

Much has been written on the history of the dandy, on the political moment of the dandy, and the dandy as a figure of modernity.[105] The most salient

---

[100] The reasons for the name change are unclear. Fenimore Cooper claimed it was to help disguise his identity when he was a fugitive following the murder of a mutineer, and this is largely supported by a letter from Jones to Franklin. A more fanciful (though discredited) tradition has him taking the name Jones as a compliment to friends with that name. See Samuel Eliot Morison, 'The Willie Jones-John Paul Jones Tradition', *William and Mary Quarterly*, 16:2 (1959), 198–206.

[101] The *OED* records 'dandy' in use in the Scottish borders at the end of the eighteenth century, and of course it appears in the colonial song 'Yankee Doodle', but it was most in vogue in London from the first decades of the nineteenth century.

[102] Leeman, *Long Road to Annapolis*, p. 13. Described thus, he is strikingly similar to one of the avatars of the Confidence-Man.

[103] Melville, *Israel Potter*, pp. 63, 90.

[104] McSweeney and Sabor (eds), *Sartor Resartus*, p. 207.

[105] Ellen Moers writes particularly of the historical moment in *The Dandy* (London: Secker and Warburg, 1960); see also chapter 9 of Elizabeth Wilson's *Adorned in Dreams* (London: Virago, 1985).

point here is in the artifice of identity that the dandy enacts. It is important to note a distinction between being 'well-dressed' and being a dandy. Someone can be well-dressed by being outfitted in a way that conforms to the rules of dress, how items and textiles are matched and arranged, how the language is grammatically correct. In not following the rules of dress, the dandy does two things. First, he draws attention to those rules, and secondly asserts a particular relation between dress and identity. With regard to drawing attention to rules, the dandy may not be 'well-dressed' at all, but he has to be someone who mixes the codes of dress and thereby asserts his freedom from those rules, simultaneously making those rules ironic. Baudelaire was particularly interested in the dandy and in the 1860s wrote of him as a figure of modernity, 'Dandyism appears especially in those periods of transition when democracy has not yet become all-powerful, and when aristocracy is only partially weakened and discredited.'[106] He also argued, 'Contrary to what a lot of thoughtless people seem to believe, dandyism . . . is not even an excessive delight in clothes and material elegance. . . . It is, above all, the burning desire to create a personal form of originality, within the external limits of social conventions. It is a kind of cult of the ego.'[107] A good contemporary example here is the British fashion designer John Galliano, whose personal style involves abrupt and clashing mixtures and traditions of clothing, and which occasionally is ill-mannered or offensive. As one critic has commented, 'the dandy is an anarchist, because he rejects *all* rules and *all* norms'.[108]

The second consequence of the dandy's drawing attention to dress is to explore or assert a specific relation between dress and identity. He is in effect, telling us that he has created his own identity, and that this identity is both malleable and multifaceted. This is what Carlyle suggests when he says that the dandy wants us above all to 'recognise his existence' and this is precisely what intrigued both Baudelaire and Sartre in their observations on the dandy: the fact that his is a created identity works to remind us that all identity is artifice. His clothes tell us that nothing is given or natural; this is why Baudelaire considered the dandy a figure of the true artist, dedicated to invention and ingenuity. Jessica R. Feldman's succinct summation of the dandy is especially relevant to Melville's depiction of Jones:

> Dandies flaunt what a culture usually attempts to ignore or hide, that the human body is never 'natural' or naked of cultural clothing, but

[106] Baudelaire, 'The Dandy', p. 421.
[107] Ibid., p. 420.
[108] Thorsten Botz-Bornstein, 'Rule-Following in Dandyism: "Style" as an Overcoming of "Rule" and "Structure"', *The Modern Language Review*, 90:2 (1995), 285.

is instead a system of signification, cultural construct. The dandy's clothing, bearing, makeup and so forth announce the necessarily 'made-up' quality of what we often take as our locus of unmediated nature, our own bodies. Once dandies discover the power of self-representation, they can no longer imagine a self independent of cultural mediation. . . . The dandy teaches us to accept ambiguity, multiplicity, and contingency – the confusing but vital making of a world, not the exploration of a given world.[109]

Just as a dandy should, Jones accepts the artifice of the world, and engages creatively with it, rather than allowing this to subdue or overwhelm him.[110] On the face of it, there is a complete contrast between the flamboyantly dressed Jones and the plainly dressed Franklin. But in fact, the dress of both is a reminder of identity as performance in modernity. Franklin, as the epitome of the self-made man, allows simple clothing to indicate different facets of his multiform identity, to present the right, apparently authentic 'self' for each occasion. Although Jones constantly represents his multiplicity of selves, the effect is the same; we dress not to reveal identity but to generate one.

In representing Jones as a dandy, though, Melville also returns to a theme long familiar in his writing, the relationship between civilized and savage. Just as he had in *Typee* and *Omoo* a decade earlier, and will do again in *Billy Budd* in 30 years' time, Melville insists on the similarities between the savage and the civilized states. The indigenous South Sea Islanders in *Typee* had their versions of the dandy, and in his representation of Jones Melville indicates that as well as being the epitome of the urban, refined, civilized man, the European dandy performs the same function as the South Sea dandy. In fact, Melville several times emphasizes the primitive or savage qualities of Jones the dandy. That first description likens Jones to a 'disinherited Indian Chief' and this is developed later, when he writes of his extensive tattoos.[111] These allusions form the basis for a typical Melvillean flourish, first invoking a contrast between the ultracivilized Paris and Jones the barbarian:

> So at midnight, the heart of the metropolis of modern civilization was secretly trod by this jaunty barbarian in broad-cloth; a sort of

[109] Jessica R. Feldman, *Gender on the Divide: The Dandy in Modernist Literature* (Ithaca, NY: Cornell University Press, 1993), pp. 270–1.
[110] Jones was not actually a pirate, since he held letters of marque authorizing his activities, but the pirate's improvised amalgamation of styles certainly parallels that of the dandy, and many cinematic representations of the pirate draw attention to this.
[111] Melville, *Israel Potter*, pp. 62–3.

prophetical ghost, glimmering in anticipation upon the advent of those tragic scenes of the French Revolution which levelled the exquisite refinement of Paris with the blood-thirsty ferocity of Borneo; showing that broaches and finger-rings, not less than nose-rings and tattooing, are tokens of the primeval savageness which ever slumbers in human kind, civilised or uncivilised.[112]

Far from an embodiment of only the civilized, the fashionable Parisian in the centre of modernity represents the most primitive and enduring of all human urges: the will to self-adornment. Melville takes this a step further when he reflects on Jones's bloody sea-battle with the *Serapis*: 'The loss of life in the two ships was about equal; one-half of the total number of those engaged being either killed or wounded.' He continues, 'In view of this battle one may well ask – What separates the enlightened man from the savage? Is civilization a thing distinct, or is it an advanced stage of barbarism?'[113]

While Melville's extensive deliberations on Franklin and Jones represent major interventions in his source material, they are by no means a digression from his characterization of Israel. The ease and confidence with which Franklin and Jones express personality through dress indicate exactly what is lacking in Israel's character. As Jones's adventures continue, Israel's changes of clothing increase, and at three particular moments Melville uses the accidents of his attire to represent Israel's overall character, as someone increasingly depersonalized. The first of these occurs when, having returned from Paris, Israel is concealed in a tiny room in Woodcock's house (another textual feature that echoes the slave narrative, and the recurring instances of enclosure make another connection between Israel and Ishmael). He endures this claustrophobic terror for three days. Eventually, convinced by now that something has happened to prevent Woodcock from releasing him, Israel manages to free himself via a secret door leading to Woodcock's bedroom. There, the funereal decor confirms that the squire has indeed died. Israel grasps the opportunity to escape from the house in clothes taken from Woodcock's closet:

> Opening the door, there hung several coats, small clothes, pairs of silk stockings, and hats of the deceased. With little difficulty Israel selected from these the complete suit in which he had last seen his once jovial friend. Carefully closing the door, and carrying the suit with him, he was returning towards the chimney, when he saw the Squire's

[112] Ibid., p. 63.
[113] Ibid., p. 130.

silver-headed cane leaning against a corner of the wainscot. Taking this also, he stole back to his cell.

> Slipping off his own clothing, he deliberately arrayed himself in the borrowed raiment; silk small-clothes and all; then put on the cocked hat, grasped the silver-headed cane in his right hand, and moving his small shaving-glass slowly up and down before him, so as by piecemeal to take in his whole figure, felt convinced that he would well pass for Squire Woodcock's genuine phantom.[114]

Notably, Israel is disguised not as the squire but as the squire's ghost, and this sense of unreality, of Israel as a phantom (not even his own), intensifies in the narrative. The euphoria he first felt after dressing in the 'borrowed raiment' is very quickly overwhelmed by his anxiety, and his sense of becoming unreal:

> [A]fter the first feeling of self-satisfaction with his anticipated success had left him, it was not without some superstitious embarrassment that Israel felt himself encased in a dead man's broadcloth; nay, in the very coat in which the deceased had no doubt fallen down in his fit. By degrees he began to feel almost as unreal and shadowy as the shade whose part he intended to enact.[115]

Israel's transformation to a ghost is confirmed when he deliberately imitates one to frighten away members of the squire's household. While becoming a phantom marks a particular stage of his depersonalization, it is swiftly followed by another. Israel eventually realizes his error in not wearing his own clothes underneath Woodcock's, and he now fears being arrested as a thief. Introduced by what is for Melville an unusual mid-chapter heading, 'An Encounter of Ghosts', Israel has a strange meeting with a 'man in black':

> [T]he phantom of Squire Woodcock . . . marched straight forward towards the mysterious stranger.
>
> As he neared him, Israel shrunk. The dark coat-sleeve flapped on the bony skeleton of the unknown arm. The face was lost in a sort of ghastly blank. It was no living man.
>
> But mechanically continuing his course, Israel drew still nearer and saw – a scarecrow.[116]

[114] Ibid., p. 75.
[115] Ibid.
[116] Ibid., p. 77.

The imagery of living death and dehumanization prefigures Israel's own depersonalization. Melville also emphasizes the improvised, makeshift and muddled identity of the scarecrow's clothing. This is dress as mixed metaphor, an ironic counterpart to the dandy's conflictual plenitude of identity. The scarecrow has been more carefully dressed as a human than seems strictly necessary for its function:

> [It] seemed to have been constructed on the most efficient principles; probably by some broken down wax-figure costumer. It comprised the complete wardrobe of a scare-crow, namely: a cocked hat, bunged; tattered coat; old velveteen breeches; and long worsted stockings, full of holes; all stuffed very nicely with straw, and skeletoned by a framework of poles. There was a great flapped pocket to the coat – which seemed to have been some laborer's – standing invitingly open.[117]

Though skeleton-like, the scarecrow is 'properly' dressed, and its pockets are not empty: containing the 'lid of an old tobacco-box, the broken bowl of a pipe, two rusty nails, and a few kernels of wheat'.[118] Israel, of course, exchanges clothes yet again, stripping the scarecrow and hiding the squire's clothes. Comically, he is then forced to act as if he were a scarecrow, in order to escape a group of farm workers who recognize the outfit.

Although it occurs at only the novel's midpoint, Israel's becoming a ghost and then a scarecrow in effect defines the rest of his life. His hiding for the three days in the squire's home, the death of the squire, the ghost clothing and the scarecrow do not appear at all in Trumbull's narrative, and are crucial to Melville's. The ghost and the scarecrow are recurring images in popular culture as well as modernist literature, representing hollowness, emptiness, the dehumanized self, the not-quite human. More immediately, Melville's dressing Israel as a scarecrow echoes Hawthorne's whimsical story 'Feathertop'.[119] Mother Rigby, a witch, brings her scarecrow Feathertop to life in order to court Polly Gookin, whose father, a magistrate, is one of her enemies. The scarecrow is alive for as long as he continues to smoke a pipe. The well-dressed scarecrow impresses the townsfolk as well as Polly, but when he and Polly look together in a mirror, his reflection shows only his actual condition as a scarecrow, 'a picture of the sordid patchwork of his real composition'.[120] His newly gained

---

[117] Ibid.
[118] Ibid.
[119] The story was first published in 1852, and then collected in the 1854 edition of *Mosses from an Old Manse*.
[120] Hawthorne, *Tales and Sketches*, p. 244.

self-knowledge, that he is a 'wretched, ragged, empty thing' undoes him, and he destroys his pipe, reverting immediately to 'a medley of straw and tattered garments'.[121] Mother Rigby decides against restoring Feathertop's humanity, commenting: 'There are thousands upon thousands of coxcombs and charlatans in the world, made up of just such a jumble of worn-out, forgotten, and good-for-nothing trash as he was! Yet they live in fair repute, and never see themselves for what they are!'[122] For all of its light-heartedness, 'Feathertop' is an astute commentary on the theme of appearance and reality, and on the power of clothes to generate an identity, with Hawthorne emphasizing Feathertop's aristocratic clothing and the impression it makes. It is also concerned with the danger of seeing oneself as one actually is. The text's central insight is far from comic, and has a special bearing on *Israel Potter*; we are all 'wretched, ragged, empty thing[s]' and only the inability to see this allows us to maintain our preferred self-image.[123]

Moreover, the scarecrow is a long-established figuration of human inadequacy or incompleteness. In 1864, Cardinal Newman famously wrote of the necessity of writing his autobiography, having been set up as a 'straw man' by those inimical to him: 'I must . . . give the true key to my whole life; I must show . . . that the phantom may be extinguished which gibbers instead of me. I wish to be known as a living man, and not as a scarecrow which is dressed up in my clothes.'[124] The scarecrow is familiar in modern literature and culture in just this way, from young Jude Fawley in *Jude the Obscure*, to Conrad's Kurtz and the 'man of patches' in *Heart of Darkness*, T. S. Eliot's Hollow Men, W. B. Yeats's use of the scarecrow as an image of his older self and of the old generally in 'Among School Children' and 'Sailing to Byzantium'. Andrew Wyeth's various paintings of scarecrows

---

[121] Ibid., p. 245.
[122] Ibid.
[123] Carlyle made a similar point in *Sartor Resartus*. Discussing the authority that clothes provide, Teufelsdröckh asks why a scarecrow dressed in the same clothes should not have the same authority: 'It will remain to be examined . . . in how far the SCARECROW, as a Clothed Person, is not also entitled to benefit of clergy, and English trial by jury: nay perhaps, considering his high function (for is not he too a Defender of Property, and Sovereign armed with the *terrors* of the Law?), to a certain royal Immunity and Inviolability; which, however, misers and the meaner class of persons are not always voluntarily disposed to grant him' (McSweeney and Sabor (eds), *Sartor Resartus*, p. 49).
[124] John Henry Newman, *Apologia Pro Vita Sua and Six Sermons*, ed. Frank M. Turner (New Haven and London: Yale University Press, 2012), p. 128. Nina Auerbach uses this quote in her study *Private Theatricals* (Cambridge: Harvard University Press, 1990) and much of her argument about the growing acceptance of the performing, multiple self in Victorian times is relevant here.

suggest human loneliness, emotional isolation and disconnection.[125] Popular images of the scarecrow typically allude to it as human-like but incomplete in some way, notably L. Frank Baum's scarecrow in Oz.

While a considerable amount of Israel's life remains after he has become a ghost and a scarecrow, it is not represented in anything like the detail that it was up to this point. The adventures with Jones and the *Serapis* battle are to come, but in them Israel is not the main focus. As noted, he does for a short time catch some of Jones's wily bravado when he ends up on the English ship, but it is insufficient to sustain him indefinitely. The image from tailoring that Melville uses emphasizes this. At the beginning of chapter 20, 'The Shuttle' he writes: 'For a time back, across the otherwise blue-jean career of Israel, Paul Jones flits and re-flits like a crimson thread. One more brief intermingling of it, and to the plain old homespun we return.'[126] Israel is blue-jean and homespun, and this brief 'intermingling' with the heroic cannot elevate him. Eventually, at his most miserable, he is not even a beggar, although he is dressed as one. Melville consistently likens Israel to a beggar, yet at the same time asserts that he is not one: 'And here it may be noted, as a fact nationally characteristic, that however desperately reduced at times, even to the sewers, Israel, the American, never sunk below the mud, to actual beggary.'[127] Although a putative source of national pride, this is also deeply ironic. Israel is in rags like the other beggars, but he lacks the ability of this 'crafty aristocracy' to represent themselves as war veterans, even though he is one. Beggars pretending to be veterans, and even 'fraudulent beggars' were real problems in Victorian London, but Israel in a sense fails even at this.[128] That is, unlike Jones or Franklin, he cannot at this point adapt his identity to his advantage. While there is some pride in this, it is primarily a failure to meet the demands of modernity.

The reviewer who complained that Melville had condensed the last 45 years of Israel's life in a few pages certainly had a point. The ending

---

[125] The most famous is probably the much-reproduced 'Benny's Scarecrow' (1955). The painting 'Dodge's Ridge' (1947) is also known as 'The Scarecrow' and was used for the cover of the 1987 Penguin Modern Classics edition of *The Sound and the Fury*. Although an unusual choice, the scarecrow connects well with Faulkner's themes; the absence of love in the Compson family and the consequent emotional and psychic damage to the brothers.

[126] Melville, *Israel Potter*, p. 131.

[127] Ibid., p. 165.

[128] Ibid. Henry Mayhew's report *London Labour and the London Poor* (1851) addressed the issue of 'dissembling beggars'; see Fabian, *The Unvarnished Truth*, pp. 44–7. The Sherlock Holmes story 'The Man with the Twisted Lip' (1891) involves a wealthy man disguising himself each day and acting as a beggar on the London streets, a fact he conceals from his family.

is abrupt, charting Israel's years in London, his eventual return to his homeland and his death. But this condensation is essential to the novel's treatment of self-estrangement. Israel has in effect disappeared from his own life, turned into no-one. The real climax was much earlier, when he became the ghost and the scarecrow, became in effect 'unreal', the depersonalized self of modernity. What he develops is akin to what later in the century will be called 'Depersonalization Disorder', or even what we might now think of as 'boredom', often considered a condition of modernity. This sense of one's own unreality was first recorded in the private journals of the Swiss academic Henri Frédéric Amiel, which were published in 1882, the year after his death.[129] Starting in the 1850s, Amiel recorded his sense of detachment, not only from others but from himself, a kind of self-estrangement that anticipates the descriptions of self-alienation in works by Sartre, Camus and Fernando Pessoa. Israel's estrangement is an actual one, since he is physically estranged from what he thinks of as his home, from whatever remains of his family, and from his fellow-countrymen. But it is also self-estrangement, and his holding on to a self defined by its past does not equip him for adapting as others do to a changed and changing environment. Men like Jones and Franklin succeed because in accepting multiplicity they can act accordingly; Israel cannot because he is preoccupied by a nostalgic longing for completeness, for who he once was. To express this, Melville must withhold Israel's subjectivity, record him only in the third person; Israel cannot articulate his condition because to do so would be to locate himself as an authority in his story.

Israel is failing in modernity. To use Anthony Giddens's well-known formulation, he is unable to keep a self-narrative going:

> A person's identity is not to be found in behaviour, nor – important though this is – in the reactions of others, but in the capacity to keep a particular narrative going. The individual's biography, if she is to maintain regular interaction with others in the day-to-day world, cannot be wholly fictive. It must continually integrate events which occur in the external world, and sort them into the ongoing 'story' about the self.[130]

---

[129] It was translated into English by Mrs Humphry Ward and published in 1885 as *Amiel's Journal*. For an account of Depersonalization Disorder, see *Feeling Unreal: Depersonalization Disorder and the Loss of the Self* by Daphne Simeon and Jeffrey Abugel (Oxford: Oxford University Press, 2006).

[130] Giddens, *Modernity and Self-Identity*, p. 54.

This is very much grounded in the ideas of Georg Simmel, and particularly his essay 'The Metropolis and Mental Life' (1903) and its examination of the problem of self in modernity and urban life: 'The deepest problems of modern life derive from the claim of the individual to preserve the autonomy and individuality of his existence in the face of overwhelming social forces, of historical heritage, of external culture, and of the technique of life.' These challenges to the self's autonomy require continual 'adjustments' to accommodate 'external forces'.[131] Without these adjustments, the self faces alienation and boredom; key aspects of Melville's representation of life in the city, notably in the characters of Israel and Bartleby. Boredom as an aspect of modernity has been much discussed, and it is notably applicable to *Israel Potter*. As one commentator asserts, 'boredom is the experience of modernity, of modern temporality, in which the conditions of possibility of experience become the conditions of its disappearance'.[132] While one study claims that Melville treated boredom more profoundly than any other nineteenth-century American artist, it is hard not to feel that 'boredom' is not quite the right term for the kind of social alienation and self-estrangement that is finally evident in *Israel Potter*.[133] At one point in his journal Amiel struggles to find analogies for his feelings: 'I can find no words for what I feel. My consciousness is withdrawn into itself; I hear my heart beating, and my life passing. It seems to me that I have become a statue on the banks of the river of time, that I am the spectator of some mystery, and shall issue from it old, or no longer capable of age.'[134] The striking image of the statue makes for a curious link with *Israel Potter*. Melville's dedication of the novel to 'His Highness, The Bunker-Hill Monument' can be read as whimsy, or as irony – the erection of a monument while the living Israel, who fought at the battle, is exiled, neglected and denied a pension. But the monument is also an analogue for Israel, immobilized, a spectator, incapable of development or self-recreation, a blue-jeaned, homespun remnant of the past, not a subject in modernity.

---

[131] *The Sociology of Georg Simmel*, trans. Kurt Wolff (New York: Free Press, 1950), p. 409.
[132] Elizabeth S. Goodstein, *Experience Without Qualities: Boredom and Modernity* (Stanford, CA: Stanford University Press, 2005), p. 6. See also Patricia Meyer Spacks, *Boredom: The Literary History of a State of Mind* (Chicago: University of Chicago Press, 1995).
[133] Paliwoda, *Melville and the Theme of Boredom*, p. 8.
[134] Henri Frédéric Amiel, *Amiel's Journal*, trans. Mrs Humphry Ward (New York and London: Macmillan, 1906), p. liii.

5

These Buttons That We Wear: *Billy Budd*

On 21 October 1805, what would become one of the most celebrated sea battles of history was fought between Britain and the combined forces of France and Spain. The battle of Trafalgar, just off the Spanish coast in the Atlantic Ocean, was a crucial victory for the British, led by Admiral Horatio Nelson on board *Victory*. The outcome cemented Britain's position as the supreme naval power, removed any remaining threat of a French invasion of England, and was a key turning-point in the Napoleonic Wars. As might be expected of such an important battle, it was commemorated enthusiastically by the victors, both immediately, and for many years afterwards. London's Trafalgar Square was first designated in 1830, with the soaring Nelson's column completed in 1843 and the fountains in 1845. It is very much the heart of the capital, and to some extent of the nation also, where Britons congregate for important events. These include all kinds of political protests and demonstrations, as well as celebrations on New Year's Eve and celebrations of sporting victories. For the British, the word 'Trafalgar', like 'Dunkirk', has a significance that makes it into a nation-defining term. It has much more resonance than, say Waterloo, the decisive land battle of the Napoleonic wars (although there is a London railway station named after it). Trafalgar resonates for two major reasons: because it includes the sense on how death of a hero, and because of British self-identification involving naval history. Trafalgar and the figure of Nelson fit into a British cultural narrative, incorporating the concept, or fiction, of naval supremacy commemorated annually at the final night of the nation's Promenade Concerts. The bicentenary of the battle of Trafalgar in 2005 was marked by a series of high-profile events, and revived a long-standing proposal for Trafalgar day to be declared a national holiday.

Nelson's heroism, unorthodox naval tactics, injured body (he had lost the sight of his right eye in 1794, and his right arm in 1797) and tragic death have also come to assume a kind of mythic status, and to be part of national folklore. Indeed, Nelson himself has come to symbolize something essentially British, and the many statues and commemorations of him similarly take on this value. Adolf Hitler's personal files revealed that he planned on moving Nelson's column from London to Berlin if his plans to invade Britain were successful. In 1966, Nelson's pillar in the heart of Dublin was blown up; it had been a prominent landmark since 1808, and for nationalists an unwelcome memory of British rule in Ireland. As might be expected, the story of Nelson's death at the battle of Trafalgar has itself become almost legendary, and its details remain familiar to the British. On the morning of battle, Nelson made his will and sent the signal 'England expects every man will do his duty' to the fleet. Early in the afternoon, he was hit on the left shoulder with a musket-ball fired by a sniper on the French ship *Redoubtable*, and the wound proved fatal. The death scene includes the heroic details of his waiting his turn for medical treatment, his courageous and realistic awareness of his impending death ('I do believe they have done it at last . . . my backbone is shot through'), his request to the ship's captain, 'Kiss me, Hardy', and his dying words 'Thank God I have done my duty.' His death on the day of battle was inspirational for numerous painters throughout the nineteenth century, and the death itself was somehow seen as redemptive, even sacrificial, a kind of martyrdom. As one twentieth-century commentator has put it: 'Nelson had been great in his life, but in his death he was sublime.[1] The death was also somehow personally redemptive, in helping to erase much of the scandal surrounding his adulterous relationship with Emma Hamilton. It was also claimed that public sadness at Nelson's death considerably outweighed the elation caused by the victorious battle. That was the mood recalled by Robert Southey in *The Life of Nelson*, a popular biography first published in 1813, and in print throughout the century:

> The death of Nelson was felt in England as something more than a public calamity; men started at the intelligence, and turned pale, as if they had heard of the loss of a dear friend. An object of our admiration and affection, of our pride and of our hopes, was suddenly taken from us; and it seemed as if we had never, till then, known how deeply we loved and reverenced him.[2]

The folkloric elements of the death include a curious detail, that on the morning of the battle, Nelson emerged from his cabin in full admiral dress. Here is Southey:

> He wore that day, as usual, his admiral's frock-coat, bearing on the left breast four stars, of the different orders with which he was invested.

---

[1] Jack Russell, *Nelson and the Hamiltons* (Harmondsworth: Penguin, 1972), p. 497.
[2] Robert Southey, *The Life of Nelson* (Hoo: Grange Books, 2005), pp. 360–1.

Ornaments which rendered him so conspicuous a mark for the enemy were beheld with ominous apprehensions by his officers. It was known that there were riflemen on board the French ships, and it could not be doubted but that his life would be particularly aimed at. They communicated their fears to each other; and the surgeon, Mr Beatty, spoke to the chaplain Dr Scott, and to Mr Scott the public secretary, desiring that some person would entreat him to change his dress, or cover the stars; but they knew that such a request would highly displease him. 'In honour I gained them', he had said when such a thing had been hinted to him formerly, 'and in honour I will die with them'.[3]

This intriguing detail has been variously taken as evidence of Nelson's vanity, a flaw in his character, or as a heroically defiant attitude towards the French. It has even been seen as the willing acceptance of a kind of martyrdom or self-sacrifice, since it was well known that some of *Redoubtable*'s crew were trained snipers and Nelson would be a key target. Southey is elaborating on an account that appeared in 1805, which included the comment: 'There can be no doubt that a deliberate aim had been taken at his lordship. He had on the insignia of the different orders conferred on him. . . . He received the musket-ball below his left shoulder through the centre of one of his decorations.'[4] In this account, and in many subsequent ones, Nelson's death is represented partly as an act of wilfulness, a direct consequence of his wearing the form of dress appropriate to his achieved status and identity.

The detail adds appeal and intrigue to an already compelling story, and this is clearly why it has persisted. It is, however, a complete fiction. The belief that Nelson wore his insignia on the day of the battle was exposed almost immediately as false by those who had been present on *Victory*. The most notable of these was Nelson's surgeon at Trafalgar, Dr Beatty, who in 1807 directly contradicted the story. Beatty wrote that Nelson wore his usual frock-coat, and added 'It has been reported, but erroneously, that His Lordship was actually requested by his Officers to change his dress, or to cover his stars.'[5] Some of this confusion may have arisen because Nelson's usual frock-coat had on it embroidered representations of his medals. That is, his *usual* dress always contained representations of the insignia. You can even go and see the coat Nelson wore at Trafalgar (with, of course, the hole made by the fatal musket-ball) on display at Britain's National Maritime

---

[3] Ibid., pp. 343–4.
[4] *The Life of Horatio Viscount Nelson* (Halifax: Nicholson, 1805), quoted in Marianne Czisnik, *Horatio Nelson: A Controversial Hero* (London: Hodder Education, 2005), p. 85.
[5] Ibid., p. 78.

Museum at Greenwich. Here is part of the museum's description of the exhibit:

> Embroidered versions of Nelson's four orders of chivalry are sewn to the front of the coat overlapping the edge of the lapel so that it could not be unbuttoned. They are: the star of the Order of the Bath, the Order of the Crescent awarded by the Sultan of Turkey, the Order of St Ferdinand and of Merit awarded by Ferdinand IV of Naples, and the German Order of St Joachim. Nelson habitually wore them on all his uniform coats.[6]

Melville's long-standing interest in the death of Nelson would not have been at all unusual, but there is at times a sense of personal identification with him, a 'peculiar emotion'.[7] During his visit to London in November 1849, he went to Greenwich and saw Nelson's death-coat: 'Went into the Painted Hall – sea-peices [sic] & portraits of naval heroes, coats of Nelson in glass cases. Fine ceiling.'[8] On his next visit to England in 1856, he saw the Nelson monument in Liverpool, prompting memories of his visit to the city in 1839: 'After dinner went to Exchange. Looked at Nelson's statue, with peculiar emotion, mindful of 20 years ago.'[9] This somewhat baroque monument, paid for by public subscription and erected in 1813, is a heroic abstraction of the death. A naked Nelson is being brought to heaven by an angelic figure, while from underneath a flag a gruesome skeleton places its right hand over Nelson's heart. Beneath Nelson lie the remnants of battle, Britannia is in mourning, and four chained figures represent the prisoners taken by Nelson in his four great victories. Around the side of the monument are the words 'England expects every man to do his duty.' Melville fictionalized his 1839 viewing in *Redburn*:

> The ornament in question is a group of statuary in bronze, elevated upon a marble pedestal and basement, representing Lord Nelson expiring in

---

[6] <http://collections.rmg.co.uk/collections/objects/71238.html> [accessed 31 October 2013].
[7] Melville, *Journals*, p. 50.
[8] Ibid., p. 23. Hawthorne also recorded seeing Nelson's coats at Greenwich, in 1855, and gives a description of the bloodstained Trafalgar coat. 'On the breast of the coat are sewn three or four orders of knighthood, the glitter of which is supposed to have drawn the enemy's aim'. Nathaniel Hawthorne, *The English Notebooks*, ed. Randall Stewart (New York: Modern Language Association of America, 1941), p. 217. It was perhaps inevitable that the author of *The Scarlet Letter* should be drawn to the sewn badges and their glitter.
[9] Melville, *Journals*, p. 50.

the arms of Victory. One foot rests on a rolling foe, and the other on a cannon. Victory is dropping a wreath on the dying admiral's brow; while Death, under the similitude of a hideous skeleton, is insinuating his bony hand under the hero's robe, and groping after his heart. A very striking design, and true to the imagination; I never could look at Death without a shudder.[10]

Melville's allusions over a long period of time indicate that for him thoughts of Nelson involve a mode of introspection, reflections on the nature of his own life and the passage of time. *Redburn* is very much part of that self-examination, and so too is *Billy Budd*, whose opening paragraphs recall an incident witnessed in Liverpool. He returns to Nelson and the death scene in writing this final work, and Southey's biography was a significant source for him. He made notes in an 1855 edition of it and directly uses details from this. Drawn as he so often was to details of dress and clothing, and how these relate to identity, Melville reflects on the motivation for Nelson's dressing in his battle honours:

> [M]artial utilitarians may suggest considerations implying that Nelson's ornate publication of his person in battle was not only unnecessary, but not military, nay, savored of foolhardiness and vanity. They may add, too, that at Trafalgar it was in effect nothing less than a challenge to death; and death came; and that but for his bravado the victorious admiral might possibly have survived the battle, and so, instead of having his sagacious dying injunctions overruled by his immediate successor in command, he himself when the contest was decided might have brought his shattered fleet to anchor, a proceeding which might have averted the deplorable loss of life by shipwreck in the elemental tempest that followed the martial one.[11]

What Melville represents as the puzzle of Nelson's choice of dress for the battle of Trafalgar touches very directly on a theme that had long preoccupied him; how to find a living, viable relation between public identity, which may be expressed as a form of duty to others, with one's sense of inner identity, which might be defined as duty to oneself or to one's feelings and conscience. While he had explored this question many times before, and typically invoked the language of clothing to do so, the question of duty is very much at the heart of *Billy Budd*, and indicates that Melville

[10] Melville, *Redburn*, p. 155.
[11] Melville, *Billy Budd*, p. 57.

became increasingly preoccupied with it as he grew older. The narrator here suggests that Nelson's alleged choice of dress represents his innate vanity and bravado, and can be seen as a failure of public duty. Melville of course knew Southey's representation of Nelson refusing to put aside the glittering medals 'In honour I gained them . . . and in honour I will die with them.' He also knew it was wrong, since he had seen the coat with its embroidered medals in 1849. But Melville needs to introduce the concept of error, of the wrong clothing in order to create a particular ambivalence about Nelson. If putting the medals aside might well have ensured his survival, as Melville's narrator suggests, it might also have represented a denial of one's actual identity, one's own sense of honour that is crucial to identity. Furthermore, in its most characteristic artistic representations, the death of Nelson is inseparable from the triumph in the battle. They are not depicted as separate events, and least of all on the Liverpool monument that so moved Melville. As he saw it, the truth offered by the monument was that the moment of victory is also the moment of death: 'Victory is dropping a wreath on the dying admiral's brow; while Death . . . is insinuating his bony hand under the hero's robe, and groping after his heart.' That is, rather than supposedly choosing the wrong clothes for the battle, Nelson has chosen exactly the right ones; those that represent the 'bravado' that is an essential component of his identity, and which challenge, or even invite, the death that is the cost of this ultimate victory. Nelson comes to represent a cluster of ideas concerning duty, sacrifice and truth to oneself. An interesting detail in the museum description of the coat that Melville had seen, is that the embroidered medals were sewn on to the coat in such a way that prevented it from being unfastened: 'orders of chivalry are sewn to the front of the coat overlapping the edge of the lapel so that it could not be unbuttoned'. That is, the coat so represents the fusion between Nelson's private and public identity that it is in effect part of his body. Melville had of course written before about self-sacrifice and of the cost of self-integrity, most notably in 'Bartleby, the Scrivener'. But he comes in *Billy Budd* to a more complex examination of forms of sacrifice, complex because it comes to include a key thematic strand of the novel, the concept of the redemptive act, and this partly develops through his reflections on Nelson.

As scholars have often pointed out, the Nelson material in *Billy Budd* is uneasily integrated into the text, and if the novel had been finished, it is uncertain whether it would have survived into the final version. What is now available to us as chapter 4 was cut out of the manuscript and uncertainly restored.[12] The Nelson material is important because it touches so directly

---

[12] Hershel Parker, *Reading Billy Budd* (Evanston, IL: Northwestern University Press, 1990), p. 164.

on the characterization of Captain Vere. This arguably makes him into the text's central character, and there has been much critical discussion over this, fuelling radically different representations of the novel. Some of these marginalize Vere altogether and locate the major thematic as the conflict between Billy and Claggart. In part these discussions turn on the nature of the text itself, and in part they arise from how the text was mediated in a particular way when it first became available in the 1920s. I now want to outline some of the compositional and textual history, to provide a sense of how these have generated varied critical interpretations.

Billy Budd is something of a literary curiosity, as well as being anomalous in Melville's oeuvre. It was composed by an author who had last published a piece of prose fiction more than 30 years earlier, and it is patently unfinished. He probably began work on it soon after he retired as a customs inspector, a position he held for almost 20 years, in December 1885. So he starts *Billy Budd* about 30 years after the publication of *The Confidence-Man* in 1857. This was not really, as it is sometimes represented, a 30-year hiatus in writing. Although he composed no prose fiction in the decades between *The Confidence-Man* and *Billy Budd*, he did write poetry, including the 2-volume epic *Clarel* (1876), one of the longest of all American narrative poems. The starting-point for *Billy Budd* was almost certainly Melville's composing sailor ballads, a mode of writing he developed in the 1880s.

Billy Budd is also a curiosity because of its very status. Melville seems to have worked at the manuscript, which consists of 351 pages, or leaves, off and on from around 1886 right up until his death in September 1891, but it remained unfinished. 'Unfinished' here does not mean incomplete. The story has a beginning, a middle and a dramatic climax, and is readable, 'finished' enough to be considered a major masterpiece. It is unfinished because Melville was considerably expanding the existing draft and taking it in new directions. Also he did not make the kind of careful revisions that would have, in his usual compositional style, resulted in a fair copy. Indeed, it was Melville's wife Elizabeth, who had often undertaken the production of the fair-copy manuscripts, who declared after his death that this was 'unfinished'. Thus, there are loose ends in the text, which Melville would likely have tidied up if he had lived; Vere's ship is first called *Indomitable*, then *Bellipotent*. More significantly, it is now generally accepted that Melville's revisions were radical because his conception of the story was changing and he was in the process of revising accordingly. Several important Melville scholars, notably the pioneers of this field, Harrison Hayford and Merton M. Sealts, Jr, have explored the manuscripts with a view to ascertaining the changing nature of the story and the possible directions that Melville was taking. Unfortunately, and in contrast to some other writers, Melville left no notes or journal entries that could be used as a guide to his intentions. In itself, the unfinished status is not necessarily an insurmountable problem for criticism. Several significant works of literature were left incomplete when their authors died; notably Charles Dickens's *Edwin Drood* and F. Scott Fitzgerald's *The Last Tycoon*. But the unfinished aspect of *Billy Budd* combined with a series of decisions by early editors, which for many years have resulted in *Billy Budd* being a highly problematic printed text, in terms of the difficulties in establishing a scholarly text reflecting the author's intentions.[13] *Billy Budd* was first published in 1924, when it was included in the thirteenth volume of a 16-volume set called *The Standard Edition of Melville's Work*, published in London by Constable. Constable began publishing this collection in 1922, with six Melville novels, and the series was completed in 1924. It was the earlier set of six books that D. H. Lawrence read for his two chapters on Melville in *Studies in Classic American Literature* (1923). It is also the set that E. M. Forster used for his comments on Melville, including some influential remarks on *Billy Budd*, in his lectures that were published in 1927 as *Aspects of the Novel*. While subsequent Melville editors and scholars have concerns about the textual accuracy of the set, its publication was a landmark event. A highly reputable publisher had brought back into print some Melville titles that had been only intermittently available. Several works, such as *The Confidence-Man* had never been reprinted since their original publication, and apart from a few stray incidences, most of his novels had been out of print since 1876.[14]

Although those who first read it could not have known this, the *Billy Budd* that appeared in volume 13 was highly problematic. It was prepared by Raymond Weaver, who had worked closely with Melville's papers for his 1921 study, *Herman Melville: Man, Mariner and Mystic*. During its preparation Weaver was shown the manuscript of *Billy Budd* by Melville's granddaughter, Eleanor Thomas Metcalf; the manuscript is now in the Houghton Library at Harvard. Weaver extracted the text of *Billy Budd* from the manuscript, but he called it a finished novel, and stated that he

---

[13] Much the same may be said of *The Last Tycoon*. Edmund Wilson undertook the production of a novel from Fitzgerald's manuscripts and notes, and his editorial interventions, including the title, have been considered highly problematic by some. In 1993 Matthew J. Bruccoli re-edited the material for the Cambridge Edition of Fitzgerald's work, radically altering Wilson's text and changing the title to *The Love of the Last Tycoon: A Western*. Other Fitzgerald texts, notably *Tender Is the Night*, are also notoriously problematic.

[14] Late in his life Melville was approached by the publisher Arthur Stedman about reprinting his work; this resulted in some of the novels, including *Moby-Dick*, being republished in 1892.

had made only slight adjustments to the manuscript. In their 1962 edition of *Billy Budd*, Harrison Hayford and Merton M. Sealts, Jr, give a detailed account of the first printed editions of the novel and the problems that these present. Weaver slightly revised the 1924 text for US publication in 1928, Hayford and Sealts comment that these two texts are 'essentially the same'.[15] In the 1940s two further editions appeared. One was based on the Constable text, but the other, edited by F. Barron Freeman in 1948, did make use of Melville's manuscript. As Hayford and Sealts indicate, while this edition included some serious errors and misconceptions, it was the first to acknowledge and confront the problems with the *Billy Budd* manuscript.[16] Freeman is also credited with the insight that the compositional process of *Billy Budd* was expansive. Freeman's was considered the standard text of *Billy Budd* until 1962, and was much reprinted in anthologies. Indeed, *Billy Budd* is one of Melville's most anthologized and widely taught texts. As with the case of 'Bartleby, the Scrivener', this is mainly because of its status as a major work of literature, but also because its relatively short length lends it more readily to the classroom than do Melville's other great, and considerably longer, achievements.

In 1962, Hayford and Sealts published their rigorously researched edition of the text. They did what no previous editors had done, thoroughly researching the manuscript and, significantly, identifying the compositional stages of the text. That is, their version was not an attempt to produce a 'finished' version of *Billy Budd* but a text that, in being faithful to the manuscript, recorded not Melville's final intentions, but the successive shifts of those intentions. Since Melville was constantly revising the *Billy Budd* manuscript, and had not finished the revisions at the time of his death, editors have two choices as to the kind of text they will produce. Usually an editor decides on the author's final intentions and edits the text accordingly. This is difficult, since it inevitably involves hard decisions about the creative spirit, and it may also require the editor to guess and even, perhaps, to introduce new material into the text to make it cohere. This practice can be deeply controversial and can cause considerable problems for scholars and critics. In editing *The Last Tycoon*, this was the practice adopted by Edmund Wilson. He silently amended what was a loose collection of material, rather than a manuscript, and provided a title that was never Fitzgerald's own. In fact, the analogy between *Billy Budd* and *The Last Tycoon* is a useful one. In both cases, 'unfinished' means not an

---

[15] Harrison Hayford and Merton M. Sealts, Jr, 'Editors' Introduction', Melville, *Billy Budd*, p. 13.
[16] Ibid., pp. 16–23.

uncompleted manuscript or draft, but a collection of material representing work in progress, incorporating revisions and recording divergent and unresolved directions. In his introduction to his edition Matthew J. Bruccoli takes issue with Wilson's choice of the word 'draft' to describe Fitzgerald's material, calling it 'inadvertently misleading': 'There is nothing that can be accurately described as "this draft": there are layers of working drafts for seventeen episodes or sections that Fitzgerald did not assemble into a single draft. . . . The whole work was still developing through a process of composition by accretion.'[17] Thus a novel that has been popular and critically acclaimed and studied for over 50 years does not really exist as the creation of F. Scott Fitzgerald, and we do not even know what title he intended for it. The full title of *Billy Budd* has been similarly problematic. The earliest editions called it *Billy Budd, Foretopman*. Hayford and Sealts realized that this proposed title had been superseded by another, *Billy Budd, Sailor (An Inside Narrative)*, and they retitled the text accordingly. This issue of the title may seem insignificant, especially as the book is typically referred to simply as *Billy Budd*. But the two titles do actually invite radically different interpretations, and these have developed into opposing positions in critical debate. The now discredited title draws attention to Billy's status and to the historical aspects of the tale, suggesting it be read within a very particular social and political context. The other invites consideration of the complex psychological aspects of the story, and its elements of secrecy and conspiracy, of the gap between the 'official' story of Billy and the one kept alive by his shipmates.

There are many more unsettled literary texts than is generally realized. When we read or watch a performance of *King Lear*, we have no certainty about whether we are experiencing Shakespeare's realized intentions. The two earliest printed editions, one published in Shakespeare's lifetime, and the other in 1623, are notably different. The 1608 printing has about 300 lines that do not appear in the 1623 version, while the later version has around 100 lines that were not in the first printing. Mostly, editors of the play will work with both the 1608 and the 1623 versions and try to produce a text based on their critical judgement, known as 'eclectic' text. An alternative is to let the two texts remain separately. This is what Stanley Wells and Gary Taylor did by including both versions in the Oxford *Complete Works of Shakespeare* (1986).

King Lear's status suggests that the textual issues may not matter greatly, as long as the play functions as a work of art, and in any case productions of

---

[17] Matthew J. Bruccoli, 'Introduction' to F. Scott Fitzgerald, *The Love of the Last Tycoon: A Western* (Cambridge: Cambridge University Press, 1993), pp. xiii–xiv.

the play will almost always involve a director editing the text. For decades, readers of *Billy Budd* have approached it without any regard at all to the textual issues. This was either because they could not have known about them, which was largely the case before 1948, or because the problems of the text seemed like a minor diversion, of interest to textual scholars rather than literary critics. E. M. Forster's influential comments on the work in *Aspects of the Novel* are, therefore, made without any sense of the text's instability. The Constable edition assured its readers that only 'slight adjustments' had been made to Melville's manuscript. The libretto which Forster wrote with Eric Crozier for Benjamin Britten's operatic version in the 1940s, similarly displays no awareness at all of the novel's textual difficulties.[18] But Forster's approach to *Billy Budd* set the tone for a good deal of later criticism. Focusing primarily on the character of Claggart, Forster saw the story as an exploration of evil, 'Evil labelled and personified'.[19] As such, Forster saw it as a good introduction to Melville's other works, arguing that this exploration of evil was a constant concern of Melville's, marking him out as a major novelist. In his Commonplace Book, Forster articulated his sense of the homoerotic element of the story, suggesting, as many critics have, that Claggart's repressed attraction to Billy, the 'handsome sailor' turns into an evil force.[20]

This approach, rooted very much in Freudian psychology, and in William Blake's representation of good, evil, innocence and repression, becomes the theme of Britten's opera. Melville's plot is revised to foreground the conflict between Claggart and Billy, and from the very opening, articulates the sense of evil. The aged Vere opens the opera, telling us that he has been shown 'much good' and 'much evil' and asserting that 'the Devil still has something to do with every human consignment to this planet of earth'.[21] One critic has stated that the opera '*Billy Budd* was, for Forster and Britten the most direct and public treatment of the homoerotically charged relationships between men they had produced.[22]

---

[18] Robert K. Martin has explored the results this reliance on a faulty text had on Britten's opera, although his own insistence on Vere as corrupt seems problematic. See Robert K. Martin, 'Saving Captain Vere: *Billy Budd* from Melville's Novella to Britten's Opera', *Studies in Short Fiction*, 23 (1986), 49–56.
[19] E. M. Forster, *Aspects of the Novel* (Harmondsworth: Penguin, 1976), p. 129.
[20] Ibid., pp. 170–1.
[21] Benjamin Britten, *Billy Budd: An Opera in Four Acts*, libretto by E. M. Forster and Eric Crozier (London: Hawkes & Son, 1952), p. 4.
[22] Mary C. Francis, 'A Kind of Voyage: E. M. Forster and Benjamin Britten's *Billy Budd*', in *Biographical Passages: Essays in Victorian and Modernist Biography*, ed. Joe Law and Linda K. Hughes (Columbia, MO: University of Missouri Press, 2000), p. 51.

Forster's comments on *Billy Budd* have helped determine a course of criticism that has been both followed and challenged ever since.[23] Certainly, there have been lively critical debates and disagreements about *Billy Budd*. The problem with this critical debate, however, is a fundamental issue. It is that positions taken depend on a kind of stabilizing of the text, and this is in actuality a text that cannot be stabilized without being represented as something that it is not. Forster and the other earliest critics on *Billy Budd* could not have been aware of the state of the manuscript when they used the Constable edition. But Freeman's 1948 edition and the work of Hayford and Sealts means that since 1962, it should be impossible for anyone approaching *Billy Budd* to be unaware of the crucial textual issues. The fundamental challenge is in offering a critical approach to a text whose very nature means that it is resistant to the stabilization on which literary criticism depends. The case of *Billy Budd* is different from that of the two versions of *King Lear*. In making assessments and critical judgements of Shakespeare's play, the two printed versions may be readily compared at key points and interpretation adjusted if a textual variant deems it necessary. But *Billy Budd* hardly exists as a text at all in the way that the *King Lear* versions do. We have a manuscript recording five years of revisions, recasting and redirections. It is perfectly possible to edit this manuscript into a readable text, and this has been done since 1924. But doing this inevitably misrepresents *Billy Budd*. To use the terms of Roland Barthes, it changes, or threatens to change, *Billy Budd* from a 'text' to a 'work'; from being a network of energies and possibilities, even contradictions, to an object, from plurality to singularity, from something to be experienced to something ready for consumption.[24]

When Hayford and Sealts published their *Billy Budd* in 1962 they actually presented two texts. The first was intended for general readers and students, and was the first 'accurate version of Melville's final novel' according to the blurb for the paperback edition. This is the version now most reprinted in anthologies and collections, including the Library of America edition in 1984, but the earlier versions are also widely reprinted. As well as the reading edition, Hayford and Sealts published a transcription of the *Billy Budd* manuscript, what is known as a genetic text. That is, rather

---

[23] See, for instance, Eve Kosofsky Sedgwick, *Epistemology of the Closet* (London: Harvester Wheatsheaf, 1991), and Thomas Dean McGlamery, *Reading a Man Like a Book: Bodies and Texts in Billy Budd* (Austin: University of Texas Press, 1996).
[24] Roland Barthes, 'From Work to Text', in *Textual Strategies: Perspectives in Poststructuralist Criticism*, ed. Josué V. Harari (Ithaca, NY: Cornell University Press, 1979), pp. 73–81.

than being edited according to the concept of the author's final intentions, it shows the act, the genesis, of the writing. A genetic text records a process, not the outcome of one. In criticism of authors whose manuscripts are available, a genetic approach can be invaluable in providing insight into the writer's creative processes and decisions. So, there are genetic editions of a variety of important texts, of Franklin's *Autobiography*, for instance, which encourages new ways of approaching and reflecting on familiar work; especially when, as in the case of Franklin, there is a long and complex compositional history.[25] Probably the most prominent current activity in genetic criticism is directed to the writing of James Joyce. This is partly because of the complex history of writing and publication of his fiction but also because seeing this process is invaluable to any understanding of his work, and of *Finnegans Wake* in particular.

The 1962 publication of the genetic text should have radically changed critical perceptions of *Billy Budd*. Indeed, it potentially could have redirected Melville studies entirely because this was the only available complete manuscript of any Melville work. But critics have found it fairly easy to ignore the genetic text, perhaps for a variety of reasons. Genetic criticism; indeed, manuscript studies, generally, are sometimes seen as a specialized area involving skills quite distinct from those of literary criticism. For some, the editor's job is to provide an authoritative text, and the critic's work starts at that point, and need not involve a return to questions of textual authority. In the case of *Billy Budd*, ironically, the simultaneous publication of the reader's text and the genetic text led to the genetic text being virtually ignored. After all, if we have the reader's text, why should we bother to look at the genetic text? The fact that the reader's text was clearly superior to earlier editions compounded this attitude: it felt as if readers at last had the real *Billy Budd*, and the availability of the genetic text seemed an irrelevance. This attitude was reinforced by the fact that the University of Chicago Press not only published the reading text and the genetic text together in one volume, but they also published the reading text by itself in a more affordable edition. Thus you could choose between a complete scholarly edition of *Billy Budd* with both texts, and a paperback of the reading text without the genetic text. It is this reader's edition that was widely distributed and remains in print.

In an important essay on *Billy Budd*, John Wenke laments the neglect of the genetic text, pointing out that it has been 'virtually unexamined over the last forty years' and argues forcefully for the necessity of including it

---

[25] J. A. Leo Lemay and P. M. Zall (eds), *The Autobiography of Benjamin Franklin: A Genetic Text* (Knoxville: University of Tennessee Press, 1981).

in critical judgements.[26] The point is, to invoke again Barthes's terms, that the reading text makes *Billy Budd* into a work, belying its actual status as a text. As Wenke puts it, 'The reading text, then, becomes what it is not – an independent and final product of artistic intention – rather than what it is – a dependent and conditional outcome of Melville's arrested compositional process.'[27] Consequently, *Billy Budd* is typically approached by reader and by critic as a stable work, ready for analysis.

As suggested earlier, *Billy Budd* is unfinished in a particular way, not only because Melville died before its completion, but also because the genetic text shows a variety of shifts in his own sense of what the text was. Hayford and Sealts formed the view that on more than one occasion Melville decided that the text was complete and began, as was his practice, to prepare a 'fair-copy' version. But he could not resist 'further revision and elaboration'.[28] It is worth remembering that Melville worked on *Billy Budd* for five years; that is, the longest he worked on any of his prose fiction. Indeed, because he began it in his retirement, it is perhaps the only fiction he produced to which he was able to devote relatively sustained, concentrated attention. Over 30 years earlier, working on *Moby-Dick*, he had complained to Hawthorne about being unable to write in 'the silent grass-growing mood in which a man ought always to compose.[29] To put the five years Melville spent on *Billy Budd* into perspective, it is estimated that it took him four months to write both *Redburn* and *White-Jacket*, both sizeable novels. *Moby-Dick* took him perhaps ten (interrupted) months. When *Mardi* is added to this list, Melville had completed four long novels between 1849 and 1851, while complaining about being unable to devote sustained time to his writing.

The time spent on *Billy Budd* is inordinately long for Melville. In five years the story grew from its seed as a sailor ballad, and changed remarkably as Melville expanded and revised, going over what he had already completed and shifting the narrative direction. Specifically, as Hayford and Sealts indicate, there was a shifting sense of the conflicts and characters that would form the novel's centre: 'In three main phases [Melville] had introduced in turn the three main characters: first Billy, then Claggart, and finally Vere. As the focus of his attention shifted from

[26] John Wenke, 'Melville's Indirection: *Billy Budd*, The Genetic Text, and "the Deadly Space Between"', in *New Essays on Billy Budd*, ed. Donald Yannella (Cambridge: Cambridge University Press, 2002). Long before that, Hershel Parker complained that the 1962 reading text was ignored by teachers and critics who preferred the older editions, since these did not require any shift from their entrenched interpretations of the novel. Parker, *Reading Billy Budd*, p. 91.
[27] Wenke, 'Melville's Indirection', p. 116.
[28] Hayford and Sealts, 'Editors' Introduction', p. 1.
[29] Melville, *Correspondence*, p. 191.

one to another of these three principals, the plot and thematic emphasis of the expanding novel underwent consequent modifications within each main phase.'[30] Some subsequent critical disagreements over the characters and conflicts of *Billy Budd* arise from this irresolution. *Billy Budd* has two major sources of conflict or tension; that between Billy and Claggart, and that of Captain Vere, which can be approached as an internalized conflict. As we have seen in the case of E. M. Forster's appraisal, the first critical approaches focused particularly on the relation between Billy and Claggart, and, as so often during the period of the Melville revival, on Melville's consideration of evil. Billy represents innocence, Claggart is evil, being a kind of analogue to Iago; and Coleridge's famous attribution of 'motiveless malignity' to Shakespeare's anti-hero may be readily applied to Claggart. As he acknowledged, Forster's emphasis on this relationship derived from Freeman's 1926 study of Melville. Freeman considered Billy an innocent, 'unpractised in the ways of life and the hearts of men', while Claggart is 'subtle, dark, demon-haunted'. *Billy Budd* for these early critics was chiefly concerned with the 'vindication of innocence'; the novel was Melville's *Paradise Regained*.[31]

This early emphasis on the relation between Billy and Claggart is understandable given the accepted idea that Melville was a writer preoccupied with evil. To creative readers such as Forster and Benjamin Britten, it also brought out the suppressed homoeroticism that is such a feature of Britten's opera, and its relative marginalization of Vere. There he occupies a kind of choric role; the real story is happening elsewhere. Certainly, much criticism since the 1940s has focused on Vere, and in some studies he occupies the text's very centre. It is Vere who must decide Billy's fate; his character is the most ambivalent. Such approaches tend to emphasize the social aspects of *Billy Budd*, stressing that it is deeply concerned with social order and with how threats to that order must be suppressed, even where this might result in injustice for an individual, or in the creation of a necessary scapegoat. A socio-historical approach is readily supported textually. At the age of 21, Billy is impressed from the merchant ship *Rights-of-Man*. Melville's references in chapter 3 to the naval mutinies at Spithead and the Nore are important both in historicizing the story, an unusual gesture in his fiction (Billy is impressed in summer 1797), and in establishing a frame of reference in which the actions of Vere in attending to the supposed conspiracy led by Billy are to be considered.

---

[30] Hayford and Sealts, 'Editors' Introduction', p. 3.
[31] John Freeman, *Herman Melville* (London: Macmillan, 1926), pp. 131, 135.

'Mutiny' may seem a rather misleading term for the labour unrest in the month-long action at Spithead (and at other places in the same year), but this is legally and technically what it was; a marked and wilful disobedience towards naval authority. It was more obviously mutiny at the Nore, where the actions involved the sailors taking over ships, blockading London port, and directly refusing orders. After the Nore mutiny 29 sailors were hanged, others were flogged, deported or received gaol sentences. While Melville had written very directly in *White-Jacket* of the injustice of the American Articles of War and the tyrannical exercise of naval authority, his treatment of these in *Billy Budd* is far less direct, and works very much to provide a historical and moral context in which the focus is very much on Vere.

As has long been known, there was also a more direct personal element in Melville addressing the themes of mutiny, authority and justice; in fact, *Billy Budd* is a highly personal book, despite its setting in the Royal Navy at the end of the eighteenth century. In November 1842, Melville's 30-year-old cousin, Guert Gansevoort, was serving as first lieutenant on the American naval brig *Somers*. While in the Atlantic en route to the West Indies, her Captain, Alexander Slidell Mackenzie, was told that twenty of the crew were plotting a mutiny. Allegedly their plan was to take over the ship, murder the captain and anyone who opposed them, and turn to piracy. After further incidents and accusations, a group of men was arrested, among them an acting midshipman, Philip Spencer; the boatswain's mate, Samuel Cromwell and Elisha Small, a common seaman. Captain Mackenzie convened a group of seven officers, including Melville's cousin, to investigate the supposed conspiracy and recommend a course of action. It was further claimed that he directed the committee, which was not officially a court-martial, to return a guilty verdict on the three accused.[32] The committee declared all three guilty, and the Captain gave the orders that resulted in their being hanged on 1 December.

When the *Somers* reached land the case was investigated by a naval court. Both this inquiry and a later court-martial upheld the verdicts and the sentences of execution. But there was much public anger and general unease about the case. It was given particular prominence because the 17-year-old Philip Spencer was the son of the then Secretary of War, John C. Spencer. Questions were raised over the proper convening of the committee, and whether it or the captain had the authority to declare death sentences and carry out the executions. The actual existence of a mutinous plot seemed to many unproven. Even if the men were guilty,

---

[32] See Parker, *Herman Melville: A Biography*, 1, p. 242.

the trial and the hangings seemed unduly hurried. After all, the United States was not at war at that time, the suspects were incarcerated, and the ship could have quickly reached the nearest port; in fact she arrived in the Virgin Islands only a few days after the trial, and was in New York about a fortnight later. The incident was much discussed in public, and there was a very strong sense that an injustice had been done. Both Mackenzie and Melville's cousin were targeted in public debate. After Mackenzie, Gansevoort was the most senior officer on board, and would have effectively led the investigating committee. James Fenimore Cooper, already engaged in a long-standing dispute with Captain Mackenzie, was particularly vocal in the many attacks on the process of the trial.[33] The controversy over the executions on the *Somers* badly affected both Captain Mackenzie and Lieutenant Gansevoort. Mackenzie died six years later, aged 45, and Gansevoort, according to several accounts, went into a decline that effectively left him a broken man. He died in 1868, at the age of 56, having left active duty in 1861. 'The experience wrecked Guert's health and drove him to alcoholism', writes Hershel Parker.[34]

In spite of their being near in age (and there being a strong family resemblance), Melville was not especially close to his cousin Guert. But the *Somers* affair made a deep and lasting impression on him. Melville had served for 14 months on a navy frigate, the *United States*, and fictionalized this experience for *White-Jacket*. Without explicitly naming the case, he refers twice to the *Somers* affair in this novel. When considering execution as a punishment listed for various transgressions under the Articles of War, White-Jacket quotes Article 19, where death is the punishment for striking a superior office. He then comments on Article 20, in which death is the punishment for falling asleep on the watch:

> Murderous! But then, in time of peace, they do not enforce these bloodthirsty laws? Do they not, indeed? What happened to those three sailors on board an American armed vessel a few years ago, quite within your memory, White-Jacket; yea, while you yourself were yet serving on board this very frigate, the Neversink? What happened to those three

[33] Parker, *Herman Melville*, 2, p. 514. A pamphlet published in 1844, titled *The Cruise of the Somers*, has been attributed to Cooper, but this is likely erroneous. Cooper's main intervention was an 'elaborate review' appended to *Proceedings of the Naval Court Martial in the Case of Alexander Slidell Mackenzie* (New York: Henry G. Langley, 1844), pp. 264–344.

[34] It is important not to overstate the representation of Guert as a failure after the *Somers* affair. In spite of Parker's characterization, he had a prominent naval career, and from 1861 he was in charge of ordnance at the Navy Yard in New York. A World War II ship, *USS Gansevoort*, was named in his honour.

Americans, White-Jacket – those three men, even as you, who once were alive, but now are dead? *'Shall suffer death!'* those were the three words that hung those three sailors.³⁵

A few pages further along, he returns to this case:

> Some may urge that the severest operations of the code are tacitly made null in time of peace. But though with respect to several of the Articles this holds true, yet at any time any and all of them may be legally enforced. Nor have there been wanting recent instances, illustrating the spirit of this code, even in cases where the letter of the code was not altogether observed. The well-known case of a United States brig furnishes a memorable example, which at any moment may be repeated. Three men, in a time of peace, were then hung at the yard-arm, merely because, in the Captain's judgment, it became necessary to hang them. To this day the question of their complete guilt is socially discussed.³⁶

Clearly, the representation of the *Somers* case in this context is one of indignation at the perceived injustice, since the punishment cited in the Articles were invoked during peace. Melville makes no mention of the alleged mutinous plot, nor of the role of any officer other than the Captain. For the purposes of *White-Jacket* and its articulation of grievance and injustice from the point of view of a common sailor, the complexities of the actual case are a distraction; White-Jacket is mainly thinking of his own vulnerability in the face of the Articles. But Melville's later reflections on the case are considerably more complex and show a marked shift of emphasis. In a poem titled 'Bridegroom Dick (1876)', published in 1888, he has Dick reminiscing on old friends. One is Tom Tight, a heavy drinker. Although Dick specifies 'Guert Gan' as a missing friend, the representation of Tight recalls Gansevoort and the *Somers*:

> Tom was lieutenant in the brig-o'-war famed
> When an officer was hung for an arch-mutineer,
> But a mystery cleaved, and the captain was blamed,
> And a rumpus too raised, though his honor it was clear.
> And Tom he would say, when the mousers would try him,
> And with cup after cup o' Burgundy ply him:

---

³⁵ Melville, *White-Jacket*, p. 294.
³⁶ Ibid., p. 303.

'Gentlemen, in vain with your wassail you beset,
For the more I tipple, the tighter do I get.'[37]

This consideration of the effects of the *Somers* case on those who survived it, rather than on injustice towards the hanged men suggests a significant shift in Melville's reflections on the affair. Now he is considering the aftermath of the case, its outcomes for the officers involved. In 1888 there had been a revival of interest in the *Somers* affair, with several articles about it appearing in prominent publications.[38] Melville's change of focus is a telling shift in itself, and because it is in some measure replicated in the process of writing *Billy Budd*. White-Jacket's perception of the case, which Melville managed from a particular point of view and in a particular narrative context, was unambiguously one of sympathy for the hanged. But as *Billy Budd* develops, Melville's own perceptions and reflections are engaged differently. While there are clearly analogies to the Somers case in the dramatic situation that Melville creates, his shifting treatment results in a complex rendering of it, and one that is not easily amenable to a simple sense of right and wrong. Of course, this shifting focus and the resulting ambivalence is manifestly present in the reading text, and forms the basis of considerable debate about *Billy Budd*. This is why the genetic text is so important, showing as it does the actuality of those shifts.

Taking into account the expansive nature of the genetic text brings Vere, and the references to Nelson, more into focus as one of the key issues of *Billy Budd*. When the narrator reflects in chapter 4 on Nelson's 'ornate publication of his person' for the battle of Trafalgar, he begins by wondering if this is a digression from the unfolding story of *Billy Budd*:

> In this matter of writing, resolve as one may to keep to the main road, some by-paths have an enticement not readily to be withstood. I am going to err into such a bypath. If the reader will keep me company I shall be glad. At the least we can promise ourselves that pleasure which is wickedly said to be in sinning, for a literary sin the divergence will be.[39]

---

[37] *Selected Poems of Herman Melville*, ed. Robert Penn Warren (New York: Barnes and Noble 1998), p. 285.
[38] See *Billy Budd, Sailor and Other Stories*, ed. Harold Beaver (Harmondsworth: Penguin, 1970), pp. 463–4.
[39] Melville, *Billy Budd*, p. 56.

The transformation of naval warfare by the introduction of gunpowder is then discussed, before Nelson's 'error' in dressing for Trafalgar is considered.[40] This continues into the brief, and similarly digressive, chapter 5, alluding to the Nore and Spithead. Both short chapters serve to introduce Captain Vere in chapter 6. It is obvious that as Melville worked on the manuscript, Vere was moving more to the centre of the action, and that the comparison with Nelson was being drafted. Chapters 4 and 5 can certainly be seen as digressive, if we make the story of Billy and Claggart the novel's centre. Also, of course, we have no way of knowing what Melville might ultimately have decided about this; he may well have located Billy as the centre of interest in the story and might eventually have cut out these chapters. As it is, we come to Vere from a direct invocation of Nelson, in particular an emphasis, which Melville knew to be erroneous, on his wearing his dress uniform and medals at the battle of Trafalgar, and with the consequent suggestion of Nelson's self-sacrificial martyrdom, his 'priestly motive'. This is the concluding paragraph of chapter 4:

> At Trafalgar Nelson on the brink of opening the fight sat down and wrote his last brief will and testament. If under the presentiment of the most magnificent of all victories to be crowned by his own glorious death, a sort of priestly motive led him to dress his person in the jewelled vouchers of his own shining deeds; if thus to have adorned himself for the altar and the sacrifice were indeed vainglory, then affectation and fustian is each more heroic line in the great epics and dramas, since in such lines the poet but embodies in verse those exaltations of sentiment that a nature like Nelson, the opportunity being given, vitalizes into acts.[41]

In foregrounding Vere with a consideration of Nelson and his appropriate clothes, Melville very quickly draws our attention to Vere's own clothing:

> Ashore, in the garb of a civilian, scarce anyone would have taken him for a sailor, more especially that he never garnished unprofessional talk with nautical terms, and grave in his bearing, evinced little appreciation of mere humor. . . . Any landsman observing this gentleman, not conspicuous by his stature and wearing no pronounced

---

[40] In the genetic text, this is one of three chapters with drafted titles, here a slight misquotation from Tennyson describing Nelson, 'The greatest sailor since the world began'. (It should be 'our world'.) For the sake of consistency, Hayford and Sealts omitted the draft chapter titles from the reading text.

[41] Melville, *Billy Budd*, p. 58.

insignia, emerging from his cabin to the open deck, and noting the silent deference of the officers retiring to leeward, might have taken him for the King's guest, a civilian aboard the King's ship, some highly honorable discreet envoy on his way to an important post.[42]

Vere is a 'gentleman' rather than a natural sailor; he has an aristocratic bearing that might mark him out as a guest on his own ship rather than the captain, and he wears no 'pronounced insignia'. In contrast to Nelson who loved such insignia, Melville represents Vere as uncomfortable in his role, and indicates that being a sailor is for him exactly that, a role, a part that has to be played. Again the contrast is with Nelson, whose Trafalgar coat could not be unbuttoned. That is, the uniform was the person, the part he played for the world and in his public duty entirely consonant with and expressive of his inner self.

In this respect, Vere is comparable to the unnamed Commodore in *White-Jacket*. Promoted from what White-Jacket thinks of as his natural (and preferred) station, the Commodore is both superfluous on the *Neversink* and, because of his rank, unable to socialize with those below his station. Seeing him as lonely and silent, White-Jacket comments: 'Truly, I thought myself much happier in that white jacket of mine, than our old Commodore in his dignified epaulets.'[43] Captain Vere's discomfort is apparent with reference back to the opening sentence of *Billy Budd*, and the description of other sailors ashore: 'In the time before steamships, or then more frequently than now, a stroller along the docks of any considerable seaport would occasionally have his attention arrested by a group of bronzed mariners, man-of-war's men or merchant sailors in holiday attire, ashore on liberty.'[44] Ashore and out of uniform, these men are instantly recognizable as sailors; in complete contrast to Vere, whom hardly anyone would take for a sailor when he is ashore and dressed as a civilian. The complexity of Vere's identity, marked by his ambivalence towards the naval uniform, is a source of discomfort and anxiety to him, as is evident from the contrast with the Anacharsis Cloots-like African sailor recalled by the narrator in the novel's second paragraph.

> In Liverpool, now half a century ago, I saw . . . a common sailor so intensely black that he must needs have been a native African of the unadulterate blood of Ham – a symmetric figure much above the

---

[42] Ibid., p. 60.
[43] Melville, *White-Jacket*, p. 22.
[44] Melville, *Billy Budd*, p. 43.

average height. The two ends of a gay silk handkerchief thrown loose about the neck danced upon the displayed ebony of his chest, in his ears were big hoops of gold, and a Highland bonnet with a tartan band set off his shapely head. It was a hot noon in July; and his face, lustrous with perspiration, beamed with barbaric good humor. In jovial sallies right and left, his white teeth flashing into view, he rollicked along, the center of a company of his shipmates. These were made up of such an assortment of tribes and complexions as would have well fitted them to be marched up by Anacharsis Cloots before the bar of the first French Assembly as Representatives of the Human Race.[45]

In *Benito Cereno*, Captain Delano is puzzled when he sees one of the crew wearing silk, and asks: 'But how come sailors with jewels? – or with silk-trimmed undershirts either?'[46] This sailor's flamboyant mixed clothing metaphors function as they do for the dandy, expressing ease with and confidence in one's identity, even if this involves complexity and contradiction. This sailor, beloved and protected by his shipmates, is also an analogue for Billy, the silk handkerchief will be echoed by the silk lining of the basket in which Billy was discovered as a baby. Although Billy is no dandy, he is shown to be comfortable in his clothing and straightforward in his self-acceptance.

Melville's emphasis on a divergence between Vere's inner identity and his uniform also makes a sharp contrast with the relative straightforwardness of the two other central characters, Billy and Claggart. Melville actually tells us very little about their dress, which is especially notable in the case of Billy, because the initial action of the novel involves Billy changing his clothes. That is, his impressment from the *Rights of Man* is a transition, a change of identity, from merchantman to a seaman in the Royal Navy. Since this requires a change of clothing, we might expect some anxiety over his shifting identity. Yet Melville does not particularly emphasize the change of clothing, suggesting that there is a stability about Billy's identity that can be sustained in spite of the change that the impressment represents. Furthermore, when Melville does refer to Billy's clothing, it is in a very particular way, indicative of his character, his origins and his relation to his shipmates. In response to a query about his origins, Billy says that he was a foundling: 'I have heard that I was found in a pretty silk-lined basket hanging one morning from the knocker of a good man's door in Bristol.'[47]

[45] Ibid.
[46] Melville, *The Piazza Tales*, p. 67.
[47] Melville, *Billy Budd*, p. 51.

The silk, as the narrator suggests, signifies his possible origins as the illegitimate son of a nobleman. Silk also suggests a feminine side to Billy's character, and a luxuriousness that could be clearly at odds with life as a common sailor. But far from creating a contradiction in Billy's identity, the silken origin seems in no way to affect his abilities as a sailor, or to hinder acceptance from his crewmates. Because silk is the preferred material for the liturgical vestments worn by priests, it may also indicate one role that Billy plays. When he is impressed Captain Graveling of the *Rights of Man* likens him to a priest:

> Before I shipped that young fellow, my forecastle was a rat-pit of quarrels. It was black times, I tell you, aboard the *Rights* here. I was worried to that degree my pipe had no comfort for me. But Billy came; and it was like a Catholic priest striking peace in an Irish shindy. Not that he preached to them or said or did anything in particular; but a virtue went out of him, sugaring the sour ones. They took to him like hornets to treacle.[48]

When celebrating the sacrifice of the mass, the priest must wear special vestments, with the liturgical calendar dictating the colours. Symbolically the role that Billy plays on the *Rights of Man* is supported and protected by the crew. Tellingly, they maintain him in his clothing: 'Some of 'em do his washing, darn his old trousers for him.'[49] That is, the image that Billy gives to them has to be stabilized through the consistency of his clothing, and repaired when necessary. This stability of identity is of course under threat when Billy must leave the *Rights of Man* and wear a uniform, adopting the rules and customs that the uniform represents. Melville draws attention to this transition as Billy leaves the *Rights of Man* and exchanges his merchantman's sea-chest for a Royal Navy sailor's bag. The *Bellipotent*'s Lieutenant Ratcliff intervenes when he sees the chest:

> 'here he comes; and, by Jove – lugging along his chest – Apollo with his portmanteau! – My man', stepping out to him, 'you can't take that big box aboard a war-ship. The boxes there are mostly shot-boxes. Put your duds in a bag, lad. Boot and saddle for the cavalryman, bag and hammock for the man-of-war's man.'[50]

---

[48] Ibid., p. 47.
[49] Ibid.
[50] Ibid., p. 48.

The transition is also marked by Billy calling out 'And good-bye to you too, old *Rights-of-Man*', an act the narrator considers 'a terrible breach of naval decorum'.[51]

The change from the merchant marine to the service is a potential threat to Billy's established identity, and this is signified by the exchange of uniforms. Unlike the officers, common sailors, and certainly an impressed one such as Billy, had no set uniform; uniforms were not standardized in the Royal Navy until 1857. During the period in which *Billy Budd* is set, a common sailor would typically wear baggy trousers and a short jacket, he would also generally wear his hair long, in a pigtail while on duty and for formal occasions. Melville notes that on the day of his execution Billy wore a white jumper and white duck trousers, duck being a hard-wearing, canvas-like linen. It was expected that the sailor's jacket would be blue, though the ship's captain could decide on a uniform for the sailors. Technically, in fact, common sailors belonged to the individual ship, rather than to the navy.[52] Hence 'bluejacket' comes to be a term for a common sailor in the Royal Navy; the *OED* dates the first printed usage of this to 1830. In *Billy Budd*, Melville uses 'bluejacket' in referring to the sailors in the *Bellipotent*, the common sailor collectively, and of Billy individually.[53] Blue is traditionally the colour that represents service and duty (in Britain the police are still colloquially – and in a double archaism – referred to as 'the boys in blue'). The description of Billy as a 'loyal bluejacket' indicates the ready conjunction of his identity with that of a sailor.[54]

What we see throughout the novel is the stability of Billy's identity. Despite his uncertain origins, he possesses a strong sense of his own selfhood. It is notable that Melville introduces and explains Billy's character very early on in the text, and that there is really no challenge to this established character, or any real development of it. Certainly, there is a crisis, and it leads to the death of Claggart and to the execution of Billy, but his established character is unaltered by this crisis; he remains the cynosure, the innocent. Certainly, Billy was the starting-point for Melville' s narrative, since it began life as a brief prose prelude Melville attached to a ballad titled 'Billy in the Darbies'.[55] In the novel, Billy is introduced with a similar vignette, as a character with

[51] Ibid., p. 49.
[52] Ibid., p. 118. See Nicholas Blake and Richard Lawrence, *The Illustrated Companion to Nelson's Navy* (London: Chatham, 2005), pp. 65–7.
[53] Melville, *Billy Budd*, pp. 51, 54, 73. Marines wore red jackets, indicating their military status.
[54] Ibid., p. 85.
[55] In British naval slang (the term is not in the *Oxford English Dictionary*), 'darbies' are irons, or handcuffs.

a fault: 'Though our Handsome Sailor had as much of masculine beauty as one can expect anywhere to see; nevertheless, like the beautiful woman in one of Hawthorne's minor tales, there was just one thing amiss in him. No visible blemish, indeed, as with the lady; no, but an occasional liability to a vocal defect.'[56] The reference is to Hawthorne's 1843 story 'The Birth-Mark', whose central character, Georgiana, is a woman of outstanding beauty that is supposedly marred by a crimson birthmark on her face, in the shape of a hand (although Hawthorne notes that some men find the birthmark is a charm that increases her attraction). Georgiana's husband, Aylmer, is a scientist who comes to be obsessed with the birthmark and after various experiments he develops a potion for its removal. Georgiana, now also obsessed with the birthmark as something detestable, resignedly drinks the potion: the mark fades, but she dies. Melville was clearly taken with the tale. It had been reprinted in the collection *Mosses from an Old Manse* that was the subject of his 1850 essay 'Hawthorne and His Mosses', and it almost certainly formed the basis for his comments on Hawthorne's abiding concern with evil: 'Certain it is, however, that this great power of blackness in him derives its force from its appeals to that Calvinistic sense of Innate Depravity and Original Sin, from whose visitations, in some shape or other, no deeply thinking mind is always and wholly free.'[57]

This sense of evil, the power of blackness, is still in Melville's mind decades later as he composes *Billy Budd*: the narrator represents Billy's one imperfection as the work of the devil: 'a striking instance that the arch interferer, the envious marplot of Eden, still has more or less to do with every human consignment to this planet of Earth. In every case, one way or another he is sure to slip in his little card, as much as to remind us – I too have a hand here.'[58] This observation has led, quite naturally, to an interpretation of *Billy Budd* as a study in evil. But it also causes something of a problem in terms of Billy's character. As Hawthorne realized, the near-perfect character, Georgina, can only generate dramatic conflict if an outside agent (here, Aylmer) interacts with her. She is content in herself and with the mark, not seeing it as an imperfection at all, until Aylmer's obsession develops. Indeed, her death is a form of sacrifice to his ideals, willingly undertaken. As such, Hawthorne's story moves to larger concerns than the presence of evil. As in other stories of his, it considers the responsibilities of transformative science and, as also recurs in a number of tales by Edgar Allan Poe, it explores the male need to control and reform

---

[56] Melville, *Billy Budd*, p. 53.
[57] Melville, *The Piazza Tales*, p. 243.
[58] Melville, *Billy Budd*, p. 53.

the otherness of the woman. In effect, Melville faces the same dramatic problem in the character of Billy. Since he is so nearly perfect, he cannot have inner conflict, at least, until interacting with some kind of external agency. This, of course, means that Claggart is essential to the plot, but it also means that in many respects Billy is what E. M. Forster would call a 'flat' character. He is not so flat as to be summed up in one sentence, one of Forster's criteria for flatness, although the narrator does explain Billy fairly fully early on in the narrative in a very few sentences.[59] What is apparent, though, is Billy's lack of development. This lack is actually intensified by Melville's use of proleptic narrative, in which events prefigure or hint at events to come. The most obvious example is inarticulate Billy's striking Red Whiskers on *The Rights of Man*; 'Quick as lightning Billy let fly his arm' prefiguring his attack on Claggart, 'quick as the flame from a discharged cannon at night, his right arm shot out, and Claggart dropped to the deck.[60] Such moments of anticipatory narrative give momentum and excitement to *Billy Budd*, as does the claustrophobic atmosphere on the ship, but they also remove complexity and change from the character of Billy. Again, while the simplicity of Billy's clothing testifies to the appealing stability of his identity, it also indicates his lack of complexity as a character.

Much the same is true of Claggart. As master-at-arms Claggart has a very different status from Billy. For one thing, he is a warrant officer rather than a commissioned officer, that is, he is directly employed by the Navy Board for a particular specialized role; the cook and the quartermaster are other examples of warrant officers on board the *Bellipotent*. As Melville notes, originally the job of the master-at-arms was to instruct sailors in weaponry, but this role changed so that by the end of the eighteenth century the master-at-arms was in effect a kind of policeman ('jaunty' the later slang for master-at-arms, derives from the French 'gendarme').[61] As 'maritime chief of police', the rattan cane that Claggart carries is more than symbolic of his authority, since it also has a literal force in being used to administer corporal punishment for offences less serious than those punishable by flogging.[62] Claggart's playfully tapping Billy with the rattan has more than a sexual connotation; it reminds us also of the power and authority that he has over Billy.[63] Although as a petty officer Claggart is low in the ship's hierarchy, he is still considerably superior to Billy. For Billy even to raise his

---

[59] Forster, *Aspects of the Novel*, p. 73.
[60] Melville, *Billy Budd*, pp. 47, 99.
[61] Ibid., p. 64. In another of the correspondences between *White-Jacket* and *Billy Budd*, Bland, the master-at-arms on the *Neversink*, is also represented as a figure of evil.
[62] Ibid., p. 67.
[63] Ibid., p. 72.

hand in violence to Claggart – never mind strike him and kill him – was, under the Articles of War, an offence punishable by death.

Like Billy, Claggart has mysterious origins, with hints of his being a Catholic French deserter, and like Billy he appears to occupy a station socially lower than his birth or background would indicate.[64] As with Billy, Melville presents Claggart's character to us before we see him in action. He is represented simply as evil, and as requiring no motivation other than the need to act out of his innate malevolence. Melville indicates that Claggart's evil is complicated by envy, reminiscent of the envy Iago admits to with regard to Cassio, 'He has a daily beauty in his life, / That makes me ugly.'[65] Melville titled the chapter sketching Claggart with a slight twist on a quotation from *Paradise Lost*, describing Satan's 'Pale ire, envy and despair'.[66] When Melville describes Claggart's having a 'disdain of innocence' that will drive him to destroy the innocence that Billy represents, there is an implicit invitation to a mode of interpretation that many critics have followed.[67] That is, Claggart is sexually attracted to Billy, but must repress this. When repressed, this passion turns into evil; this had been explored by Blake in *Songs of Innocence and Experience*; another of the texts that, like *Othello* and *Paradise Lost*, resonates throughout *Billy Budd*. This is very much the approach to *Billy Budd* that Forster and his contemporaries developed and is central to Britten's opera: the intricate relation between repression and malevolence. As such, there is a good deal of textual support for this Freudian account of *Billy Budd*, and it is notable that the first publication of *Billy Budd* was during the period that Freud's ideas were very current, his books becoming widely available in English translation. For instance, the playful tap with his cane that Claggart gives to Billy is sexual, and the insistence on Billy's feminine beauty also supports the idea of a sexual attraction. These aspects of *Billy Budd*: men without women; relationships intensified in an enclosed, even claustrophobic space, is the dramatic basis of Britten's opera, and also of other creative interpretations, notably Claire Denis's 1999 film *Beau Travail*, set in Djibouti among French Legionnaires, and using snatches from Britten's opera in its soundtrack.

Claggart's furtiveness is established early on in the novel, and is reinforced by the brief description of Claggart's clothing. Like the common

---

[64] Ibid., pp. 64–5.
[65] William Shakespeare, *Othello*, 5, i, 19–20.
[66] As noted above, Hayford and Sealts omitted draft chapter titles from the reading edition. As they point out in their note to p. 137, Melville has used 'pale' as if it were an adjective; in Milton's line it is a noun, meaning darkness or gloom: 'his face / Thrice chang'd with pale, ire, envy and despair' (John Milton, *Paradise Lost*, 4, 114–15).
[67] Melville, *Billy Budd*, p. 78.

sailors, the master-at-arms would have had no special uniform, although the cane does represent his official status. In the very brief sketch of Claggart's dress, Melville emphasizes his neatness: 'That Claggart's figure was not amiss, and his face, save the chin, well molded, has already been said. Of these favorable points he seemed not insensible, for he was not only neat but careful in his dress.'[68] 'Careful' carries connotations of caution, watchfulness, of someone on guard against self-revelation, while the emphasis on neatness does have a suggestion of a repressed nature; it forms another contrast with the dandiacal handsome sailor in Liverpool, with his earrings and silk adornment. More explicitly, Melville writes of Claggart's attitude to Billy:

> When Claggart's unobserved glance happened to light on belted Billy rolling along the upper gun deck in the leisure of the second dogwatch, exchanging passing broadsides of fun with other young promenaders in the crowd, that glance would follow the cheerful sea Hyperion with a settled meditative and melancholy expression, his eyes strangely suffused with incipient feverish tears. Then would Claggart look like the man of sorrows. Yes, and sometimes the melancholy expression would have in it a touch of soft yearning, as if Claggart could even have loved Billy but for fate and ban.[69]

'Promenading' the deck was a common activity during the short (2 hour rather than 4) early evening dogwatches, though the term carries connotations of leisure, display and parading, the actions of the boulevardier or dandy. The 'ban' is generally taken as a reference to the outlawing of homosexual acts; section 28 of the Articles of War relevant to the *Bellipotent* specifically forbade 'unnatural and detestable' sexual acts (specified as buggery and sodomy), and these offences were punishable by death. At the time when Forster and Britten encountered *Billy Budd*, homosexuality was criminal in British civil law. Hence the situation of Billy and Claggart has a special, if somewhat covert relevance to them, and they could use this to generate a dramatic tension in the operatic version.

This representation of the tension of *Billy Budd* is important, and it is worth recalling that the novel deals a good deal generally with secrecy, suggestion, subversion and covert acts. Its post-1962 subtitle, an 'inside' narrative, indicates something unofficial, or anti-official, about the story of Billy himself and how that story is mediated, specifically counter

---

[68] Ibid., p. 77.
[69] Ibid., pp. 87–8.

to the laconic account of the conspiracy and the hanging given in the official record of the naval chronicle.[70] At the same time, though, the idea of Claggart attempting to destroy Billy because of a repressed, distorted love is at odds with Melville's representation of him elsewhere. Melville typically refers to Claggart as someone who, is in effect, predestined to do evil. It is simply his nature; like the scorpion, be cannot help but sting, it is what it does.[71] The references in *Billy Budd* to Calvinism reinforce this idea. Claggart acts not out of will, or choice, or unconscious motivation, but because it is his predestined fate; just as 'fate' forbids him to love Billy. It is his nature. Linking with the connotations of his careful neatness of dress, Melville describes Claggart as someone whose outward rationality and control mask an internal irrational malevolence: 'Now something such an one was Claggart, in whom was the mania of an evil nature, not engendered by vicious training or corrupting books or licentious living, but born with him and innate, in short "a depravity according to nature"'.[72] Claggart has no motive, unconscious or not; he is simply acting out who he is destined to be. Melville's invocation of Hawthorne's 'The Birth-mark' is here especially significant. You cannot remove or disguise a mark that has been put there by providence, just as you cannot avoid what has been predestined for you, just as the Calvinists believed that original sin could not be sacramentally erased. This version of Claggart is clearly at odds with a more complex study of his motivations, and, recalling that this is an unfinished text, it may be that Melville would have revised a final version in only one or other of these directions. As it stands, though, the emphasis on Claggart as acting out an evil disposition actually works against there being much dramatic tension in the novel. There can be no doubt that evil will destroy innocence and, although we are prepared for it, the main plot surprise is that Billy, as innocence, destroys Claggart. The dramatic intensity of *Billy Budd* has several sources, but it does not derive from any inner struggle in the characters of Billy or Claggart.

When Melville refers to Billy as a 'loyal bluejacket', he suggests the easy transition Billy has made to the service of the royal navy, but that transition will result in his death.[73] The relation between loyalty and self-sacrifice is an obvious theme in 'The Birth-Mark', as Georgina sacrifices herself to the will of Aylmer. Loyalty and self-sacrifice were of course also intimately linked in Melville's representation of the death of Nelson, in which Nelson adorns

---

[70] Ibid., pp. 130–1.
[71] Ibid., p. 78.
[72] Ibid., p. 76. In their note on this passage Hayford and Sealts note the echo of Plato's phrase 'natural depravity'.
[73] Ibid., p. 73.

himself 'for the altar and the sacrifice'.[74] Billy is not self-sacrificial in the way that Georgina is. He does not choose to die, his killing of Claggart is involuntary, and though he accepts his punishment he has in no way sought it. But it is easy to represent his death as sacrificial, because the execution serves a larger purpose than simply retribution for the death of Claggart. Melville's historical contextualization, invoking the recent mutinies and the current state of being at war, indicates there is a political, as well as a judicial, necessity for the execution, and it must fall to Vere to sacrifice Billy. There is, though, as Melville was well aware, a whole series of stories from the classics and from mythology in which sacrifice ensures victory. *Billy Budd* is in fact one of Melville's most allusive texts in terms of classical mythology.[75] This further dimension of sacrifice allows for a reading of *Billy Budd* in which Billy is the chosen victim, whose death is an appeasement to the gods. The representation of Nelson's death had made it similarly sacrificial; without his death there was to be no victory. Among the more obvious classical parallels is the story of Agamemnon and his daughter Iphigenia. In one version of this story, the goddess Artemis, Apollo's twin sister, demands that Agamemnon sacrifice Iphigenia so that the Greek fleet, becalmed by her at Aulis, could sail to make war on Troy. Sacrifice is a common element in many forms of worship and ritual, and there are many allusions to these in *Billy Budd*, aligned with the classical references. Billy is referred to as 'Apollo with his portmanteau' and the *Agamemnon* is mentioned as the former ship of the Dansker. This was the ship captained by Nelson for three years (reputedly his favourite) and she was involved in the Spithead and Nore mutinies.[76] The most sustained reading of the mythological sacrifice theme in *Billy Budd* is provided by H. Bruce Franklin. Noting that *Billy Budd* is 'a story about Britain and its navy' Franklin explores Melville's allusions to the ancient British religion, Druidism.[77] In one account of the Druids that Melville may have known, the most important British god was Hu, the 'Celtic Apollo', known also as Beli and Budd.[78] In effect, Franklin argues, Billy is the sacrificial victim, the Druids being notorious for rituals that involved human sacrifice. He is chosen for his innocence, and his death will result eventually in peace. The description of Billy's death conflates

[74] Ibid., p. 58.
[75] See Gail H. Coffler, *Melville's Classical Allusions* (Westport, CT: Greenwood Press, 1985).
[76] Melville, *Billy Budd*, pp. 48, 69. It was fairly common in this period for Royal Navy ships to bear classical names; contemporaneous with the *Agamemnon*, for example, were *Leda, Virago, Vulcan, Ariadne, Apollo, Acasta, Jupiter* and *Leander*.
[77] H. Bruce Franklin, *The Wake of the Gods* (Stanford, CA: Stanford University Press, 1963), p. 193.
[78] Ibid., p. 195.

aspects of Druidism with Christian symbolism. The narrator tells us that the hanging of Billy from the main yard, that is, on the lowest horizontal spar of the main mast, was unusual: 'the execution by halter of a military sailor was generally from the foreyard. In the present instance, for special reasons the mainyard was assigned.'[79] As Franklin among others points out, the hanging from the main yard intensifies the growing association of Billy with Christ, since this mast, the central of the *Bellipotent*'s three, makes an analogy with Christ's being crucified on the central of three crosses, between the two thieves.[80] The language used to describe that death also carries forward the Christian symbolism:

> The hull, deliberately recovering from the periodic roll to leeward, was just regaining an even keel, when the last signal, a preconcerted dumb one, was given. At the same moment it chanced that the vapory fleece hanging low in the East was shot through with a soft glory as of the fleece of the Lamb of God seen in mystical vision, and simultaneously therewith, watched by the wedged mass of upturned faces, Billy ascended; and, ascending, took the full rose of the dawn.
>
> In the pinioned figure arrived at the yard-end, to the wonder of all no motion was apparent, none save that created by the slow roll of the hull in moderate weather, so majestic in a great ship ponderously cannoned.[81]

Billy's ascension and the near-miraculous lack of muscular spasms climax the religious symbolism, which is carried forward into the future as Billy's crewmates venerate his memory: 'The spar from which the foretopman was suspended was for some few years kept trace of by the bluejackets. Their knowledges followed it from ship to dockyard and again from dockyard to ship, still pursuing it even when at last reduced to a mere dockyard boom. To them a chip of it was as a piece of the Cross.'[82] This last comment is of special importance, emphasizing once more how much *Billy Budd* is an 'inside narrative', exploring the conflict between 'knowledges', between the official record of Billy and the personal, sacred, memory of his crewmates.

While Franklin's mythic framing of *Billy Budd* may seem now rather overly schematic, especially for an unfinished text, the representation of Billy as sacrificial is important. So too is what lies beyond his recognition of the

[79] Melville, *Billy Budd*, p. 123.
[80] Franklin, *The Wake of the Gods*, p. 199.
[81] Melville, *Billy Budd*, p. 124.
[82] Ibid., p. 131.

Druidical and Christian elements of this story of a Briton; that the language of *Billy Budd* stretches from the world of fact into the world of myth. Early on, the narrator tells us that this narrative is not a romance: 'The avowal of such an imperfection in the Handsome Sailor should be evidence not alone that he is not presented as a conventional hero, but also that the story in which he is the main figure is no romance.'[83] Billy is no conventional hero. He commits no heroic act but is rather the victim of malevolence and his death is sacrificial. But *Billy Budd* is far from being the non-romance that is here suggested. In spite of its historical contextualization and its grounding in the factual, *Billy Budd* is a strikingly non-realistic text. Melville offers very little in the way of the details of navy life during the Napoleonic wars. A simple contrast with the representation of the period in the series of Aubrey–Maturin novels by Patrick O'Brian, with their meticulous, even ponderous, detail, brings out this point sharply. *Billy Budd* is somewhere between realism and romance; again, perhaps, indicative of Melville's shifting intentions as to this work. Early on Billy is described as the story's 'main figure', but the implications of this are unclear. He is the main figure in that he is the centre of the dramatic conflict that emerges, but in some regard both he and Claggart are too straightforward as characters, lacking internal conflict, to form the centre of interest. As Melville worked again and again on the *Billy Budd* manuscript the character of Vere increasingly engaged his imagination. In some respects this is hardly surprising. The involvement of Guert in the *Somers* case strongly corresponds to the position of Vere. But more significantly, Vere is the only character who must struggle internally, whose character is in conflict with itself. Billy and Claggart lack this inner conflict and while they create the external dramatic tension of *Billy Budd*, Vere's ambiguities create their own inner tension.

As already noted, Melville's introduction of Vere includes a remark about his clothing; when he is ashore, no-one would consider him a sailor. The sea, Melville suggests, is a profession for Vere, it is not a calling that engages or expresses his true self. Since professionalization and bureaucracy are key aspects of the modern, he is another Melville character ill-equipped for modernity. That is, as a professional he is filling a role in which actions must be determined by duty rather than by the self. His fellow-officers see him as different, a man apart who is 'lacking in the companionable quality, a dry and bookish gentleman'.[84] Although a highly capable seaman, his disinterested intellect and considered pedantry mean that he lacks the heroic qualities of focus and self-engagement that mark out the truly great

[83] Ibid., p. 53.
[84] Ibid., p. 63.

captain. Typically, Melville's imagined conversation about Vere involves a textural metaphor: "'Vere is a noble fellow, Starry Vere. 'Spite the gazettes, Sir Horatio" (meaning him who became Lord Nelson) "is at bottom scarce a better seaman or fighter. But between you and me now, don't you think there is a queer streak of the pedantic running through him? Yes, like the King's yarn in a coil of navy-rope?'"[85] Navy rope, defined as cordage over 1 inch in diameter, was usually made by spinning hemp fibres to make yarns. These were then tarred and twisted the opposite way to form strands, the number of twists determining the strength of rope needed. The inclusion of a non-tarred coloured yarn meant that the rope's origin could be identified; this was important should the rope prove defective, and to identify it as the property of the crown. This piece of yarn was generally known as rogue's yarn.[86] Here the image is one of intimate entanglement: Vere's sense of duty is so strong that it is inseparably fused into his identity as a sailor. Although he famously sent the message about duty, Nelson's attitude to conventions and regulations was more flexible, and his bold originality was key to his successes.

Melville had used this thread imagery before to indicate inseparability. In *Israel Potter* he wrote of Israel's life being for a time entangled with that of John Paul Jones: 'For a time back, across the otherwise blue-jean career of Israel, Paul Jones flits and reflits like a crimson thread. One more brief intermingling of it, and to the plain old homespun we return.'[87] There is also an impossible tangling of ropes in *Benito Cereno*: 'a combination of double-bowline-knot, treble-crown-knot, back-handed-well-knot, knot-in-and-out-knot, and jamming-knot'.[88] On the face of it, Vere's absolute obedience to duty and regulation removes any tension from the decision to hang Billy. Having had this established as a key characteristic, we do not expect Vere to swerve from it, and we have been told that he is someone who never tolerates 'an infraction of discipline'.[89] Furthermore, the application of the Articles of War seems also unproblematic; the offence is clear, and England is at war. But there is a conflict within Vere, and it arises from his very sense of the uniform. Wearing the uniform, he assumes the identity that it confers, but this is different from his civilian, private self. Vere ashore and out of the uniform, it is implied, would act differently, bringing sympathy, mercy and a consideration of the circumstances to bear on the case. Although there is a

---

[85] Ibid.
[86] William Falconer, *An Universal Dictionary of the Marine* (London: Thomas Cadell, 1784), p. 266.
[87] Melville, *Israel Potter*, p. 131.
[88] Melville, *The Piazza Tales*, p. 76.
[89] Melville, *Billy Budd*, p. 60.

gap between law and 'natural justice', in the role of captain he must insist on allegiance to the book of law, and it is his duty to persuade his fellow-officers to overcome their human scruples regarding Billy's case. He is reluctantly obedient to modernity:

> But your scruples: do they move as in a dusk? Challenge them. Make them advance and declare themselves. Come now: do they import something like this: If, mindless of palliating circumstances, we are bound to regard the death of the master-at-arms as the prisoner's deed, then does that deed constitute a capital crime whereof the penalty is a mortal one. But in natural justice is nothing but the prisoner's overt act to be considered? How can we adjudge to summary and shameful death a fellow-creature innocent before God, and whom we feel to be so? – Does that state it aright? You sign sad assent. Well, I too feel that, the full force of that. It is Nature. But do these buttons that we wear attest that our allegiance is to Nature? No, to the King. Though the ocean, which is inviolate Nature primeval, though this be the element where we move and have our being as sailors, yet as the King's officers lies our duty in a sphere correspondingly natural?[90]

According to a long-held belief, the practice of wearing of buttons in the Royal Navy was initiated by Nelson, who insisted on his sailors having them sewn on their sleeves to prevent them from wiping their noses there (some of a crew could be as young as 9 years old, and naval dress had no pockets in which to store a handkerchief). Although this is not actually the case, navy buttons do not for the most part function as buttons; they have a symbolic purpose only. In fact, the practice of having ornamental sleeve buttons spread into civilian clothing, and is now a staple of any dress or sporting jacket. So, while they denote Vere's deep sense of obedience to the strict rules of his chosen office, the 'buttons' he alludes to also suggest his considerable discomfort in this role, and the sharp division between it and his natural, internal sympathies. The naval buttons are an important symbol of his office, but they are symbolic, in no way 'natural'. They represent duty and allegiance in a professional who must obey the uniform, but this uniform may also act, as it does for Vere, to conceal or suppress true inner identity. As Alison Lurie remarks, to put on a uniform 'is to give up one's right to act as an individual – in terms of speech, to be partially or wholly censored'.[91] Vere articulates this when he speaks about members of

[90] Ibid., p. 110.
[91] Lurie, *The Language of Clothes*, pp. 17–18.

his own crew perhaps having a conscience that is at odds with their role as sailors of the King: 'In His Majesty's service – in this ship indeed – there are Englishmen forced to fight for the King against their will. Against their conscience, for aught we know. Though as their fellow-creatures some of us may appreciate their position, yet as navy officers, what reck we of it? Still less recks the enemy.'[92] Modernity demands obedience to professional duty, not to conscience. Vere's position is also practical and contextual, and Melville's references to the Nore are significant in the provision of context. Vere rejects the suggestion that Billy might be found guilty but shown clemency and not be executed. To the crew, clemency would seem an act of cowardice, suggesting the officers are afraid of the sailors.

It is here that the earlier contrast made between Vere and Nelson becomes more fully apparent. Nelson's clothes for Trafalgar were correct, in that his identity was fully invested in them. They entirely expressed who he was; there was no confusion between the uniform and his self. But, he had also made that uniform his own, individuated it, as it were, by tailoring it according to his own will. His dress represented a fusion of inner identity with public duty. Unlike Vere he would never inflexibly follow the rules laid down by the uniform but, through initiative and expediency, would find a form of accommodation between his will and his 'buttons'. Vere, though, while acknowledging the disconnection between his self and his uniform, and perceiving this as a condition of service, can find no such accommodation of the two. Billy is 'a martyr to martial discipline' but also to Vere's inability to find reconciliation or even commonality between his heart and the duty his buttons represent. This divided Vere is apparent in his ambivalent name, which suggests truth and fidelity, but also unpredictability and uncertainty, someone liable to 'veer': 'Was he unhinged?' wonders the ship's surgeon.[93]

Vere's statement of allegiance to the King is telling. Throughout *Billy Budd* Melville repeatedly insists on this allegiance, reminding us of the regal power and authority that lies above the ship. Billy has entered the 'King's service', having been surrendered 'to the King' by his merchant captain; Charles Dibdin's song 'And as for my life, 'tis the King's!' is invoked; Claggart is introduced as someone who has 'volunteered into the King's Navy'; at the arraignment Billy swears 'I have eaten the King's bread and I am true to the King.'[94] This repeated insistence on the ultimate authority of the King has several effects. For one thing, it reminds us that the story is set on a British

---

[92] Melville, *Billy Budd*, p. 112.
[93] Ibid., p. 102. See Nicholas Royle, *Veering* (Edinburgh: Edinburgh University Press, 2011), p. 166.
[94] Melville, *Billy Budd*, pp. 44, 48, 55, 65, 106.

rather than an American ship. This may seem unnecessary, but it is crucial for considering the nature of authority in a monarchy. Allegiance is not to God or to conscience, but to the King, and the King's will is expressed in the Articles of War. A more significant effect of the insistence of the King's authority is in, again, contextualizing the character of Vere. It is important to remember that even as he reminds his officers of their allegiance to the King, to their buttons, Vere as Captain is himself the representative of the King on this ship. This is partly why conspiracy, mutiny and sedition are such serious offences, punishable by death. They are actually treasonous, resisting not the authority of an individual captain, but that of the Crown. This aspect of Vere's role intensifies the division within himself. It is not that the King is elsewhere; he is here in the persona of the King. Thus, his recognition of a conflict between 'Nature' and 'the King' is also the identification of an internalized struggle between two selves: between his instinctual self and his self as representative.

To express Vere's crisis in this way is inevitably to invoke Shakespeare, whose history plays so often focus on the dilemma of a King as both human and ordained by God into some state beyond the human. This is particularly explored in *Richard II*, where the deposed Richard finds himself in a condition without identity. Who, or what, is a King who is no longer a King?

> I have no name, no title;
> No, not that name was given me at the font,
> But 'tis usurp'd. Alack the heavy day,
> That I have worn so many winters out,
> And know not now what name to call myself![95]

In his copy of the play, Melville marked up the 'mirror scene' in which Richard calls for a looking-glass and examines his face.[96] Seeing in the glass only what he was when he was King, there being no other identity for him, he violently dashes the mirror to the ground: 'For there it is, crack'd in an hundred shivers. / Mark, silent king, the moral of this sport – / How soon my sorrow hath destroy'd my face.'[97]

[95] William Shakespeare, *Richard II*, 4, i, 255–9.
[96] Matthiessen, *American Renaissance*, p. 449. Matthiessen suggests that Melville refers to the mirror scene when Ahab dashes the quadrant to the deck in *Moby-Dick*. He also proposes (p. 502) that Melville's preoccupation with the Fall in *Billy Budd* echoes a speech in *Richard II* which Melville had underlined, when the Queen, on hearing of Richard's deposition, responds: 'What Eve, what serpent, hath suggested thee / To make a second fall of cursed man?' (Shakespeare, *Richard II*, 3, iv, 75–6.)
[97] Shakespeare, *Richard II*, 4, i, 289–91.

Richard is in effect destroyed by this lack of private identity. Vere is not destroyed because his public duty and his private identity may coexist, even though they are in conflict with one another. Vere does die, though, giving his life to his duty. The dramatic events of *Billy Budd* take place while the *Bellipotent* is on a cruise, that is, she is sailing independently and alone over a specified region, rather than undertaking defined duties as part of the fleet. It was on these cruises that captains and crews hoped to encounter enemy ships with valuable cargo which, if captured as prizes, would generate significant profits for all crew members, shared out according to a set formula. While returning to the fleet, the *Bellipotent* encounters the French line-of-battle ship the *Athée*. In the ensuing engagement, Vere is mortally wounded, and again the death of Nelson is invoked:

> Captain Vere, in the act of putting his ship alongside the enemy . . . was hit by a musket ball from a porthole of the enemy's main cabin. More than disabled, he dropped to the deck and was carried below to the same cockpit where some of his men already lay. The senior lieutenant took command. Under him the enemy was finally captured, and though much crippled was by rare good fortune successfully taken into Gibraltar, an English port not very distant from the scene of the fight.[98]

While Melville sets up the similarities with the death of Nelson, he introduces significant differences. Nelson dies on his ship during the battle, behaving as an admiral should. He is a leader to the last at the scene of battle, a martyrdom which will be imaginatively commemorated in numerous works of art. Although *Billy Budd*'s narrator wonders what might have happened had Nelson not been wounded, the glory of the death is still paramount; he issued 'nothing less than a challenge to death; and death came'; the victory is 'crowned' by his 'glorious death'.[99] However, Vere does not die on board his ship, but ashore, in Gibraltar:

> He lingered for some days, but the end came. Unhappily he was cut off too early for the Nile and Trafalgar. The spirit that 'spite its philosophic austerity may yet have indulged in the most secret of all passions, ambition, never attained to the fulness of fame.

---

[98] Melville, *Billy Budd*, p. 129. This 'rare good fortune' is evidence for the argument that Billy has been sacrificed to the gods to ensure victory; the fact that the defeated ship is the Atheist is also relevant.

[99] Ibid., pp. 57, 58.

Not long before death, while lying under the influence of that magical drug which, soothing the physical frame, mysteriously operates on the subtler element in man, he was heard to murmur words inexplicable to his attendant: 'Billy Budd, Billy Budd'. That these were not the accents of remorse would seem clear from what the attendant said to the *Bellipotent*'s senior officer of marines, who, as the most reluctant to condemn of the members of the drum-head court, too well knew, though here he kept the knowledge to himself, who Billy Budd was.[100]

The difference between Vere at sea in uniform and Vere on land has already been noted. On duty he is true to his uniform, but on land, where no-one would guess he is a sailor, a more complex and ambivalent character emerges. This ambivalence extends to our interpretation of these dying words. Not only does Melville's syntax become distorted, but once more in this narrative he emphasizes the uncertain, the hidden, the occluded and the conspiratorial. The name means nothing to Vere's attendant, and when he reports them to the man who knows what they mean, their significance is not divulged. While the narrator tells us that the name is not spoken in the 'accents of remorse', the effect of the syntax is to maintain the suggestion that they could be. Since he is drugged, dying and ashore, we might expect Vere's words to represent regret. He has done his naval duty, been true to the buttons, but when not wearing that uniform he expresses the human regret that he necessarily suppressed formerly. Both the ambiguity and the repetition suggest that Vere does not know what he means any more by the name. The profound ambivalence of his identity ultimately makes him powerless to maintain a singularity of vision, of self-judgement.

A recurring theme in *Billy Budd* is redemption after transgression, the possibility of restitution. This was evident in the public treatment of Nelson, whose death and victory exonerated his scandalous personal life. It is also apparent when the narrator reflects on the Spithead and Nore rebellions:

> At all events, of these thousands of mutineers were some of the tars who not so very long afterwards – whether wholly prompted thereto by patriotism, or pugnacious instinct, or by both – helped to win a coronet for Nelson at the Nile, and the naval crown of crowns for him at Trafalgar. To the mutineers, those battles and especially Trafalgar were a plenary absolution and a grand one.[101]

---

[100] Ibid., p. 129.
[101] Ibid., pp. 55–6.

Whatever their motivation, the mutineers achieve a kind of redemption, an absolution through their later actions. The reclamation of innocence, after an experience of evil, was from the very earliest criticism taken to be a major concern of *Billy Budd*. This mostly arises from a direct contrast with *Moby-Dick*, in which no such redemption seemed available or possible. As noted earlier, Freeman suggested it was Melville's *Paradise Regained*, whereas *Moby-Dick* was his *Paradise Lost*; *Moby-Dick* 'ends in darkness and desolation' but *Billy Budd* 'ends in a brightness of escape'.[102] Freeman linked this redemptive theme with the circumstances of Melville's life and his changing attitudes, so different from when he wrote *Moby-Dick*, arguing that *Billy Budd* shows 'the striking security of Melville's inward peace . . . in his last days he re-enters an Eden-like sweetness and serenity . . . and sets his brief, appealing tragedy for witness that evil is defeat and natural goodness invincible in the affections of man'.[103] Auden's celebrated poem 'Herman Melville' focuses mostly on the provenance of *Billy Budd* and shares with Freeman these two related insights: the novel is concerned with redemptive innocence, and it reflects a freshly gained serenity in Melville's personal life. That the poem's sentiments so closely match Freeman's comments suggests that his book, and Forster's representation, were its direct sources. Auden's poem begins 'Towards the end he sailed into an extraordinary mildness' and continues:

> Goodness existed: that was the new knowledge.
> His terror had to blow itself quite out
> To let him see it.[104]

Billy Budd is born in Melville's 'exultation and surrender'; that is, from acceptance of providence and God's will rather than rebellion against these.

There are two major problems with this representation of *Billy Budd*. First, it makes too much of a contrast with *Moby-Dick*, as if Melville had written little of substance in the almost 40 years between that and this last work.[105] Secondly, in placing Billy at the centre of the narrative, it privileges the death, occluding the aftermath of the execution and the prominence given to Vere. Given the text on which this approach was based it necessarily

---

[102] Freeman, *Herman Melville*, pp. 131, 135.
[103] Ibid., pp. 135–6.
[104] W. H. Auden, *Collected Poems* (London: Faber and Faber, 1976), p. 200.
[105] This is the attitude that Freeman encouraged. Of the fiction written after 1851, only *Pierre* and *Billy Budd* are treated substantially; the other work is bundled together under a chapter titled 'Other Prose'.

cannot account for the developing nature of the manuscript, where Vere gained prominence. Even the last line of Auden's poem, in which Melville 'sat down at his desk and wrote a story' is also misleading, suggesting that *Billy Budd* is a completed story written straightforwardly with one theme in mind. Melville actually returned to this desk repeatedly over five years, rewriting a story that developed in different ways until he died with it unfinished. However, the assumptions made by Freeman and by Auden invite us to recall the composition of *Billy Budd*. It is in many ways Melville's most personal work. Not personal in the use of autobiographical material, which he had done so often before, from his first two novels right through to *Redburn* and *White-Jacket*, and more obliquely in *Israel Potter*. There is a very different kind of self-examination apparent in *Billy Budd*, and this was prolonged throughout the abnormally long period of its composition. It is autobiographical in terms of being an intense retrospective self-examination, an inside narrative, rather than in being factually rooted in Melville's own experience. The dedication to Jack Chase, the shipmate who Melville knew 40 years before and whom he made heroic in *White-Jacket*, suggests how deeply and how far Melville is reaching back into his own life. On the inside of his writing-desk while working on *Billy Budd* he had pasted a translated quotation from Friedrich von Schiller's historical drama *Don Carlos*; 'Keep true to the dreams of thy youth.' Melville had probably known this quotation since reading *Don Carlos* early in the 1860s. He may also have come across it in Carlyle's *Life of Friedrich Schiller*, where Carlyle commented on the line's 'pathetic wisdom'.[106] There is even in *Billy Budd* a coy reference to Melville himself, 'a writer whom few know'.[107] *Billy Budd* is not an autobiography in a generic sense, but it grows out of the autobiographical impulse, in exactly the terms that Roy Pascal used for the motivation of self-writing: 'The autobiography is the means to review one's life, to organize it in the imagination, and thus to bring the past experience and the present self into balance. The object is not so much to tell the truth about oneself, as to come to terms with oneself.'[108] As a late work, *Billy Budd* might also be about being true to oneself, as in the fuller quotation from *Don Carlos*:

> Tell him that when he is a man and King
> He must respect the dreams he had when young,

---

[106] Parker, *Herman Melville*, 2, p. 437; Thomas Carlyle, *The Life of Friedrich Schiller* (London: Taylor and Hessey, 1825), p. 105.
[107] Melville, *Billy Budd*, p. 114.
[108] Roy Pascal, *Design and Truth in Autobiography* (London: Routledge, 1960), p. 59.

And guard his sacred gentleness of heart
Against the disenchanting touch of reason.[109]

In *Billy Budd*, Vere is of course the only character who lives beyond early manhood, the man old enough to be Billy's father. He is thus the only character who can offer a parallel to the retrospective vision that Melville is himself providing in the text. Nelson, Vere, Melville: a shifting triad of identities being explored in the text. Melville reminding us of Nelson writing his brief will just before his last battle; telling us of Vere's last reported words, 'Billy Budd, Billy Budd'.[110] 'It may seem strange' Melville wrote in *Moby-Dick*, 'that of all men sailors should be tinkering at their last wills and testaments, but there are no people in the world more fond of that diversion'.[111] *Billy Budd*, at which Melville was 'tinkering' for more than five years, and which he perhaps he did not want to complete, is not a will. But it is a form of legacy, an act of claiming identity which is often a motivation for late works. As such, Vere is Melville's autobiographical focal point. He may have been a divided man, yet he performed his duty to the point of self-sacrifice.

---

[109] Friedrich Schiller, *Don Carlos*, trans. Hilary Collier Sy-Quia and Peter Oswald (Oxford: Oxford University Press, 1996), p. 161. The speaker is the Marquis of Posa, here advising the Queen about the Prince, Don Carlos.
[110] Melville, *Billy Budd*, pp. 58, 129.
[111] Melville, *Moby-Dick*, p. 227.

Bibliography

Abbott, H. Porter, 'Autobiography, Autography, Fiction: Groundwork for a Taxonomy of Textual Categories', *New Literary History*, 19:3 (1988), 597–615.
Amiel, Henri Frédéric, *Amiel's Journal*, trans. Mrs Humphry Ward, New York and London: Macmillan, 1906.
Anderson, Charles Roberts, *Melville in the South Seas*, New York: Columbia University Press, 1939.
Arac, Jonathan, *Commissioned Spirits: The Shaping of Social Motion in Dickens, Carlyle, Melville, and Hawthorne*, New Brunswick: Rutgers University Press, 1979.
Arvin, Newton, *Herman Melville: A Critical Biography*, New York: William Sloane Associates, 1950.
Atwood, Margaret, *The Handmaid's Tale*, London: Cape, 1986.
Auden, W. H., *Collected Poems*, London: Faber and Faber, 1976.
Auerbach, Nina, *Private Theatricals: The Lives of the Victorians*, Cambridge: Harvard University Press, 1990.
Baker, Anne, 'What to Israel Potter Is the Fourth of July? Melville, Douglass, and the Agency of Words', *Leviathan: A Journal of Melville Studies*, 10:2 (2008), 9–22.
Barthes, Roland, 'From Work to Text', in *Textual Strategies: Perspectives in Poststructuralist Criticism*, ed. Josué V. Harari, Ithaca, NY: Cornell University Press, 1979, 73–81.
Baudelaire, Charles, *Selected Writings on Art and Artists*, trans. P. E. Charvet, Harmondsworth: Penguin, 1972.
Bennett, Anthony, 'Rivals Unravelled: A Broadside Song and Dance', *Folk Music Journal*, 6:4 (1993), 420–45.
Bercaw Edwards, Mary K., *Cannibal Old Me: Spoken Sources in Melville's Early Works*, Kent, OH: Kent State University Press, 2009.
— 'Questioning *Typee*', *Leviathan: A Journal of Melville Studies*, 11:2 (2009), 24–42.
Bercovitch, Sacvan, *The Puritan Origins of the American Self*, New Haven: Yale University Press, 1975.
Berman, Marshall, *All That Is Solid Melts into Air: The Experience of Modernity*, Harmondsworth: Penguin, 1988.
Bishop, Elizabeth, *The Complete Poems 1927–1979*, New York: Farrar Straus Giroux, 1984.
Blake, Nicholas and Richard Lawrence, *The Illustrated Companion to Nelson's Navy*, London: Chatham, 2005.
Boswell, James, *The Life of Samuel Johnson*, London: Oxford University Press, 1966.

Botz-Bornstein, Thorsten, 'Rule-Following in Dandyism: "Style" as an Overcoming of "Rule" and "Structure"', *The Modern Language Review*, 90:2 (1995), 285–95.
Bradbury, Ray, *Green Shadows, White Whale: A Novel of Ray Bradbury's Adventures Making Moby Dick with John Huston in Ireland*, London: HarperCollins, 1992.
Branch, Watson G. (ed.), *Melville, The Critical Heritage*, London: Routledge and Kegan Paul, 1974.
Britten, Benjamin, *Billy Budd: An Opera in Four Acts*, libretto by E. M. Forster and Eric Crozier, London: Hawkes & Son, 1952.
Bryant, John, *The Fluid Text: A Theory of Revision and Editing for Book and Screen*, Ann Arbor: University of Michigan Press, 2002.
—, *Melville Unfolding: Sexuality, Politics, and the Versions of Typee*, Ann Arbor: University of Michigan Press, 2008.
Buchan, John, *The Complete Richard Hannay*, London: Penguin, 1992.
Calder, Alex, '"The Thrice Mysterious Taboo": Melville's *Typee* and the Perception of Culture', *Representations*, 67 (1999), 27–43.
Cameron, Sharon, *Impersonality: Seven Essays*, Chicago and London: University of Chicago Press, 2007.
Carlyle, Thomas, *The French Revolution: A History*, 2 volumes, London: Chapman and Hall, 1896.
—, *The Life of Friedrich Schiller*, London: Taylor and Hessey, 1825.
—, *Sartor Resartus*, ed. Rodger L. Tarr and Mark Engel, Berkeley: University of California Press, 2000.
—, *Sartor Resartus*, ed. Kerry McSweeney and Peter Sabor, Oxford: Oxford University Press, 2008.
Carter, Angela, *Shaking a Leg: Journalism and Writings*, London: Chatto & Windus, 1997.
Cavallaro, Dani and Alexandra Warwick, *Fashioning the Frame: Boundaries, Dress and the Body*, Oxford and New York: Berg, 1998.
Chacko, David and Alexander Kulcsar, *Beggarman, Spy: The Secret Life and Times of Israel Potter*, Cedarburg, WI: Foremost Press, 2010.
Clark, Kenneth, *The Nude: A Study in Ideal Form*, London: Folio Society, 2010.
Coffler, Gail H., *Melville's Classical Allusions: A Comprehensive Index and Glossary*, Westport, CT: Greenwood Press, 1985.
Colchester, Chloë (ed.), *Clothing the Pacific*, Oxford and New York: Berg, 2003.
Conrad, Joseph, *Heart of Darkness*, Harmondsworth: Penguin Books, 1981.
Cook, Jonathan A., 'Introduction to Melville's Marginalia in Nathaniel Hawthorne's *Mosses from an Old Manse*', <http://melvillesmarginalia.org/UserViewFramesetIntro.php?id=16> [accessed 31 October 2013].
Corbey, Raymond, 'Alterity: The Colonial Nude', *Critique of Anthropology*, 8:3 (1988), 75–92.
Cotkin, George, *Dive Deeper: Journeys with Moby-Dick*, New York and Oxford: Oxford University Press, 2012.

Crane, Stephen, *Prose and Poetry*, New York: Library of America, 1984.
Crick, Bernard, *George Orwell: A Life*, Harmondsworth: Penguin Books, 1992.
Crook, William Pascoe, *An Account of the Marquesas Islands 1797–1799*, ed. Greg Dening, H.-M. Le Cleac'h, Douglas Peacocke and Samuel Greatheed, Tahiti: Haere Po Editions, 2007.
Cumming, Mark (ed.), *The Carlyle Encyclopedia*, Cranbury, NJ: Fairleigh Dickinson University Press, 2004.
Czisnik, Marianne, *Horatio Nelson: A Controversial Hero*, London: Hodder Education, 2005.
Dana, Richard Henry, Jr, *Two Years before the Mast and Other Voyages*, New York: Library of America, 2005.
Davidmann, Sara, *Crossing the Line*, Stockport: Dewi Lewis, 2003.
Davis, Fred, *Fashion, Culture and Identity*, Chicago: University of Chicago Press, 1992.
Defoe, Daniel, *Robinson Crusoe*, ed. J. Donald Crowley, Oxford: Oxford World's Classics, 1990.
Delbanco, Andrew, *Melville: His World and His Work*, New York: Knopf, 2005.
De Man, Paul, *The Rhetoric of Romanticism*, New York: Columbia University Press, 1984.
Dening, Greg, *Beach Crossings, Voyaging across Times, Cultures and Self*, Philadelphia: University of Pennsylvania Press, 2004.
—, *Islands and Beaches: Discourse on a Silent Land: Marquesas 1774–1880*, Carlton: Melbourne University Press, 1980.
Derrida, Jacques and Anne Dufourmantelle, *Of Hospitality*, trans. Rachel Bowlby, Stanford, CA: Stanford University Press, 2000.
Dickens, Charles, *Oliver Twist*, Bloomsbury: Nonesuch Press, 1937.
Doctorow, E. L., *All the Time in the World*, London: Little, Brown, 2011.
—, *The Lives of the Poets*, London: Picador, 1985.
Douglass, Frederick, *Narrative of the Life of Frederick Douglass*, Harmondsworth: Penguin, 1986.
Doyle, William, *Aristocracy and Its Enemies in the Age of Revolution*, Oxford: Oxford University Press, 2009.
—, *The Oxford History of the French Revolution*, Oxford: Oxford University Press, 2002.
Dryden, Edgar A., *Monumental Melville: The Formation of a Literary Career*, Stanford, CA: Stanford University Press, 2004.
Duban, James, *Melville's Major Fiction: Politics, Theology, and Imagination*, Dekalb: Northern Illinois University Press, 1983.
Edmond, Rod, *Representing the South Pacific: Colonial Discourse from Cook to Gaugin*, Cambridge: Cambridge University Press, 1997.
Ellis, William, *Polynesian Researches during a Residence of Nearly Eight Years in the Society and Sandwich Islands*, 2 volumes, New York: J. and J. Harper, 1833.

Emerson, Ralph Waldo, *Selected Journals 1820-42*, New York: Library of America, 2010.
—, *Selected Journals 1841-47*, New York: Library of America, 2010.
Emmers, Amy Puett, 'Melville's Closet Skeleton: A New Letter about the Illegitimacy Incident in *Pierre*', *Studies in the American Renaissance* (1977), 339-43.
Fabian, Ann, *The Unvarnished Truth: Personal Narratives in Nineteenth-Century America*, Berkeley and London: University of California Press, 2000.
Falconer, William, *An Universal Dictionary of the Marine*, London: Thomas Cadell, 1784.
Fanon, Frantz, *The Wretched of the Earth*, trans. Constance Farrington, New York: Grove Press, 1963.
Faulkner, William, *Novels 1942-1954*, New York: Library of America, 1994.
Feldman, Jessica R., *Gender on the Divide: The Dandy in Modernist Literature*, Ithaca, NY: Cornell University Press, 1993.
Fender, Stephen, *Plotting the 'Golden West': American Literature and the Rhetoric of the California Trail*, Cambridge: Cambridge University Press, 1981.
Fenske, Mindy, *Tattoos in American Visual Culture*, New York and Houndmills: Palgrave Macmillan, 2007.
Finkelstein, Joanne, *The Fashioned Self*, Cambridge: Polity Press, 1991.
Fitzgerald, F. Scott, *The Love of the Last Tycoon: A Western*, Cambridge: Cambridge University Press, 1993.
Flügel, J. C., *The Psychology of Clothes*, London: Hogarth Press, 1930.
Forster, E. M., *Aspects of the Novel*, Harmondsworth: Penguin, 1976.
Foucault, Michel, *Discipline and Punish: The Birth of the Prison*, trans. Alan Sheridan, Harmondsworth: Penguin, 1979.
—, *The Foucault Reader*, ed. Paul Rabinow, New York: Pantheon Books, 1984.
Fox, George, *The Journal*, ed. Nigel Smith, London: Penguin, 1998.
Francis, Mary C., 'A Kind of Voyage: E. M. Forster and Benjamin Britten's *Billy Budd*', in *Biographical Passages: Essays in Victorian and Modernist Biography*, ed. Joe Law and Linda K. Hughes, Columbia, MO: University of Missouri Press, 2000, 44-64.
Franklin, Benjamin, *The Autobiography of Benjamin Franklin: A Genetic Text*, ed. J. A. Leo Lemay and P. M. Zall, Knoxville: University of Tennessee Press, 1981.
—, *Autobiography, Poor Richard and Later Writings*, New York: Library of America, 1987.
Franklin, H. Bruce, *In the Wake of the Gods: Melville's Mythology*, Stanford, CA: Stanford University Press, 1963.
Freeman, John, *Herman Melville*, London: Macmillan, 1926.
Frey, James, *A Million Little Pieces*, New York: Random House, 2003.
Gates, Henry Louis, Jr, 'Critical Fanonism', *Critical Inquiry*, 17:3 (1991), 457-70.

Gates, Henry Louis, Jr, and Nellie McKay (eds), *Norton Anthology of African American Literature*, New York and London: Norton, 1997.

Gell, Alfred, *Wrapping in Images: Tattooing in Polynesia*, Oxford: Clarendon Press, 1993.

Giddens, Anthony, *Modernity and Self-Identity: Self and Society in the Late Modern Age*, Cambridge: Polity Press, 1991.

Giddens, Anthony and Christopher Pierson, *Conversations with Anthony Giddens*, Cambridge: Polity Press, 1998.

Gilman, William H., *Melville's Early Life and Redburn*, New York: New York University Press, 1951.

Goffman, Erving, *The Goffman Reader*, ed. Charles Lemert and Ann Branaman, Oxford: Blackwell, 1997.

Goodstein, Elizabeth S., *Experience Without Qualities: Boredom and Modernity*, Stanford, CA: Stanford University Press, 2005, p. 6.

Hammett, Dashiell, *Complete Novels*, New York: Library of America, 1999.

Hardy, Thomas, *The Mayor of Casterbridge*, London: Macmillan, 1963.

Harrison, Henrietta, 'Clothing and Power on the Periphery of Empire: The Costumes of the Indigenous People of Taiwan', *Positions: East Asia Cultures Critique*, 11:2 (2003), 331–60.

Hawthorne, Nathaniel, *The English Notebooks*, ed. Randall Stewart, New York: Modern Language Association of America, 1941.

—, *Novels*, New York: Library of America, 1983.

—, *Tales and Sketches*, New York: Library of America, 1982.

Hay, Sheridan, *The Secret of Lost Things*, New York: Doubleday, 2006.

Hayford, Harrison, 'The Significance of Melville's "Agatha" Letters', *ELH, A Journal of English Literary History*, 13 (1946), 299–310.

Hayford, Harrison and Hershel Parker, *Melville's Prisoners*, Evanston, IL: Northwestern University Press, 2003.

Hearst, Patricia, *Every Secret Thing*, Garden City, NY: Doubleday, 1982.

Higgins, Brian and Hershel Parker (eds), *Herman Melville: The Contemporary Reviews*, Cambridge: Cambridge University Press, 1995.

Hillway, Tyrus, *Herman Melville*, Boston: G. K. Hall, 1979.

Hollander, Anne, *Seeing through Clothes*, New York: Viking Press, 1978.

Howard, Leon, *Herman Melville: A Biography*, Berkeley: University of California Press, 1958.

Hughes, Clair, *Dressed in Fiction*, New York and Oxford: Berg, 2006.

—, *Henry James and the Art of Dress*, New York: Palgrave, 2001.

Hughes, Henry (ed.), *Melville and the Marquesas*, special issue of *Leviathan: A Journal of Melville Studies*, 11 (2009).

Hunt, Alan, *Governance of the Consuming Passions*, Basingstoke: Macmillan, 1996.

Jacobs, Harriet, *Incidents in the Life of a Slave Girl*, The Schomburg Library of Nineteenth Century Black Women Writers, New York and Oxford: Oxford University Press, 1988.

James, Henry, *Essays, American and English Writers*, New York: Library of America, 1984.
—, *Novels 1881–86*, New York: Library of America, 1985.
Joyce, James, *Ulysses*, Richmond: Alma Classics, 2012.
Keating, Peter, *Into Unknown England, 1866–1913: Selections from the Social Explorers*, Manchester: Manchester University Press, 1976.
Kelley, Wyn (ed.), *A Companion to Herman Melville*, Malden, MA: Blackwell, 2006.
—, *Herman Melville: An Introduction*, Malden, MA: Blackwell, 2008.
Keyssar, Alexander, *Melville's Israel Potter: Reflections on the American Dream*, Cambridge: Harvard University Press, 1969.
Kuhn, Cynthia and Cindy Carlson (eds), *Styling Texts: Dress and Fashion in Literature*, Youngstown, NY: Cambria Press, 2007.
Lawrence, D. H., *Studies in Classic American Literature*, Harmondsworth: Penguin, 1977.
Leeman, William P., *The Long Road to Annapolis: The Founding of the Naval Academy and the Emerging American Republic*, Chapel Hill: University of North Carolina Press, 2010.
Lejeune, Phillipe, 'The Autobiographical Contract', in *French Literary Theory Today*, ed. Tsetavan Todorov, trans. R. Carter, Cambridge: Cambridge University Press, 1982.
Levine, Robert S. and Samuel Otter (eds), *Frederick Douglass and Herman Melville: Essays in Relation*, Chapel Hill: University of North Carolina Press, 2008.
Leyda, Jay (ed.), *The Melville Log*, 2 volumes, New York: Harcourt Brace and Co., 1951.
London, Jack, *Novels and Social Writings*, New York: Library of America, 1982.
Lurie, Alison, *The Language of Clothes*, New York: Random House, 1981.
McGlamery, Thomas Dean, *Reading a Man Like a Book: Bodies and Texts in Billy Budd*, Austin: University of Texas Press, 1996.
McNeil, Peter, Vicki Karaminas and Catherine Cole (eds), *Fashion in Fiction: Text and Clothing in Literature, Film and Television*, New York and Oxford: Berg, 2009.
Marr, Timothy, *The Cultural Roots of American Islamicism*, Cambridge and New York: Cambridge University Press, 2006.
Martin, Robert K., 'Saving Captain Vere: Billy Budd from Melville's Novella to Britten's Opera', *Studies in Short Fiction*, 23 (1986), 49–56.
Matthiessen, F. O., *American Renaissance: Art and Expression in the Age of Emerson and Whitman*, London: Oxford University Press, 1976.
Maugham, W. Somerset, *Collected Stories*, New York and London: Knopf, 2004.
Melville, Herman, *Billy Budd, Sailor: An Inside Narrative*, ed. Harrison Hayford and Merton M. Sealts, Jr, London and Chicago: Chicago University Press, 1962.

—, *Billy Budd, Sailor and Other Stories*, ed. Harold Beaver, Harmondsworth: Penguin, 1970.
—, *Clarel: A Poem and Pilgrimage in the Holy Land*, ed. Harrison Hayford, Alma A. MacDougal, Hershel Parker and G. Thomas Tanselle, Evanston, IL: Northwestern University Press, 1991.
—, *Collected Poems of Herman Melville*, ed. Howard P. Vincent, Chicago: Packard and Company, 1947.
—, *The Confidence-Man: His Masquerade*, ed. Harrison Hayford, Hershel Parker and G. Thomas Tanselle, Evanston, IL: Northwestern University Press, 1984.
—, *Correspondence*, ed. Lynn Horth, Evanston, IL: Northwestern University Press, 1993.
—, *Israel Potter, His Fifty Years of Exile*, ed. Harrison Hayford, Hershel Parker and G. Thomas Tanselle, Evanston, IL: Northwestern University Press, 1982.
—, *Journals*, ed. Howard C. Horsforth and Lynn Horth, Evanston, IL: Northwestern University Press, 1989.
—, *Mardi and A Voyage Thither*, ed. Harrison Hayford, Hershel Parker and G. Thomas Tanselle, Evanston, IL: Northwestern University Press, 1970.
—, *Moby-Dick, or, The Whale*, ed. Harrison Hayford, Hershel Parker and G. Thomas Tanselle, Evanston, IL: Northwestern University Press, 1988.
—, *Omoo: A Narrative of Adventures in the South Seas*, ed. Harrison Hayford, Hershel Parker and G. Thomas Tanselle, Evanston, IL: Northwestern University Press, 1968.
—, *The Piazza Tales, and Other Prose Pieces, 1839–1860*, ed. Harrison Hayford, Alma A. MacDougall and G. Thomas Tanselle, Evanston, IL: Northwestern University Press, 1987.
—, *Pierre; or, The Ambiguities*, ed. Harrison Hayford, Hershel Parker and G. Thomas Tanselle, Evanston, IL: Northwestern University Press, 1971.
—, *Redburn,'His First Voyage*, ed. Harrison Hayford, Hershel Parker and G. Thomas Tanselle, Evanston, IL: Northwestern University Press, 1969.
—, *Selected Poems of Herman Melville*, ed. Robert Penn Warren, New York: Barnes and Noble, 1998.
—, *Typee, A Peep at Polynesian life*, ed. Harrison Hayford, Hershel Parker and G. Thomas Tanselle, Evanston, IL: Northwestern University Press, 1968.
—, *White-Jacket; or, The World in a Man-of-War*, ed. Harrison Hayford, Hershel Parker and G. Thomas Tanselle, Evanston, IL: Northwestern University Press, 1970.
Moers, Ellen, *The Dandy: Brummell to Beerbohm*, London: Secker & Warburg, 1960.
Morison, Samuel Eliot, 'The Willie Jones-John Paul Jones Tradition', *William and Mary Quarterly*, 16:2 (1959), 198–206.
Morris, Oswald, *Huston, We Have a Problem: A Kaleidoscope of Filmmaking Memories*, Lanham, MD: Scarecrow Press, 2006.

Murray, Henry A., Harvey Myerson and Eugene Taylor, 'Allan Melvill's By-Blow', *Melville Society Extracts*, 61 (1985), 1–6.
Newberry, Frederick, 'A Red-Hot "A" and a Lusting Divine: Sources for *The Scarlet Letter*', *The New England Quarterly*, 60 (1987), 256–64.
Newman, John Henry, *Apologia Pro Vita Sua and Six Sermons*, ed. Frank M. Turner, New Haven and London: Yale University Press, 2012.
Oliver, Douglas, *Polynesia in Early Historic Times*, Honolulu: Bess Press, 2002.
Orwell, George, *Down and Out in Paris and London*, London: Secker and Warburg, 1986.
—, *Nineteen Eighty-Four*, Harmondsworth: Penguin, 1974.
Otter, Samuel, *Melville's Anatomies*, Berkeley: University of California Press, 1999.
Paliwoda, Daniel, *Melville and the Theme of Boredom*, Jefferson, NC: McFarland, 2010.
Parini, Jay, *The Passages of Herman Melville*, Edinburgh: Canongate, 2012.
Parker, Hershel, *Herman Melville: A Biography*, 2 volumes, Baltimore and London: Johns Hopkins University Press, 1996, 2002.
—, *Reading Billy Budd*, Evanston, IL: Northwestern University Press, 1990.
Pascal, Roy, *Design and Truth in Autobiography*, London: Routledge, 1960.
Paston, George, *At John Murray's*, London: Murray, 1932.
Picardie, Justine, *My Mother's Wedding Dress: The Fabric of Our Lives*, London: Picador, 2005.
Plath, Sylvia, *Collected Poems*, London: Faber and Faber, 1988.
Pratt, Mary Louise, *Imperial Eyes: Travel Writing and Transculturation*, London: Routledge, 1992.
Ra'ad, Basem L., '"The Encantadas" and *The Isle of the Cross*: Melvillean Dubieties, 1853–54', *American Literature*, 63 (1991), 316–23.
Rampersad, Arnold, *Melville's Israel Potter: A Pilgrimage and Progress*, Bowling Green, OH: Bowling Green University Popular Press, 1969.
Rapport, Michael, *Nationality and Citizenship in Revolutionary France: The Treatment of Foreigners 1789–1799*, Oxford: Clarendon, 2000.
Renker, Elizabeth, *Strike through the Mask: Herman Melville and the Scene of Writing*, Hampden Station, MD: Johns Hopkins University Press, 1996.
Reynolds, David S., *Beneath the American Renaissance: The Subversive Imagination in the Age of Emerson and Melville*, New York: Knopf, 1988.
Ribiero, Aileen, 'On Englishness in Dress', in *The Englishness of English Dress*, ed. Christopher Breward, Becky Conekin and Caroline Cox, New York and Oxford: Berg, 2002, 15–27.
Ricoeur, Paul, *History and Truth*, trans. Charles A. Kelbley, Evanston IL: Northwestern University Press, 1973.
Rowlandson, Mary, *Narrative of the Captivity and Restoration of Mrs Mary Rowlandson*, Minneapolis: Filiquarian Publishing, 2008.

Royle, Nicholas, *Veering: A Theory of Literature*, Edinburgh: Edinburgh University Press, 2011.
Russell, Jack, *Nelson and the Hamiltons*, Harmondsworth: Penguin, 1972.
Samson, John, *White Lies: Melville's Narratives of Facts*, Ithaca, NY: Cornell University Press, 1989.
Sanborn, Geoffrey, *The Sign of the Cannibal: Melville and the Making of a Postcolonial Reader*, Durham, NC: Duke University Press, 1998.
—, *Whipscars and Tattoos: The Last of the Mohicans, Moby-Dick, and the Maori*, New York and Oxford: Oxford University Press, 2011.
Sartre, Jean-Paul, *Being and Nothingness: An Essay on Phenomenological Ontology*, trans. Hazel E. Barnes, London: Routledge, 2000.
Schiller, Friedrich, *Don Carlos and Mary Stuart*, trans. Hilary Collier Sy-Quia and Peter Oswald, Oxford: Oxford University Press, 1996.
Sealts, Merton M., Jr, *The Early Lives of Melville: Nineteenth-Century Biographical Sketches and Their Authors*, Madison: University of Wisconsin Press, 1974.
—, *Melville's Reading: Revised and Enlarged Edition*, Columbia: University of South Carolina Press, 1988.
—, *Pursuing Melville: 1940–1980*, Madison: University of Wisconsin Press, 1982.
Sedgwick, Eve Kosofsky, *Epistemology of the Closet*, London: Harvester Wheatsheaf, 1991.
Sedgwick, William Ellery, *Herman Melville: The Tragedy of Mind*, Cambridge: Harvard University Press, 1944.
Shurtleff, Nathaniel (ed.), *The Records of the Governor and Company of the Massachusetts Bay in New England*, 5 volumes, New York: AMS Press, 1968.
Simeon, Daphne and Jeffrey Abugel, *Feeling Unreal: Depersonalization Disorder and the Loss of the Self*, Oxford: Oxford University Press, 2006.
Simmel, Georg, *The Sociology of Georg Simmel*, trans. Kurt Wolff, New York: Free Press, 1950.
Smith, Sidonie, *Where I'm Bound: Patterns of Slavery and Freedom in Black American Autobiography*, Westport, CT and London: Greenwood Press, 1974.
Southey, Robert, *The Life of Nelson*, Hoo: Grange Books, 2005.
Spacks, Patricia Meyer, *Boredom: The Literary History of a State of Mind*, Chicago: University of Chicago Press, 1995.
Spark, Clare L., *Hunting Captain Ahab: Psychological Warfare and the Melville Revival*, Kent, OH: Kent State University Press, 2006.
Sponsler, Claire, *Drama and Resistance: Bodies, Goods, and Theatricality in Late Medieval England*, Minneapolis: University of Minnesota Press, 1997.
Spufford, Margaret, *The Great Reclothing of Rural England*, London: Palgrave Macmillan, 2003.

Steedman, Carolyn, *Landscape for a Good Woman*, London: Virago, 1996.
Steiner, Franz, *Taboo*, London: Routledge, 2004.
Stevens, Wallace, *The Collected Poems*, New York: Knopf, 1981.
Stevenson, Robert Louis, *Dr Jekyll and Mr Hyde and Other Stories*, Harmondsworth: Penguin, 1979.
Symons, Julian, *Thomas Carlyle: The Life and Ideas of a Prophet*, London: House of Stratus, 2001.
Temple, Gale, 'Fluid Identity in *Israel Potter* and *The Confidence-Man*', in *A Companion to Herman Melville*, ed. Wyn Kelley, Malden, MA: Blackwell, 2006, 451–66.
Thomas, Nicholas, 'The Case of the Misplaced Poncho: Speculations Concerning the History of Cloth in Polynesia', in *Clothing the Pacific*, ed. Chloë Colchester, Oxford and New York: Berg, 2003, pp. 79–96.
Thomas, Nicholas, Anna Cole and Bronwen Douglas (eds), *Tattoo: Bodies, Art and Exchange in the Pacific and the West*, London: Reaktion, 2005.
Thomson, Shawn, *The Fortress of American Solitude: Robinson Crusoe and Antebellum Culture*, Madison and Teaneck: Fairleigh Dickinson University Press, 2009.
Vincent, Howard P., *The Tailoring of Melville's White-Jacket*, Evanston, IL: Northwestern University Press, 1970.
Voltaire, *Letters Concerning the English Nation*, ed. Nicholas Cronk, Oxford: Oxford University Press, 1999.
Wallace, Robert K., *Douglass and Melville: Anchored Together in Neighborly Style*, New Bedford: Spinner Publications, 2005.
Weaver, Raymond, *Herman Melville: Man, Mariner and Mystic*, New York: George H. Doran, 1921.
Welters, Linda and Abby Lillethun (eds), *The Fashion Reader*, New York and Oxford: Berg, 2007.
Wenke, John, 'Melville's Indirection: Billy Budd, The Genetic Text, and "the Deadly Space Between"', in *New Essays on Billy Budd*, ed. Donald Yannella, Cambridge: Cambridge University Press, 2002, 114–44.
White, Joanna, 'Marks of Transgression: The Tattooing of Europeans in the Pacific Islands', in *Tattoo: Bodies, Art and Exchange in the Pacific and the West*, ed. Nicholas Thomas, Anna Cole and Bronwen Douglas, London: Reaktion, 2005, 72–89.
Whitman, Walt, *Complete Poetry and Collected Prose*, New York: Library of America, 1982.
Wilde, Oscar, *The Picture of Dorian Gray*, London: Penguin Classics, 2003.
Williams, Raymond, *The Long Revolution*, Harmondsworth: Penguin Books, 1975.
Wilson, Elizabeth, *Adorned in Dreams: Fashion and Modernity*, London: Virago, 1985.
Winters, Yvor, *In Defense of Reason*, Chicago: Swallow Press, 1943.

Worth, Rachel, 'Rural Working-Class Dress, 1850–1900: A Peculiarly English Tradition?' in *The Englishness of English Dress*, ed. Christopher Breward, Becky Conekin and Caroline Cox, New York and Oxford: Berg, 2002, 97–112

Wright, Richard, *Later Works*, New York: Library of America, 1991.

Wu, Duncan (ed.), *Romanticism: An Anthology*, Oxford: Blackwell, 1994.

Young, Philip, *The Private Melville*, University Park: Pennsylvania State University Press, 1993.

Index

Abbott, H. Porter 90, 153n. 79
abolition of slavery 147–8
Alger, Horatio 155
Allen, Ethan 132, 158
Amiel, Henri Frédéric, 168–9
Anderson, Charles 89
Arac, Jonathan 47n. 21
Arvin, Newton 131n. 1
Atwood, Margaret 23–4, 24n. 46
 The Handmaid's Tale 23–4, 24n. 46
Auden, W. H. 209–10
 'Herman Melville' 209–10
Auerbach, Nina 166n. 124
Austen, Jane 87
Auster, Paul 15–16
autobiographical pact 89

Baker, Anne 148n. 63
Barbie doll 123
Barnum, P. T. 122
Barthélemy, Jean-Jacques 40
Barthes, Roland 182, 184
Baudelaire, Charles 2–3, 161
Baum, L. Frank 167
Beaumont, Gustave de 45n. 17
Beethoven, Ludwig van 43n. 11
 Fidelio 43n. 11
Bennett, Anthony 95n. 25
Bentley, Richard 79, 80–1
Bercovitch, Sacvan 154
Berman, Marshall 3n. 6, 64, 143–4
Bishop, Elizabeth 80, 85n. 1
 'Exchanging Hats' 80
 'In the Waiting Room' 85n. 1
Bismarck Otto von 46n. 18
Blake, William 181, 197
 Songs of Innocence and Experience 197
boredom 53, 168–9
Boswell, James 20, 33n. 75

Botz-Bornstein, Thorsten 161n. 108
Bradbury, Ray 76n. 106
Britten, Benjamin 181, 185, 197–8
Brönte, Charlotte 149
 Jane Eyre 149
Browne, Thomas 45
Bruccoli, Matthew J. 178n. 13, 180
Bryant, John 21, 86, 88
Buchan, John 141
Byron, Gordon Lord George 20, 87, 90
 Memoirs 20

Calder, Alex 119n. 91
Camus, Albert 168
captivity narrative 90, 92, 120–1
Carlson, Cindy 24n. 48, 26n. 52, 34n. 77
Carlyle, Thomas 2, 4, 29, 31n. 66, 39–40, 41–2, 44–59, 66, 67, 69, 73, 74, 77, 78, 79, 83, 85, 109–10, 111, 160, 161, 166n. 123, 210
 History of the French Revolution 39
 Life of Friedrich Schiller 210
 'Occasional Discourse on the Nigger Question' 46n. 18
 On Heroes and Hero-Worship 42n. 8, 47, 52
 Sartor Resartus 2, 29, 31, 41, 44–59, 66, 73, 85, 109–10, 122, 160, 166n. 123
 'Shooting Niagara' 46n. 18
Carter, Angela 56–7
Chacko, David 132n. 4
Clark, Kenneth 108
Clifford, John H. 12–13, 19, 21
Cloots, Anacharsis 39–44, 160, 191–2
Coffler, Gail H. 200n. 75
Colchester, Chloë 101, 104n. 52
Cole, Catherine 34n. 77

Coleridge, Samuel Taylor 155–6, 185
  Biographia Literaria 155–6
Conrad, Joseph 96, 166
  Heart of Darkness 96, 166
Cook, Captain James 90, 95n. 26, 119, 121
Cook, Jonathan A. 19n. 37
Cooper, James Fenimore 59, 69, 82, 101, 158n. 93, 159n. 97, 160n. 100, 187
  History of the Navy of the United States 158n. 93, 159n. 97
  The Last of the Mohicans 101
  The Pilot 158n. 93
  The Red Rover 82
Corbey, Raymond 107n. 58
Costentenus, Captain 122
Cotkin, George 76n. 106
Cowper, William 111
  The Iliad 111
Craford, Hester 23n. 44
Crane, Stephen 128–9
  The Open Boat 128–9
Crick, Bernard 126n. 109
Crook, William Pascoe 102–3
Crozier, Eric 181
Cumming, Mark 42n. 8, 48n. 25
Czisnik, Marianne 173

Dana, Richard Henry 45n. 17, 59–60, 65, 68, 69, 70, 70n. 89, 71, 77, 87, 125, 125–6, 127, 129
  Two Years Before the Mast 59–60, 65, 70n. 89, 71, 87, 125, 125–6, 127, 129, 148
Dandy, The 2–3, 32, 34, 44, 65–6, 140, 145–6, 159–65, 192, 198
Darwin, Charles 87
  The Voyage of the Beagle 87
Davidmann, Sara 140
Davis, Fred 30n. 64, 58n. 61
De Man, Paul 90
Defoe, Daniel 17, 30, 90, 97–8
  Robinson Crusoe 17, 30, 90, 97–8

Delano, Amasa 132, 192
Dening, Greg 102n. 47
Denis, Claire, 197
  Beau Travail 197
Depersonalization Disorder 168
Derrida, Jacques 29, 31
Dickens, Charles 30–1, 178
  Edwin Drood 178
  Oliver Twist 30–1
Doctorow, E. L. 16, 56n. 52
  'The Leather Man' 56n. 52
  'Wakefield' 16
Douglass, Frederick 122n. 96, 148–50
  Narrative of the Life of Frederick Douglass 148–50, 151
  North Star 122n. 96, 148
  'What to the Slave is the Fourth of July?' 151
Doyle, Arthur Conan 167n. 128
  'The Man with the Twisted Lip' 167n. 128
Doyle, William 39n. 2, 40n. 6
dress codes 41, 100
Druids, The 200
Dufourmantelle, Anne 29n. 61
Dumas, Alexandre 16
  The Return of Martin Guerre 16
Duplessis, Joseph-Siffred 152n. 72
Duyckinck, Evert 42, 68–9, 81

Edmond, Rod 102, 116–17, 128
Edwards, Mary K. Bercaw 89n. 11
Eliot, T. S. 7, 166
  'The Hollow Men' 166
Ellis, William 92, 103–5, 112–13, 121
  Polynesian Researches 92, 103–5, 112–13, 121
Emerson, Ralph Waldo 6, 10, 31, 45–6, 48–9, 147n. 59
  'Address 'to the citizens of Concord' 147n. 59
  'The Divinity School Address' 46
  'The Over-Soul' 46
  'The Poet' 46

Representative Men 46
'Self-Reliance' 46
Emmers, Amy Puett 13n. 20
Enlightenment, The 151–2, 156–7

Fabian, Ann 135, 150n. 69, 167n. 128
Fanon, Frantz 100
 The Wretched of the Earth 100, 101
fatal impact theory 101–2, 117
Faulkner, William 31–2, 35, 167n. 125
 Intruder in the Dust 31–2, 35
 The Sound and the Fury 167n. 125
Feldman, Jessica R. 161–2
Fender, Stephen 60n. 64
Fenske, Mindy 123n. 99
Finkelstein, Joanne 108
Fitzgerald, F. Scott 178, 178n. 13, 179–80
 The Last Tycoon 178, 178n. 13, 179–80
 Tender is the Night 178n. 13
Flügel, J. C. 27, 78–9
Fluid text 86
Forster, E. M. 178, 181–2, 185, 196–8, 209
 Aspects of the Novel 178
 Billy Budd libretto 181–2, 196–8
Foucault, Michel
 Discipline and Punish 40
 'What is Enlightenment' 2
Fox, George 54–7, 58, 73
Francis, Mary C. 181
Franklin, Benjamin 36, 132, 136–7, 143–4, 151–8, 159, 162, 163, 167, 168, 183
 Autobiography of Benjamin Franklin 153–7, 183
 Poor Richard's Almanack 155
 Way to Wealth 153
Franklin, H. Bruce 200–1
Fraser, James 48
Frederick II (the Great) 46n. 18
Freeman, F. Barron 179, 182
Freeman, John 185, 209–10

Freud, Lucian 108n. 65
Freud, Sigmund 181, 197
Frey, James 89
 A Million Little Pieces 89
Fugitive Slave Act 147–8

Galliano, John 161
Gansevoort, Guert 186–9
Gansevoort, Peter 8, 44
Gates, Henry Louis Jr 102, 148n. 60
Gaultier, Jean Paul 1, 65–6
Gell, Alfred 122n. 97
genetic text 182–4, 189–90
George III 132, 146
Giddens, Anthony 3, 57, 57n. 55, 168–9
Gilman, William H. 66n. 79
Goffman, Erving 107
 Asylums 107
Goodstein, Elizabeth S. 169
Goswami, Joy 100
Greene, Richard Tobias (Toby) 89, 89n. 11
Grey, Zane 101
 The Vanishing American 101

Hamilton, Emma 172
Hammett, Dashiell 15
 The Maltese Falcon 15
Hardy, Thomas 20, 144, 166
 'The Dorsetshire Labourer' 144n. 44
 Jude the Obscure 166
 The Mayor of Casterbridge 144
Harper, Fletcher 18–19, 91
Harris, John 102n. 47
Harrison, Henrietta 99
Hatch, Agatha 12–14, 16–17, 21
Hathorne, William 23n. 44
Hawthorne, Nathaniel 3, 5–29, 31, 33–4, 38, 47, 63–4, 68, 90–1, 133, 165–6, 174n. 8, 184, 195, 199
 Friendship with Melville 5–21, 33–4, 47, 68

works:
  'The Artist of the Beautiful' 19
  'The Birth-Mark' 195, 199
  The Blithedale Romance 9
  'The Custom-House' 10–11, 14, 27
  'Endicott and the Red Cross' 27
  'Ethan Brand' 11
  Fanshawe 9
  'Feathertop' 165–6
  'The Gentle Boy' 11
  The House of the Seven Gables 9, 10
  Life of Franklin Pierce 9
  Mosses from an Old Manse 7, 9, 19n. 37, 165n. 113, 195
  'My Kinsman Major Molineux' 16, 63–4
  The Scarlet Letter 8, 9, 10, 11, 22–9, 174n. 8
  Twice Told Tales 9, 14
  'Wakefield' 14–16, 21–2
Hay, Sheridan 20
  The Secret of Lost Things 20
Hayford, Harrison 18n. 31, 88n. 6, 177–8, 179–80, 182–5, 190, 197n. 66, 199n. 72
Hearst, Patricia 121n. 94
  Every Secret Thing 121n. 94
Heckerling, Amy 1
  Clueless 1
Hemingway, Ernest 20
Hillway, Tyrus 52
Hitler, Adolf 172
Hollander, Anne 108n. 64
Household, Geoffrey 141
  Rogue Male 141
Howard, Leon 132
Hughes, Clair 34n. 77, 35
Hunt, Alan 24n. 49
Huston, John 76n. 106

Irving, Washington 87, 135
  Bracebridge Hall 87
  'Rip Van Winkle' 135

Jacobs, Harriet 148–50
  Incidents in the Life of a Slave Girl 148–50
James, Henry 11, 27–8, 29, 34, 35–7
  The Awkward Age 37
  The Golden Bowl 37
  Hawthorne 11, 27–8
  The Portrait of a Lady 35–7
  What Maisie Knew 37
Johnson, Samuel 33n. 75
Jonah, book of 139
Jones, John Paul 65, 135n. 17, 136–7, 143–4, 147, 158–63, 167, 168, 203
Joyce, James 55, 183
  Finnegans Wake 183
  Ulysses 55

Karaminas, Vicki 34n. 77
Keating, Peter 127
Keyssar, Alexander 131n. 1
'The King of the Cannibal Islands' 94
King Philip's War 26, 120
Kuhn, Cynthia 24n. 48, 26n. 52, 34n. 77
Kulcsar, Alexander 132n. 4

Langsdorff, Georg H. 121
  Voyages and Travels in Various Parts of the World 121
Lauren, Ralph 55
Lawrence, D. H. 8, 106, 156, 178
  Studies in Classic American Literature 8, 156, 178
Leeman, William 159, 160
Lejeune, Phillipe 89
Levine, Robert S. 148
Leyda, Jay 87n. 3, 133, 134
London, Jack 125–6
  People of the Abyss 125–6
London Missionary Society 92, 102
Longfellow, Henry Wadsworth 6
Lowry, Malcolm 20
  Ultramarine 20
Lurie, Alison 34–5, 73, 204

McGlamery, Thomas Dean 182n. 23
McKee, David 115
Mackenzie, Alexander Slidell 186–7
McLoughlin, Coleen 66n. 78
McNeil, Peter 34n. 77
Mansfield, Katherine 96n. 31
   'The Garden Party' 96n. 31
Marlboro Man 123n. 99
Marr, Timothy 32, 82n. 123
Martin, Robert K. 181n. 18
Mather, Increase 26
Matteson, Tompkins Harrison 28
Matthiessen, F. O. 47, 206
Maugham, W. Somerset 105
   'Rain' 105
Mayer, Ruth 26n. 52
Mayhew, Henry 167n. 128
Melville, Elizabeth 6, 17, 18, 70n. 88, 177
Melville, Gansevoort 86, 87, 88, 91
Melville, Herman, works
   'Agatha' 12–14, 16–21, 22–8, 32, 38, 57, 69
   'Bartleby, the Scrivener' 1, 9, 16, 32, 53, 69, 97, 132, 134, 169, 176, 179
   Battle-Pieces 8, 19
   'The Bell-Tower' 9
   Benito Cereno 9, 132, 148, 192, 203
   Billy Budd, Sailor 2, 3, 4, 9, 32, 43–4, 52n. 36, 65, 73, 74, 86, 132, 162, 175–211
   'Billy in the Darbies' 194
   'Bridegroom Dick' 188–9
   Clarel 8, 82, 131, 177
   The Confidence-Man 8, 9, 42–3, 155n. 83, 156, 157, 160n. 102, 177, 178
   'The Encantadas' 20
   'Hawthorne and His Mosses' 7, 47, 195
   The Isle of the Cross 17–18, 19–20
   Israel Potter 1, 2, 9, 16, 36, 38, 65, 72, 80, 124, 131–69, 203, 210
   Mardi 11, 17, 41, 45, 47, 52, 67, 68, 71, 80n. 114, 131, 136, 136n. 21, 184
   Moby-Dick 4, 5, 6, 7, 9, 10, 11–12, 16, 17, 19, 42, 42n. 9, 43, 44, 47, 52–3, 58, 60, 68, 69, 76n. 106, 77, 90–1, 124, 125n. 105, 133, 134, 135, 139, 178n. 14, 184, 206n. 96, 209, 211
   'My jacket old' 82
   'Norfolk Isle and the Chola Widow' 20
   Omoo 2, 11, 17, 19, 41, 45, 47, 67, 69, 83, 85, 86, 87n. 3, 91–3, 95–6, 102, 117, 121–4, 128, 129–30, 133, 162
   'The Paradise of Bachelors and the Tartarus of Maids' 83
   'The Piazza' 64
   The Piazza Tales 9, 20, 132n. 3
   Pierre 6–7, 9, 11, 13n. 20, 17, 18, 19, 52, 83, 131, 133, 134, 136
   Redburn 2, 19, 45n. 15, 59–70, 74, 75, 77–9, 80, 80n. 114, 81–3, 87, 131, 134, 136, 174–5, 184, 210
   Typee 1, 2, 3, 4, 11, 17, 19n. 36, 20–1, 29, 30, 32, 41, 45, 47, 58–9, 67, 69, 74, 83, 85–130, 133, 136, 148, 162
   White-Jacket 1, 2, 17, 19, 37, 45, 57–8, 68, 69–83, 87, 134, 136, 184, 186, 187–9, 191, 196n. 61, 210
Melville, Thomas 56
Merle, Hugues 28n. 59
Metcalf, Eleanor Thomas 178
Milnes, Richard Monckton 45n. 17
Milton, John 111, 185, 197n. 66
   Paradise Lost 111, 197, 209
   Paradise Regained 185, 209
Modernity 2–3, 15–16, 29, 34, 49, 53, 56–7, 64, 100–1, 112–13, 134, 143–5, 153–4, 160–2, 167–9, 204–5

Moers, Ellen 160n. 105
Morison, Samuel Eliot 160n. 100
Morrison, Jim 56
'Mother Hubbard' 105
Moxon, Edward 45n. 17
Mr Benn 114–15, 126
Munroe, James 48
Murray, Henry A. 13n. 20
Murray, John 48, 80, 87–8, 91
muumuu 105
Myerson, Harvey 13n. 20

Nabokov, Vladimir 50n. 30
   Pale Fire 50n. 30
nakedness 26–7, 29–30, 36–7, 55, 97–8, 106–13, 129, 161–2
Napoleonic Wars 171–5, 202
Nelson, Horatio 171–7, 189, 190–1, 199–200, 203, 204–5, 207–8, 211
Newberry, Frederick 23n. 44
Newman, John Henry 166

O'Brian, Patrick 202
O'Brien, Flann 50n. 30
   The Dalkey Archive 50n. 30
   The Third Policeman 50n. 30
Oliver, Douglas 95n. 26
Olympic Games 41
Orientalism 93, 107
Orwell, George 23–4, 125–7, 129
   Down and Out in Paris and London 125–7
   Nineteen Eighty-Four 23–4
Ossian 45
Otter, Samuel 122n. 97, 148n. 61

Paine, Thomas 40
Paliwoda, Daniel 53, 169
Parker, Hershel 7, 12, 13, 18, 19, 32, 45, 82n. 123, 87n. 3, 89n. 11, 91, 94n. 24, 132, 133, 155n. 85, 176, 184n. 26, 186, 187, 210
Pascal, Roy 210

Pessoa, Fernando 168
Peterson, T. B. 133n. 9
Picardie, Justine 57n. 54, 66n. 78
Pierce, Franklin 9
Pierson, Christopher 57n. 55
Pirate, The 162n. 110
Plath, Sylvia 20, 107
   The Bell Jar 20
   'Tulips' 107
Poe, Edgar Allan 16, 195
Potter, Israel 132n. 4, 134, 135–7, 151, 158
Pound, Ezra 7
Pratt, Mary Louise 107
pursuit narrative 140–2
Putnam, George 19, 132, 137

Quakers (Society of Friends) 43, 56, 152, 157n. 89

Ra'ad, Basem L. 20
Rabelais, François 45
Rampersad, Arnold 131n. 1
Rapport, Michael 39, 40
Renker, Elizabeth 83
Reynolds, David S. 79n. 113
Ribiero, Aileen 145, 146
Ricouer, Paul 85, 127
Robertson, James 12–13, 17, 18–19, 21, 29, 32
Rogers, Samuel 45n. 17
Rolling Stones, The 56–7
romance 10–11, 14, 22–3, 64, 114, 202
Romanticism 49, 52, 56, 115, 155–6
Rooney, Wayne 66n. 78
Roosevelt, Theodore 60
Rossetti, Dante Gabriel 143
Routledge, George 133
Rowlandson, Mary 120–1
   Narrative of the Captivity and Restoration of Mrs. Mary Rowlandson 120–1
Royle, Nicholas 205n. 93
Russell, Jack 172

Said, Edward 93
Samson, John 135n. 17
Sanborn, Geoffrey 93n. 20, 95n. 25, 107n. 59, 125n. 105, 127
Sartre, Jean-Paul 141, 161, 168
scarecrows 165–8
Schiller, Friedrich 210–11
  Don Carlos 210–11
Scott, Sir Walter 87
Sealts, Merton M. Jr 42n. 8, 90n. 14, 177–8, 179–80, 182–5, 190, 197n. 66, 199n. 72
Sedgwick, Eve Kosofsky 182n. 23
Sedgwick, William Ellery 135
Selkirk, Alexander 98n. 39
Shakespeare, William 14, 43n. 11, 107, 180, 182, 185, 197, 206–7
  Cymbeline 43n. 11
  King Lear 107, 180, 182
  Othello 185, 197
  Richard II 206–7
  The Tempest 14
  The Winter's Tale 14
Shaw, George Bernard 55
  In Good King Charles's Golden Days 55
Shaw, Lemuel 12, 45, 78, 79, 148
Shuvaprasanna 100
Simeon, Daphne 168n. 129
Simmel, Georg 169
slave narrative 72, 148–51, 163
Smart, Christopher 33n. 75
Smith, Sidonie 150
smock-frock 143–4
Somers affair 186–9, 202
Southey, Robert 172–3, 175, 176
  The Life of Nelson 172–3, 175, 176
Spacks, Patricia Meyer 169n. 132
Sponsler, Claire 111–12
Spufford, Margaret 143
Stedman, Arthur 178n. 14
Steedman, Carolyn 142
Steiner, Franz 119n. 91

Sterne, Laurence 45, 48
  The Life and Opinions of Tristram Shandy 48
Stevens, Wallace 111n. 71
  'Disillusionment of Ten O'Clock' 111n. 71
Stevenson, Robert Louis 106
  The Ebb-Tide 106
  In the South Seas 106
Stowe, Harriet Beecher 127n. 113, 147n. 59
  Uncle Tom's Cabin 127n. 113, 147n. 59
sumptuary laws 23–7, 40–1, 112, 115
Swift, Jonathan 48, 107
  Gulliver's Travels 107
  A Tale of a Tub 48
Symons, Julian 49

taboo 118–20
tattooing 86, 99, 106, 109–12, 115–16, 121–5, 160, 162
Taylor, Eugene 13n. 20
Taylor, Gary 180
Temple, Gale 155, 158n. 91
Tennyson, Alfred 16, 20, 190n. 40
  'Enoch Arden' 16
Thomas, Nicholas 104
Thomson, Shawn 98n. 36
Thoreau, Henry David 147n. 59
  'Slavery in Massachusetts' 147n. 59
Tocqueville, Alexis de 45n. 17
  Democracy in America 45n. 17
Took, Horne 151
Trafalgar, Battle of 171–7, 189–91, 205, 208
Transcendentalism 49, 50, 52, 56
transvestitism 43n. 11, 80, 115, 140
Trumbull, Henry 132n. 4, 135, 136–8, 142n. 39, 145–6, 150, 151, 158, 165

uniform 4, 24n. 46, 41, 44, 56, 59, 65, 70–1, 73–4, 94, 95, 106, 110, 160, 190–4, 198, 203–6, 208–9

Vincent, Howard P. 37n. 84
Voltaire (François-Marie Arouet) 40, 55
  Letters Concerning the English Nation 55

Wallace, Robert K. 122n. 96, 148n. 61
Walters, William 28n. 59
Ward, Mrs Humphry 168n. 129
Weaver, Raymond 178–9
Wells, H. G. 93
  The Time Machine 93
Wells, Stanley 180
Wenke, John 183–4
White, Joanna 122n. 97, 124n. 102
Whitman, Walt 32, 43, 46–7
  'Carlyle from American Points of View' 47
  'Death of Thomas Carlyle' 46
Wilde, Oscar 153
  The Picture of Dorian Gray 153
Wiley, John 88
Wilkes, Charles 92
  Narrative of the United States Exploring Expedition 92
Williams, Raymond 150
Wilson, Edmund 178n. 13, 179–80
Wilson, Elizabeth 3, 26, 27, 160n. 105
Winchester, Simon 105n. 54
Winters, Yvor 158
Wordsworth, William 111
  White Doe of Rylstone 111
Worth, Rachel 144
Wright, Richard 15
  The Outsider 15
Wycherley, William 43n. 51
  The Plain Dealer 43n. 51
Wyeth, Andrew 166–7

Yeats, W. B. 166
  'Among School Children' 166
  'Sailing to Byzantium' 166
Young, Philip 13n. 20
Young, William 158

www.ingramcontent.com/pod-product-compliance
Lightning Source LLC
Chambersburg PA
CBHW062148300426
44115CB00012BA/2049